How to Improve Your Study Skills

Second Edition

Marcia J. Coman · Kathy L. Heavers

NTC Publishing Group
a division of NTC/CONTEMPORARY PUBLISHING COMPANY
Lincolnwood, Illinois USA

Executive Editor: Marisa L. L'Heureux
Editor: Sue Schumer
Cover illustration: Ophelia Chambliss
Design Manager: Ophelia Chambliss
Production Manager: Margo Goia

Acknowledgments begin on page 212, which is to be considered an extension of this copyright page.

Library of Congress Cataloging-in-Publication Data

Coman, Marcia J.
    How to improve your study skills / Marcia J. Coman, Kathy L.
Heavers. — 2nd ed.
       p.   cm.
    Includes index.
    ISBN 0-8442-5886-5
    1. Study skills — Handbooks, manuals, etc.   I. Heavers, Kathy L.
II. Title.
LB1049.C5816   1997
371.3'028'1—dc21   97-16138
                                            CIP

7 8 9 0 CU 0 9 8 7 6 5 4 3 2 1

Contents

Increasing Speed   73   **UNIT 6**

Reading for Enjoyment   151

UNIT 10

Preface

How to Improve Your Study Skills, Second Edition, was written because, as experienced teachers, we came to realize that many students didn't know how to study—they had never been taught a sequential, systematic study procedure. As educators who shared a classroom, we developed our own course of study to address this lack of instruction.

From the time students begin content area studies, they are expected to absorb large amounts of information by listening, taking notes, and comprehending what they read. All these skills are necessary for both educational success and satisfaction in the workplace. Students often lack the ability to make the connections between knowledge of the subject matter and how to use it in other areas of their lives. Instructors often assume that upper-level students have good study skills. This is not always true. They may never have been taught the hows and whys of studying and thus never make those critical connections.

This book is a step-by-step plan for improving student skills and confidence in the areas of reading comprehension and speed. It also introduces strategies for gathering and organizing the information necessary for success. The book provides a series of exercises for use by students who want to build their study skills. The exercises may be used successfully as either an independent study for students working on their own or in a teacher-directed classroom setting. The activities can be worked through sequentially, or students can focus on specific units and strategies to achieve their own studying goals.

ORGANIZATION

The text is divided into twelve units. Each unit focuses on an area critical to building good study skills.

Unit 1 "Getting Started" establishes rapport with students by highlighting reading habits and a general inventory of personal study preferences—students' likes and dislikes. Students become familiar with diverse ways of learning. For many, this is a comforting revelation. Specific strategies are discussed for maximizing the "differences."

Unit 2 "Developing Study Skills" addresses the often false assumption that students beyond grade school have learned and are using good study techniques. The unit covers such vital tools as how to preview the text, tips for improving concentration, control of time, study settings, and techniques for setting goals and planning. Students learn how and why good study habits are tied to good grades.

Unit 3 "Note Taking" provides students with several options in note-taking methods and teaches shortcuts that can be used with any note-taking technique. The exercises in this unit are aimed at streamlining the note-taking process, making students better, more efficient note takers.

Unit 4 "Taking Tests" covers a skill apart from learning course material—test taking. Students need to know that doing well on a test depends not only on their mastery of material covered, but also on knowing how to take a test. Unit 4 focuses on what test taking involves as well as supplying students with mental preparation tips for taking tests.

Unit 5 "Improving Your Understanding" establishes that, if students are to improve their comprehension, they must first learn to use a repertoire of strategies in comprehension monitoring. Unit 5 demonstrates several techniques that will help students improve their understanding of what they read.

Unit 6 "Increasing Speed" presents a number of activities that focus specifically on improving reading speed. Units 5 and 6 go hand in hand, presenting many activities and exercises that motivate students to work at improving both speed and comprehension.

Unit 7 "Skimming and Scanning" introduces students to the concept of flexible reading rates. Unit 7 builds on that concept by introducing the skills of skimming and scanning. Skimming is used to preview, review, or gain an overview of material, while scanning allows students to quickly obtain specific pieces of information. Both strategies conserve time and effort.

Unit 8 "Using the Dictionary" seeks to heighten students' awareness of the wonders of the dictionary. This unit helps students learn how to locate words quickly and how to determine correct definitions, spellings, and pronunciations. Activities help students decipher other information found in a dictionary entry, such as etymologies, inflected forms, variant spellings, and homographs. This unit provides an in-depth look at a rather commonplace old friend.

Unit 9 "Exploring the Library/Media Center" acquaints students with the materials and services available to them in the library/media center. The library and staff provide form and structure for those seeking knowledge and information in our hi-tech world of rapidly accumulating data. Students will learn of the potential resources for acquiring information, from call numbers to the Internet.

Unit 10 "Reading for Enjoyment" presents strategies that inspire even reluctant readers to read for enjoyment. Today the flood of statistics, information, and entertainment presented by computers, CD-ROMs, television, and videos make reading for pleasure a rarity, but learning how to read for enjoyment is still important.

Unit 11 "Getting It Together" addresses long-term planning for all students, whether they are headed for post-secondary education, military service, or the job market. This unit takes students through an analysis of their interests, potential careers that fit those interests, promising careers for the near future, a comparison of salaries, and the use of various sources to research careers. After completing the activities, students will know the steps involved in researching careers and what factors to consider when selecting a career.

Unit 12 "Summing It Up" brings closure to the material covered in the text. Students prepare for and complete a worktext review. In order to complete the review successfully, students must apply a variety of skills learned in previous units. Students can focus on their individual progress over the course of study and see concrete evidence of their improvement. They are also asked to evaluate each individual unit's effectiveness for them. This becomes a meaningful, thought-provoking exercise since students seldom are given an opportunity to judge and express their feelings about a text.

FEATURES

The materials in *How to Improve Your Study Skills, Second Edition,* present a wide variety of interesting activities. Each of these activities aids in developing study skills and enhancing reading ability, both necessary tools for success in school and beyond. Important thinking skills are integrated and developed throughout the book. Students will enhance comprehension, relate and apply information to their own needs and goals, and evaluate their improvement. All activities feature clear instructions and a hands-on approach to learning and practice.

Each unit outlines specific strategies and provides ample practice opportunities. Unit reviews and individual student progress records conclude each chapter. A worktext review brings closure to the book and reinforces the student's individual progress. This is a book that shows students how to achieve the best results from reading, studying, and research.

Marcia J. Coman
Kathy L. Heavers

UNIT

1

Getting Started

Do you know that, when you take a test, you are not only being tested on your knowledge of a subject but on your test-taking techniques as well? Many students feel nervous about taking tests, and their anxiety makes it difficult for them to concentrate or remember.

After you study a subject, do you find you can't recall much about it? If this has happened to you, you'll be eager to learn the simple techniques that will help you study more efficiently and effectively. *Where*, *when*, and *how* you study affect your ability to recall information.

When you take notes, do you try to include only the important things, or do you race to record everything your instructor says? In class, some students scribble away in their notebooks, only to find later that they can't decipher what they wrote.

Most people would like to be able to read faster and to understand and remember material better. Are you a slow reader, or do you read everything from paperback mysteries to your science textbook at the same rate? Can you read at speeds of one thousand words per minute or more?

Suppose you have just been given an assignment involving research. Where do you begin? Because they don't know how to use them, many people think of the dictionary as a bulky book of words and their meanings and the newspaper as a collection of comics, sports, and classified ads. But these two resources, as well as the media center library, are great sources of information; we just have to learn how to use them well.

Each year, the American College Test Program publishes a survey of students in which approximately 35 percent respond that they need additional help in reading, and 45 percent request further development of their study skills. Would you place yourself in these percentages?

Information now being published predicts that the average person will have to retrain for a new job five times during his or her working life span and that 56 percent of the jobs people will hold in the year 2005 do not even exist today. With so much change in your future, you need to acquire skills involving how to learn, how to study, how to research, and how to read with more speed and better comprehension.

How to Improve Your Study Skills addresses each of these skills in very special ways. Written by instructors, and used, tested, and revised by students and instructors, this book is a compilation of techniques that people have discovered really work.

We believe you will find that you can use these basic techniques every day to improve your abilities in all the areas we discussed. And we believe that you will find the materials in this book easy to adapt to your particular learning style and reading and study habits.

Remember, some of the greatest and most beneficial skills you can acquire— the ones that will help you throughout your life— are skills that focus on the abilities to learn, study, research, and read with appropriate speed and comprehension. This text was written to help you develop and sharpen those essential skills.

ACTIVITY 1.1

Introductions

You have enrolled in this class because you want to improve your study skills. So how do you go about it? The activities in Unit 1 will help acquaint you with your instructor and your classmates. You can ask questions about what you will be doing in class and how it will help you. At the same time, you will learn what your instructor's expectations are for the class. As you, your fellow students, and your instructor continue your discussion, you may be surprised to notice that you already feel more prepared and comfortable in this new environment.

Your instructor may begin by introducing himself or herself and asking you to do the same. Besides giving your name, mention your year in school and any hobbies, activities, or part-time jobs you have. After you know a little bit about your instructor and the other students, you will naturally want to learn more about the class itself. Throughout the class, there will be many opportunities for you to take part in discussions and develop your interpersonal communication skills.

ACTIVITY 1.2

Interest Inventory

You have characteristics, interests, and habits that make you special. Sometimes, writing about yourself helps you become more aware of your talents and unique abilities. For example, why are you taking this class? In what subjects are you strongest? In what areas would you like to improve? Are you the reader you would like to be? Knowing the answers to questions such as these will help you become a better student. Your answers will also aid your instructor in identifying your strong and your not-so-strong areas.

On a separate sheet of paper, answer the following questions in the Interest Inventory. When you have finished, you'll know yourself a little better.

Interest Inventory

1. What do you like to do in your spare time?
2. What do you consider as career possibilities?
3. List your favorite subjects in school.
4. List your least favorite subjects.
5. Imagine a free day. What would you do with it?
6. If you could be anyone in the world, who would you be?
7. What is the title of the best book you've ever read?
8. What is (are) your favorite type(s) of book(s)?
9. Have you read any books for pleasure during the past year? How many? List their titles.
10. Do you read a newspaper (or part of one) daily? If you do, which one(s)? Which part(s)?
11. Do you read comic books? If you do, which one(s)?
12. What are your favorite TV programs?
13. Are you employed part-time? Describe what you do during the week from 4:00 PM until you go to bed.
14. Would your describe yourself as a leisure-time reader? Do you read frequently, sometimes, or never?
15. Do you have a library card? Do you use the library often, sometimes, or rarely?
16. How could this class promote your own reading for enjoyment?
17. Is there specific information you need on reading or study skills right now? If so, what is it?
18. On a separate sheet of paper, reconstruct a class schedule like the one below, and fill it out for the classes in which you are currently enrolled.

Hour	Name of Class	Instructor	Level of Difficulty for You Most Difficult = 1, Least Difficult = 5
1			
2			
3			
4			
5			
6			
7			
8			
9			

19. What are your plans after graduating from high school (college, vocational or trade school, armed forces, job)?

Discovering How You Know Things

Now that you have finished the Interest Inventory and have detailed for your instructor and for yourself a little bit of who you are, let's take getting started one step further by discovering how you personally know things. In other words, *how* is it that you know what you already know?

All people are different—you have known that for years. Dr. Howard Gardner's Theory of Multiple Intelligences helps explain why. This Harvard researcher's work is an exciting shift in theory about how people know what they know and is changing traditional educational thinking across the country. Gardener's research says that there is no one way of learning that is superior to another. There are many ways by which people know, understand, and learn about their environment. In the words of Dr. Thomas Armstrong, Multiple Intelligence educator, "It's not how smart you are, but how you are smart that you need to find out."

In this activity, you can get a glimpse of your most effective ways of thinking. Complete this checklist of preferences. Place a check beside the categories that seem to best represent the way you are. Don't spend too much time thinking about your choices.

I am Verbal/Linguistic:

___✓___ I love words.

___✓___ I like to write.

_____ I appreciate jokes, riddles, and tongue twisters.

___✓___ I define some of the words I use regularly because my friends ask me to.

___✓___ I love to spend time talking with my friends.

___✓___ I like to read for pleasure.

___✓___ I do not have a problem with spelling.

___✓___ I have an excellent memory for trivia.

___—___ I find English, social studies, and history are easier than math and science.

I am Logical/Sequential:

___✓___ I like to figure things out.

_____ I find my favorite questions are *why, what if…*, and *how do you….*

___✓___ I usually have a reason for what I do.

___✓___ I am interested in patterns and sequences.

___✓___ I find that math and science are my favorite subjects.

___✓___ I often compute math problems in my head.

_____ I enjoy using computers.

_____ I find that chess, logic problems, and Rubik's Cube are fun for me.

_____ I enjoy finding logical flaws in what people say and do.

_____ I want movies and stories to have logical beginnings, middles, and endings.

I am Visual/Spatial:

_____ I can often see clear visual images in my head.

_____ I seldom get lost in unfamiliar territory.

_____ I doodle a lot while I'm listening to the teacher.

_____ I get feedback that my friends think I'm artistic.

_____ I am sensitive to and appreciate color.

___✓___ I often see what I'm reading as a movie or video in my head.

_____ I find that maps and jigsaw puzzles intrigue me.

_____ I find that geometry is easier than algebra.

_____ I often daydream.

_____ I can imagine a place or event when hearing about it.

I am Body/Kinesthetic:

_____ I have a hard time sitting still.

_____ I like lots of activity.

___✓___ I notice that people say I talk with my hands.

___✓___ I always "show" people how to do something.

_____ I am a hands-on learner.

___✓___ I am well coordinated.

___✓___ I like to challenge myself physically.

_____ I enjoy doing things outdoors.

_____ I prefer to use word processors rather than write by hand.

_____ I find adventurous activity exciting.

I am Musical/Rhythmic:

___✓___ I can always hear the beat in a piece of music.

___✓___ I play a musical instrument.

___✓___ I frequently listen to music on the radio or compact disks.

___✓___ I find that song lyrics often stick in my head.

_____ I compose music.

___✓___ I feel that music is a very important part of my life.

___✓___ I like to sing.

___✓___ I always hear the "off key" notes in a performance.

___✓___ I often tap my foot or pencil or hum while working on other things.

___✓___ I know the tunes to many musical pieces.

I am Interpersonal:

_____ I have many friends.

_____ I get feedback that indicates my advice is valued.

_____ I spend lots of time on the phone.

_____ I enjoy extracurricular activities in school, church or synagogue, and community.

_____ I like being with people better than being alone.

_____ I am thought of as a leader in my group.

_____ I prefer to participate in team sports.

_____ I like to work with others on projects.

_____ I think crowds of people are fun.

_____ I don't enjoy video games and solitaire as much as social outings with my friends.

I am Intrapersonal:

_____ I prefer to work alone.

_____ I usually have strong opinions.

_____ I regularly spend time alone thinking.

_____ I am usually self-motivated.

_____ I sometimes feel people think I'm "different."

_____ I keep a diary or journal of life's happenings.

_____ I have a time-consuming solitary hobby.

_____ I often wish I were finished with school.

_____ I have specific life goals.

_____ I am usually an independent thinker.

Count the number of checks you have in each category. Each of us possesses all of the different ways of thinking in varying degrees, but five or more checks in any one category indicate the ways you know, think, and learn most comfortably. There is no bad or good score. This activity should give you one more piece of information as to who you are and how you differ from the person sitting next to you. Look at your rating on this checklist as one additional piece of valuable information in your self-assessment as you get started on your quest to become a better student.

ACTIVITY 1.4

Identifying Your Personal Learning Style

In the previous exercise, you discovered that all of us acquired our knowledge in unique ways. In this activity, you will discover more specifically how we learn things and see that we each learn things in different ways. You will learn how you personally learn best. Why is this important? Let's assume you are an auditory learner, which means you learn best by hearing things. But currently when you study, you read and reread the material in your notes and in your book. You have completely missed *your personal* learning style, and the material is not going to sink in and stay with you nearly as well.

If you are an auditory learner, you should go into a room and shut the door when you study to eliminate distracting noises, and you should say your notes aloud to yourself so that you can hear them. Or you could recite the important information into a tape recorder and play it back so that you hear it. The point is that you need to *hear* the material; otherwise, you have completely missed your learning style.

There are several types of learning styles, and auditory is only one. There are visual learners who remember best by seeing and kinesthetic learners who learn best by doing. There are also those who learn best by writing, speaking, or reading. Each of these types of learners retain, retrieve, and reproduce information best by studying in different ways. As you read about the various learning styles in the following list, look for any categories that describe you.

Check the items that apply to you.

I am an auditory learner:

_____✓_____ I can follow directions given by my instructor fairly easily.

_____✓_____ I could remember what to get at the store if someone told me. I wouldn't need to write it down.

_____ I like to study with other people; I can hear them discuss the information.

_____ I can remember things better if I repeat them aloud to myself several times.

_____ I do better in class if an instructor lectures than if I read the material myself.

_____ I retain information better if someone quizzes me and I respond out loud.

_____ I can easily remember a joke when someone tells it to me.

I learn best, retain information longer, and reproduce the information more accurately if I can hear it.

I am a visual learner:

_____ I close my eyes as I try to learn things.

_____ I prefer to watch demonstrations of the things I need to learn rather than simply hearing, reading about, or doing them.

_____ I solve simple math problems in my head by seeing the numbers.

_____ I learn better and remember more by seeing videos or movies relating to the topic rather than listening to a lecture.

_____✓_____ I look at the ceiling as I memorize things.

_____ I like to close my eyes and practice seeing the information in my head.

I learn best, retain information longer, and reproduce the information more accurately if I see it or picture it in my head.

I am a kinesthetic learner:

_____ I like to build, design, or create things.

_____ I get most out of doing experiments in class.

_____ I remember best when I type my notes or use a computer.

_____ I like classes in which we do activities or projects rather than read, write, or talk about topics.

_____ I like to move around during class.

___/____ I learn facts better by having information on flash cards, shuffling them, and then matching them up again as compared to rereading the information or listening to it a second time.

I learn best, retain information longer, and reproduce the information more accurately if I am involved in handling the material and doing something.

My strongest learning style is speaking:

_____ I remember best if I move my lips or say things aloud as I try to memorize.

___/____ I find myself saying the information in my head as I write it down.

_____ I like to give a speech rather than write a report on the material.

_____ I would remember a friend's telephone number fairly well if I repeated it out loud several times; I would not need to write it down.

_____ I don't remember my notes very well if I just reread them; I remember them better if I say them aloud.

___/____ I remember better if I can attend class and discuss the material or ask questions about it.

I learn best, retain information longer, and reproduce the information more accurately if I talk about it.

My strongest learning style is writing:

___/____ I can't remember well unless I write things down.

_____ I remember really well if I recopy my notes.

_____ I find myself writing lists of things people tell me to do as opposed to relying on memory.

_____ I prefer to do written reports as opposed to speeches or demonstrations.

_____ I like to write to people instead of calling them on the phone.

___/____ I keep track of assignments best when I write them down.

I learn best, retain information longer, and reproduce the information more accurately if I write it down.

My strongest learning style is reading:

___/____ I remember better if I read a chapter than if I listen to a lecture on it.

___/____ I remember well if I reread my notes; I don't need to retype, rewrite, or say them aloud in order to remember them.

_____ ✓ I prefer to read instructions myself rather than have someone read them to me, tell me what to do, or show me how to do something.

_____ ✓ I like to spend my time reading assignments as opposed to doing projects.

_____ ✓ I would remember information better if I read it than if someone told me about it.

I learn best, retain information longer, and reproduce the information more accurately if I see it and read it myself.

Most people do not have just one learning style. They may have one style that is stronger than another, but it is not uncommon to have several learning styles, strengths, or tendencies. Let's see which learning style(s) best fits you.

1. Count the number of checks in each area. Which area(s) appears to be the primary way(s) in which you learn?

2. Which area(s) appears to be the secondary way(s) in which you learn?

3. In order for you to learn, remember, retrieve, and accurately reproduce information best, describe how you should study.

If you approach studies using your preferred learning style(s), you should be able to study for the same amount of time (or less), remember more, get better grades, raise your level of self-confidence, and reduce your anxiety as you tackle classroom life.

Developing Study Skills

Were you ever taught *how* to study? Instructors often assume that students beyond grade school know and use good study techniques. You may know some people who seem to be able to do more in less time and get good grades besides. How do they do it?

In this unit you will learn some simple techniques that good students consider most important when studying. Now you can discover some of their secrets.

Previewing Your Textbook

Learn to preview your textbook and you will be on your way to becoming a better student. By spending no more than five minutes the first day of class to preview each of your new texts, you can determine what material will be covered in the book, how familiar you are with the material, and how difficult the material will be for you. In addition, you will discover the book's format and the aids included to make your job as a student easier.

You can practice the technique now. Using a separate sheet of paper and this textbook, answer the following questions. Your answers will become your five-minute preview of this text.

1. List the title of the text. *How to improve your study skills*
2. List the author(s). *Corman, Heavers*

3. What is the text's most recent copyright date? 1998

4. Read the preface or introduction. Summarize in a few sentences what the book is going to be about.

5. Read the table of contents. How many units are in the text? How many pages are in the text? List the title of the unit that sounds most interesting to you.

6. Thumb through the book. Are there pictures? Graphics? Maps? Charts? Illustrations? Questions at the end of the chapters? Pages with a lot of white space?

7. Evaluate the difficulty of the text; how hard do you think this text will be for you to read and understand?

8. Turn to the end of the text. What appendixes does it have?

ACTIVITY 2.2

What Is Previewing?

Now that you have actually previewed a textbook, read the following article, "How to Preview Your Textbook." Using a separate sheet of paper, start a section of notes and entitle this section, "Study Skills"—Previewing Your Textbook." Answer the following questions:

1. What is previewing your text?
2. List the seven steps in previewing your text.
3. What is the value of previewing your text?

How to Preview Your Textbook

The difference between being a good student or being a poor one sometimes hinges on whether you know how to study. There are some very basic study techniques that require only a short amount of time to learn but that result in tremendous benefits. Previewing your text is one of these techniques.

Previewing your text involves looking at a book before a class begins to determine what the text contains. This process will take no more than five minutes, but in that amount of time, you will gain much useful information. Your preview can reveal what material will be covered in the book and in the class, how familiar you are with that material, and how difficult that material will be for you to read and understand. You will be able to determine the following: the format of the book; the location of the study aids, pictures, charts, and graphs used throughout; and your level of interest in the material. Equipped with this information, you are a more informed and prepared student already, and you will save yourself study time later on.

The first step in previewing your text is to look at the title, author, and date of publication, or copyright date. The copyright date is important because it not only tells you how current the information is but also how popular the book has been. A book that has been printed and reprinted several times is usually a very popular one.

Next, read the preface or introduction. It usually discusses the scope of the book and explains why the author or authors wrote it.

Third, find the table of contents and read the chapter or unit titles, main headings, and subheadings included within. Turn these into questions so that you can read with a purpose to find the answers.

Next, flip through the book, looking at any charts, pictures, captions, and graphs. These items provide additional information about the subject and also affect your interest in reading the text.

Fifth, evaluate the difficulty of the material. How much do you already know about the subject? How much does it interest you? Is the print large or small? How much white space does a typical page have? Are there many pictures, charts, graphs, and illustrations? These factors all determine the level of difficulty of the text and the amount of material you will have to read.

Next, know your purpose for reading the text. Are you required to read it for class? Will the teacher test you on its contents? Or is it just a supplement to the teacher's notes? Knowing your purpose is crucial in determining how and at what rate you should read the text.

Last, go to the back of the book to see what study aids are included. Does the text include a glossary of words and their meanings to help you with vocabulary? Is there an index listing names, events, terms, and the pages on which these items can be found? Better yet, does the appendix have solutions to problems you may have been asked to solve? Obviously, all these materials will help you as you read the text, *if you know they are there*. If you don't spend time previewing your text, however, you may not discover them.

Study-Setting Worksheet

ACTIVITY 2.3

Take a look at where you study, how you study, and what your "study center" consists of. How strong is your power of concentration in this environment? It may surprise you to learn that your study center, your study environment, and your method of studying directly affect your concentration and comprehension.

For a few minutes, think about your own study situation and environment. Then, on a separate sheet of paper, make a worksheet like the one below and list the conditions that make it hard for you to concentrate. Be honest—no one will deduct points if your study area is a disaster! Be sure to leave room to jot down later your solutions to any problem conditions.

Conditions That Make It Hard for Me to Concentrate	Ways I Can Improve Those Conditions

Study-Setting Worksheet

Tips on Concentration

Read the following article, "Tips on Concentration." Then, add to the notes on study skills you began in Activity 2.2 at least seven tips for improving your study environment, study techniques, and concentration.

Tips on Concentration

Think about your usual study environment. Are you sprawled on your bed with the stereo blaring, books and papers scattered around you? Are you trying not to spill your soda as you retrieve that elusive pencil? Or is your study environment, perhaps, flat on your stomach on the floor, in front of the TV, with the dog licking your ear and your brothers playing video games nearby? If this sounds at all familiar, you may find concentration—or the lack of it—one of your biggest hindrances to effective studying.

"But," you ask, "how can I concentrate better?" The following tips have been gathered from students who have learned to do so.

Study in the same place every day. Psychologically, this establishes a pattern that your brain will respond to automatically when you settle down in that spot day after day. When your study place is your bed, the desire to study is in conflict with the desire to sleep, a conflict that often causes problems for many students.

In spite of what you may think, studying in a quiet place is more beneficial than being surrounded by music or other noise. From experience, you know you can learn to block certain sounds from your consciousness, such as the exasperated tone of a parent's voice calling or the rumble of passing traffic. But having a quiet area is critical, because comprehension rates zoom downward in direct relationship to the amount of sound in your environment. Some experts assert that noise can actually cut comprehension in half!

Since your primary occupation at this time is that of student, make your "office" a study center. Gather together all the equipment you need to do your work. Face a blank wall if possible; don't let distractions creep in to break your concentration. After all, this is where you do your work.

Good lighting and ventilation are primary requirements when you set up your study area. Invest in a desk lamp that will eliminate glare and uneven lighting. Open the window a crack, even in chilly weather, to fend off stuffiness and the yawns that quickly follow.

Find a working surface that is large enough for your needs, and clear it of any clutter. Be sure to provide room for the supplies you need—perhaps just a shoe box on the floor beside your working area.

Note, too, that your eyes will see more easily and become less tired if you prop your book up at a thirty-degree angle, rather than leave it flat on the desktop. You can hold your book at an angle, use other texts as a support, or build a book rest.

You will concentrate better if you have only one task before you at a time; too many tasks may overwhelm you. Always complete one task before beginning another. Avoid the urge to get something to eat or to call a friend. Instead, use these well-known stalling techniques as rewards for yourself when you have completed a task. With a definite plan of attack, you will finish all your assignments sooner.

Learning to concentrate is hard work, but the payoff is better grades. Good students have mastered this skill. You can too!

Solutions to Study-Setting Problems

Now, consult your list of conditions that make it hard for you to concentrate (Activity 2.3) and think of some practical solutions to your problems. List the solution opposite the corresponding problem.

For the next week, put your solutions into practice. See how successful you are and be persistent—remember, it takes time to change habits. Then evaluate what solutions did and did not work for you. Decide what permanent changes you can make to improve your study setting.

Where Does Your Time Go?

It seems we never have enough time to accomplish what we want to. Are you good at disciplining yourself to use your time wisely? Each day, how do you spend the sixteen hours you are not in school?

Consider the fact that the average kindergarten graduate has already seen more than five thousand hours of television by age five or six. That is more than it takes to get a bachelor's degree from college! How much time do you spend in front of the television? Perhaps you don't realize where your time really does go.

On the other hand, you might know someone who *always* comes to class prepared, who studies sufficiently for *every* exam, who carefully prepares *each* written assignment, and who comprehensively reads the text material. Do you envy that person as you scramble before class to get your work done, however haphazardly? If only you had more control of your time....

Tracking Your Time

To help you pinpoint what you really do with your time, on a separate sheet of paper make a chart like the one that follows and complete it according to your schedule for one typical day in your school week.

Start with the time you generally wake up, and continue to identify how you spend your time throughout the day, right up until when you usually go to bed. Include hours spent dressing, eating, traveling to and from school, attending classes, visiting, exercising, working, studying, watching TV, talking on the phone, sleeping, and so on. Make sure your log represents a twenty-four-hour period.

Time	Activity	Time	Activity

Now answer on your own paper the following summary questions:

1. How much time do you use to eat and dress? 2 hr
2. How much time do you spend traveling to and from school? 30 min a day
3. How many hours do you attend classes? 3
4. How much time do you spend exercising? 1
5. How much time do you spend watching TV, visiting, or just relaxing? 1
6. How many hours do you work at a part-time job? 5 hrs a day
7. How many hours do you sleep? 6

ACTIVITY 2.7

Controlling Your Time

What did you discover when you made the chart in Activity 2.6 to determine how you spend your time? Many people feel that they waste time, but they do not know how to correct the problem. The following article, "Tips for Control of Your Time," will give you some time-budgeting suggestions. Read it and answer the questions at the end, writing the questions and the answers in your notes.

Tips for Control of Your Time

Controlling your time is somewhat like learning to budget your money. At first, the money always runs out before the month ends, but with practice and planning, your money-management skills increase. The same is true for budgeting your time. Improving your time-management skills involves just a few simple steps.

If you want to be in control of your time, you need a plan. Your survival depends on having one. Figure out your priorities; think about the things you must accomplish and decide approximately how much time you need to do them. Write these tasks down; they provide a guide, or budget, for spending your hours and minutes.

Consider your prime time and downtime. Are you most alert in the early, mid, or late morning; early, mid, or late afternoon; or early, mid, or late evening? You should plan your study time accordingly, because you will accomplish far more if you study when your concentration abilities are sharp.

Plan for breaks to rest your mind and eyes. Some research suggests taking breaks of approximately ten minutes every hour and/or scheduling these breaks between tasks if possible.

Professor Claude Olney of Arizona State University developed a program called *Where There's a Will There's an A*. He suggests studying in "short bursts." To demonstrate this technique in his video, he slowly reads off a series of unrelated numbers to students and then asks them to recall the first number, some subsequent numbers, and the last number. Everyone can remember the first and last numbers, but very few recall the middle numbers. Studying, he says, is the same: You remember well what you go over at the beginning of your study session and also what you cover at the end, but you lose a lot in the middle. The answer, he says, is to shorten those study sessions so that you have lots of firsts and lasts.

Using Olney's "short bursts" techniques, substitute several short periods of time for the "ten minutes every hour" mentioned earlier. You will find, he says in the video, this usually results in spending less time studying with better results. Ten, fifteen, twenty, or even thirty minute study sessions can even be carried out when you find yourself on the bus or waiting in line. He calls this "studying smarter not harder."

Whichever method you use, either hourly breaks or short bursts, you still need to consider your personality. If you like structure, set up your time budget in an exact time frame. It will make you feel very organized and self-disciplined. If, on the other hand, you dislike rigid time limits, plan your sequence without specific time allotments.

Either approach can be successful, but remember that a time budget, like a budget of dollars and cents, must be somewhat flexible. It is sometimes hard to judge how long a task will take. If you can't meet the time requirement that you have allowed, revise your schedule. Because unexpected things come up, try to have some time in reserve, if possible.

If your out-of-school life is always in a state of chaos, devote a few minutes daily to planning your tasks. By having some plan, whether it be closely structured or more loosely organized, you will know the satisfaction that comes from gaining more control of your time.

Answer the following questions in your notes:

1. In order to plan your time, what do you need to write down? *schedual*
2. What do you consider to be your prime time? Why do you think this is your prime time? *11 right after school before work*
3. What do you consider to be your downtime? Why should you avoid studying then? *4 so I actuallay get a break*
4. Which technique would work best for you: studying for longer periods of time with short breaks in between or studying for short bursts with longer breaks in between? Why would this technique be better for you? *beter in tune with notes*
5. Think about your schedule. Will more structure and a more exact time frame be the best scheduling technique for you, or will a more loosely arranged one be better? Why? *loosely, plans + needs change*

Study Sequence

In addition to listing the tasks you need to do and determining how much time you will need to complete them, you also need to think of the order in which you do them. This called your *study sequence*.

When it's time to study, what do you tackle first? The book at the top of the pile? Or the first book that falls out of your backpack? Maybe you start with the subject you have the first hour in the day and just keep going. Determining what to study first in such ways as these is problematic because you may run out of time or energy and never get to that all-important assignment, the one that matters the most. Consider your own personality and the following study-sequence options instead:

- **Hardest to Easiest**   Some students prefer to study the hardest subject first and get them out of the way. That leaves the easiest subjects for when they are tired and their attention span is winding down.

- **Easiest to Hardest**   Other students prefer to study easiest to hardest. Doing the easier subjects gives them a jump start. It gets them going, and they can see they are getting a lot accomplished quickly. They are encouraged by this and have a more positive mind-set when approaching the harder subjects.

- **Most Important to Least Important**   This sequence is for the students who do not like that all-important assignment hanging over their heads. Instead of constantly being stressed by the thought that they might never have enough time "to get the big one done," they approach the most important assignment first. Completing it first reduces pressure, and they can relax and finish the rest of the subjects in the time that remains. If they do run out of time, at least the big one is done!

- **Least Important to Most Important**   Other students prefer to clear their minds of all the clutter by getting the least important assignments out of the way and then focusing all their attention on the most important task. To them, this is the least stressful way to study.

- **Alternating Activities**   Still others like variety when they study. They choose to do some heavy reading that involves deep concentration for maximum comprehension and then follow that with lighter, more activity-oriented work like drawing a map or inputting some notes on the computer. The advantage of this study sequence is the change of pace.

In order to determine the study sequence that best suits you, consider the circumstances and your personality.

- **Circumstances**   Some nights you may need to tackle the most important assignments first. Maybe it's quarter or semester exam time, and you are really struggling with math. You need to do well on the test, so math becomes the top priority. Other times you may find the doldrums have set in, and you need a change of pace. Alternating activities is the answer for those study sessions.

- **Personality**   Your personality plays a big part in your selection of study sequence. What stresses you the most—quantity? If so, get a lot of the easier or less important assignments out of the way so you can focus on the one big task. Do hard classes give you the most anxiety? If that is the case, do the hardest subjects first so that you can relax as you complete the easier ones.

The top of the pile or the first thing that falls out of your backpack is not a choice for study sequence. Looking at your personality in general or circumstances on a particular night and then selecting a study sequence will result in better use of study time and improved grades.

Answer the following questions in your notes:

1. List the choices for study sequence and explain each.
2. Explain which study sequence would work best for you and why.
3. Explain under what circumstances you might switch to another study sequence and what it would be.

Budgeting Your Time

Having completed Activities 2.6 and 2.7, can you see any areas where you might be able to adjust your present schedule in order to use your time more efficiently? List them on a separate sheet of paper. Then create another chart like the one in Activity 2.6 for a schedule in which you will plan ahead. For the next week you are to create a new budget for your time. Keep in mind the best ways to use your time; your goal is to be more efficient.

At the end of one week, evaluate your new schedule. Did you succeed in using your time more to your advantage? If you found you were more prepared and less rushed, you will probably be eager to make your trial schedule changes permanent.

Sizing Up Your Instructor

"That instructor doesn't like me." "I can't do anything right in his class." "I never know what to expect in her class." Do you recall making similar remarks? If so, maybe you never ask yourself what your instructor expects.

Instructors are as different from one another as you are from your friends. Some are very relaxed in their approach while others rely on lots of structure. Some are very explicit in what they expect from students and what kinds of tests they give. Others may not be so direct.

If you want to learn as much as you can and have the best possible grades, it's your job as a student to understand the expectations of each of your instructors. This process doesn't take long, and it's not difficult either. Use your powers of observation, and if you still aren't sure, ask your instructor.

To begin, in the first days of class, spend a few minutes thinking about your instructor's expectations regarding the following: your behavior, participation, and note taking; his or her method of grading and testing; and, finally, the appropriate techniques you can use to study for that instructor's class. You will be amazed at the results! Not only will you know how to tailor your studying to each class and its instructor's expectations, you will also earn better grades and waste less time.

Next, select the instructor or class that you find most difficult. Remember, the purpose of this exercise is to guide you through an evaluation of your instructor's expectations about you as a student. Once you determine what those expectations are, you can adjust your efforts accordingly and thereby minimize your study time and improve your grade.

On a separate sheet of paper, list the expectations of your instructor, as you understand them, in each of the following areas. Be sure to allow enough room to write.

Instructor's Expectations of My Behavior and Participation:

1. At the beginning of the hour—
2. During the hour—
3. At the end of the hour—
4. In general—

Instructor's Expectations in the Areas of:

1. Note taking—
2. Study techniques—
3. Tests—
4. Grades—

Accuracy of Instructor's Expectations

Take your list of perceived expectations (Activity 2.10) to the instructor you selected and ask him or her to read it to see how accurate you were.

If you were good at predicting what your instructor wants, you are off to a strong start in his or her class. If, on the other hand, you don't yet have a very clear picture of what is expected, ask your instructor specific questions about each area on your expectations list until you understand what he or she wants. Learn now—not after a test. Surprises aren't fun when grades are involved.

The SQ3R Method

An important part of improving your study skills is finding a dependable study technique. Some of you may have already discovered a method that gives you good results, but others may have no system at all...and have grades that show it. If you haven't had the opportunity to develop a study technique yet, the SQ3R method may be for you.[1] Add notes on SQ3R to the section on study skills information that you began in Activity 2.2.

SQ3R

As students, most of you know it is not enough simply to read an assignment. The act of reading does not ensure that you will remember what you have read. Perhaps you daydream while you read, or maybe you are surrounded by background noise, commotion, or interruptions. In any case, you can't recall a thing about what you have just read. Does this scenario sound familiar?

You need to be an active participant as you read and study. You can do so by practicing a technique that involves you in the learning process—SQ3R. Many of you already use part of the SQ3R technique if you preview material. You carry it even further if, as you read, you try to find answers to questions about the materials. Both the previewing and questioning techniques are important steps in SQ3R, but there is more to it. See Figure 2.1.

S = Survey.   The S in SQ3R stands for *survey*, which means *previewing*, a concept you are familiar with. The steps in the survey are simple and take very little time. They are as follows:

---

[1]SQ3R was developed in 1941 by Francis Robinson. It is a popular and successful study technique.

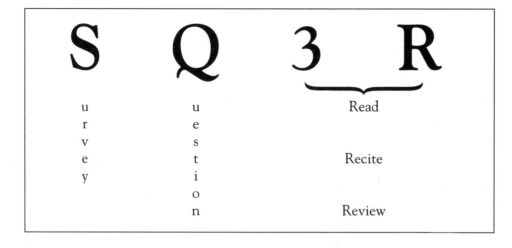

FIGURE 2.1
SQ3R Technique

1. Look at the title.
2. Read the first paragraph or introduction.
3. Read the first sentence of each of the other paragraphs.
4. Read the last paragraph or conclusion.

The survey step in SQ3R helps you in four ways:

1. You get a glimpse of the contents of the material without having to read every word.
2. You get a feel for your familiarity with the material.
3. You can estimate the amount of time you should set aside for covering the material.
4. You may actually double your comprehension when you do read the entire selection.

Surveying the material accomplishes these steps in a matter of minutes!

Q = Question.   In order to become actively involved in the actual reading process, you need to read with a purpose. That is, you need to read to answer questions. Look to the following sources for *questions* you can answer as you read:

1. questions listed at the end of the chapter;
2. questions provided by your instructor;
3. headings you turn into questions; and
4. questions on worksheets, quizzes, or tests.

Knowing the questions before you actually read the selection helps you read with a purpose. You will be an involved reader, and your comprehension and retention of the material will be greatly improved. Better yet, after you finish reading the selection, you will find you know the answers to the questions you had as you were reading.

R = Read.   *Read* the material as an active reader with the goal of answering questions as you go along. You'll be surprised at how much more you'll get out of your reading assignment, and you'll feel good when your reading reveals answers.

R = Recite.   The next step is to *recite* the answers to your questions. Recite aloud to another person or quietly to yourself what you have read. Studies show that students tend to forget as much as 80 percent of what they have learned from reading within two weeks after studying. But when students recite immediately after reading, they forget only 20 percent during the same time period.

Recite what you have read and then write it down, if necessary. This proves that you understand and comprehend what you have read—that you have been actively involved in the reading process. You know you have read because you can recite the answers to questions.

R = Review.   After a few hours, or even a couple of days, *review* the answers to your questions. This step will keep the material fresh in your mind and retain it and recall it accurately for longer periods of time.

In addition, using the SQ3R method will save you from test anxiety and late-night or all-night crash study sessions. SQ3R helps you learn and retain the material so that you can approach a test with confidence.

ACTIVITY 2.13

Practice with SQ3R

Learning anything new takes some practice before it feels comfortable; the SQ3R technique for studying is no exception. Start by trying the SQ3R method on a chapter from a textbook that is difficult for you. Use your notes and think about what you are doing and why you are doing it.

Next, give yourself a long-term trial with SQ3R. Commit to using this technique for two weeks as you study one subject that gives you difficulty. Be conscientious and follow the procedure steps exactly. SQ3R is used successfully by many students—see if it is a technique that will work for you.

Following is a review of what you have learned in Unit 2 on developing study skills. Try to remember the major points that were covered. On a separate sheet of paper, answer the following questions:

I. Multiple Choice (1–5)

Number your paper from one to five. Place the letter of the correct answer beside the corresponding number.

1. In what order should you study subjects?

    A. Hardest or least interesting to easiest or most interesting?

    B. Alternate types of activities.

    C. First things first, in order of descending importance.

    D. Any of the above.

2. What is the benefit of a study budget or a time sheet?

    A. Sets immediate goals.

    B. Helps concentration because you are working against the clock.

    C. Helps resist distractions.

    D. All of the above.

3. How long should a break be?

    A. Five minutes.

    B. Ten minutes.

    C. Fifteen minutes.

    D. As long as you need it to be.

4. What did the article you read say about taking breaks?

    A. They are optional and not really important.

    B. They are a waste of times and should be omitted.

    C. They are absolutely essential to maintain your concentration.

    D. They should be taken frequently; every thirty minutes is best.

5. Your study schedule should be:

    A. Very rigid. If you do not follow it carefully you'll never develop any self-discipline.

    B. Flexible. You'll become frustrated and easily discouraged if it is too rigid and you can't live up to it.

    C. Quickly disposed of. A study schedule forces you to be too organized and has very little benefit.

    D. Made out for weeks in advance. Careful planning never hurt anyone.

II. Listing (6–17)

6.–12. Number your paper from six through twelve. Read the questions below carefully, choose one of the two questions, and write the correct answers.

    A. List seven tips concerning the setting or environment in which you should study if you wish to get maximum comprehension.

    B. List the seven steps in previewing your text.

13.–17. Explain what the five letters in SQ3R stand for.

III. Short Essay (18)

18. Choose one of the following topics and write your answer in paragraph form.

    A. Describe what is involved in previewing your text and discuss the benefits you found when you previewed three of your texts.

    B. Discuss the value of creating a good study setting, explain the changes you made in your study setting, and conclude by discussing how these changes have helped you improve your concentration.

    C. Explain the steps in SQ3R and discuss how this technique will be beneficial to you.

Note Taking

Almost anyone would agree: Note taking can be a real chore! Some instructors talk so fast, you can't begin to keep up. Others wander from one subject to the next until you can't even remember the points they are trying to make. A fast talker leaves your hand numb from writer's cramp. A disorganized speaker leaves you dizzy with confusion—and with few notes in your notebook. You need a better, more efficient method for taking notes.

Notes and note taking are personal. No two students take notes in the same way, although each is trying to pick out the same main points from a lecture. Whether you consider yourself a skilled or unskilled note taker, your note taking can improve. You can learn to be more flexible and concise.

Unit 3 will give you experience using several methods of taking notes, as well as some shortcuts you can use—regardless of the type of note-taking technique you favor. The exercises in this unit will help you streamline your note taking; in other words, they will help you develop skills that will make it easier to take notes efficiently. And, because you will soon be an efficient note taker, the notes you take will be more useful to you, too.

Evaluating Your Present System

ACTIVITY 3.1

This activity lets you evaluate your own note-taking techniques and illustrates a concise method for taking notes in the future. For those of you who have trouble deciding what to include in your notes, practice picking out the main points and subpoints from the material.

Part One

First, read the following selection entitled "Evaluating Your Present System." As you read, use your standard note-taking technique to take notes on a separate sheet of paper. When you finish, compare your notes with those in the answer key in the Appendix at the end of this unit.

Evaluating Your Present System

Lectures given by instructors are fleeting things. The ideas and concepts presented, unless captured on paper by students taking notes, are quickly confused or forgotten. In order to recall a lecture's main points, you must develop good note-taking skills.

First, you have to concentrate on the lecture. You cannot be thinking about your plans for the evening, tomorrow's dance, or your next car repair. Next, you must learn to pick out the speaker's important points and to exclude the insignificant details. To do this, listen for signal words such as, *the three main reasons are...* and *first, next, last.* Third, you should develop a system for taking notes. Many students use an outline form because it is simple and straightforward. Fourth, you need to find ways to streamline your note-taking system; that is, don't miss an important point because you fall behind as you write. Last, you need to review your notes soon after taking them to fill in any additional information and to refresh your memory on the major points.

Part Two

Compare the notes you took with the outline provided in the answer key in the Appendix. How did you do?

1. Did you use complete sentences? Complete sentences waste time. Be brief, using only key words.
2. Did you use an outline form, or any form at all? Would you describe your notes as clear or confusing?
3. Did you capture the main point and all the subpoints? Signal words in this selection such as *first, next, third, fourth,* and *last* should help you recognize the subpoints.
4. Did you use any abbreviations or shortcuts while taking your notes? If not, you will want to focus on streamlining your note taking.

ACTIVITY 3.2

Note-Taking Questionnaire

This activity uses a survey to give you insight into your thoughts about note taking, your individual note-taking practices, and your weaker areas in note taking. Take a minute to complete the following survey. Your responses will help you gain the most from this unit by emphasizing specific goals for you.

On a separate sheet of paper, number from one to ten. Leave enough room to make comments for each question.

Note-Taking Questionnaire

1. When do you take notes? In class? While studying?

2. Do you find it difficult to take notes while studying? If so, why?

3. Do you ever borrow notes from someone else? If so, are they easier or harder to use than your own?

4. Do you find it difficult to take notes in class? If so, why?

5. Do you write complete sentences when you take notes?

6. List the instructors who expect you to take notes.

7. Do you take notes in those instructors' classes?

8. Do you have trouble picking out main ideas from material?

9. Do you use any shortcuts in taking notes? If so, what are they?

10. Do you feel that taking notes or not taking notes affects the grade you earn?

Outlining

ACTIVITY 3.3

The first note-taking technique presented in this unit is outlining, the most widely used method of taking notes. Outlining provides you with a well-organized set of notes to study from because it forces you to seek out the main idea and to recognize supporting details, eliminating unnecessary information. Once mastered, outlining can be a valuable tool for making you a better student.

Activity 3.3 introduces you to the basics of outlining. It focuses on recognizing main ideas from paragraphs and writing them in proper outline form. Once you have completed this activity, you will have a good understanding of what outlining involves.

If you are not new to outlining, sharpen your skills by reviewing the technique. To help you practice, your instructor may want to provide additional exercises.

Number from one to seven on a separate sheet of paper, leaving room for your comments. Read "The Basics of Outlining" as you follow these directions carefully.

1. Read the first two paragraphs in the article.

2. Answer questions 1 to 4.

3. Read the next paragraph.

4. Answer questions 5 to 6.

5. Read the following two paragraphs.

6. Answer question 7.

7. Read the remainder of the selection and compare your answers to those in the Appendix at the end of this unit.

The Basics of Outlining

One of the most important skills to develop early in your school career is that of taking notes in an organized manner. In many classes, note taking is required. Learning to take organized notes is essential because information is more easily remembered if it is structured when written down.

One of the first steps toward developing an organized note-taking system is being able to recognize the author's main idea; that is, you must clearly understand the point or central thought the author is communicating. That main idea is the topic sentence, and all the other sentences in the paragraph help support it.

```
I. Topic Sentence
  A. Major Point
    1. Subpoint
      a. detail
```

1. In the first paragraph, what is the main idea or topic sentence?
2. Where in the paragraph is the main idea or topic sentence located?
3. Find the main idea or topic sentence in the second paragraph.
4. Where is it located?

You will discover that a paragraph's main idea or topic sentence may be found in a number of different positions in the paragraph. Most frequently, it is the first sentence of the paragraph; the author wants to begin with his or her main idea and use all the other sentences to develop that main idea. The second most frequent location for the topic sentence is the last sentence of the paragraph. By placing the main idea at the end, the author can present a number of details first and then tie them together or sum them up with the topic sentence. Sometimes the main idea may be stated in the first sentence and restated in the last sentence. And occasionally, the main idea may be sandwiched somewhere between the first and last sentences, or split between two sentences. Finally, the topic sentence may be missing altogether! Obviously, topic sentences that are the first or last sentences of a paragraph will be easiest to find. Locating those floating in the middle of a paragraph or split between sentences takes practice.

5. On your paper set up the outline form shown below:

    I.

        A.

        B.

        C.

        D.

        E.

        F.

What is the main idea or topic sentence in the previous paragraph? Write it beside Roman numeral I.

6. What are the six major points in the previous paragraph? Using the capital letters A through F, list each one.

One of the most widely used methods of note taking—the outline—is preferred by many students because its format follows a specific structure and is concise. Notes taken in this manner are well organized and easily remembered.

7. On a separate sheet of paper, copy the outline form shown below:

I.

    A.

    B.

    C.

    D.

Write the main idea for the previous paragraph beside Roman numeral I and the major points beside the capital letters A through D.

Because outlines have specific structures, as mentioned earlier, you'll find outlining an easy technique to learn. Always write the main idea or topic sentence of a paragraph beside a Roman numeral. Then list each of the major points—those that provide information about the topic—beside a capital letter. Subpoints describe the major points and are listed beside numbers. Finally, supporting details that define, explain, give examples of, give proofs of, or give opinions about the subtopics are placed next to lowercase letters. The paragraph's ideas are thus placed in order of importance. Look at the following example:

I. Main idea or topic sentence

    A. Major points providing information about the topic

        1. Subpoints that describe the major points

            a. Supporting details for the subpoints

Now check your answers for questions one through seven with the answers given in the Appendix at the end of this unit. How accurate are your outlines?

ACTIVITY 3.4

More Practice with Outlining

Now that you are familiar with outlining, try your hand at outlining the main ideas and major points in Paragraph One and Paragraph Two.

As you read Paragraph One and Paragraph Two, take notes on a separate sheet of paper, keeping in mind three goals as you write:

1. Your notes should be clear and concise.

2. Your notes should include the paragraphs' main ideas and major points.

3. Your notes should use shortcuts such as abbreviations, technical symbols, and personal shorthand.

Paragraph One

There are three reasons for learning to take good notes. First, note taking helps you pay attention. While you are writing, you are concentrating, and your mind wanders less. You stay with the subject. Second, note taking helps you remember. In their book *Note Taking Made Easy*, Judi Kesselman-Turkel and Franklynn Peterson state that note taking is a muscle activity, and that our muscles "remember" better than our heads. They give as an example a sixty-eight-year-old man who climbed on a bike for the first time in forty years and, after a few shaky starts, was able to ride off down to the corner. Third, note taking helps you organize ideas. You lean to sort out and write down the main points and subpoints in an organized fashion.

Paragraph Two

In order to keep your mind from wandering when taking notes, there are several steps you can take. First, you can choose your seat carefully. Sit in one of the first few rows, away from distracting doorways and windows. Next, avoid friends, especially friends who capture your attention when you should be listening. In addition, avoid thinking of personal matters. Keep your thoughts on what the speaker is saying and not on your affairs outside of class. Last, stay awake and alert. Take your coat or sweater off if you are too warm, and sit up, with your pen held ready to write. You need to be an active listener.

Now compare your notes with the answers in the Appendix at the end of this unit. How well do your notes match those outlines?

ACTIVITY 3.5

Signal Words

In this activity, you will continue to improve your note-taking skill and efficiency. Begin by reviewing your outlines from Activities 3.1, 3.3, and 3.4, and add three new note-taking terms to your vocabulary: signal words, full signals, and half signals.

Signal words are extremely helpful tools for picking out important details. They serve as flags to indicate main points in sentences or paragraphs. There are two types of signal words: full signals and half signals. *Full signals* are obvious flags, words such as *the first, the second,* and *the third. Half signals* are less obvious; they are words such as *the next, the last, in summary,* and *therefore.*

After writing these terms and their definitions in your notes, look back at More Practice with Outlining (Activity 3.4) and list on a separate sheet of paper the full signals used in Paragraph One and Paragraph Two. Can you find any half signals? List them. Check your answers with those in the Appendix at the end of this unit.

ACTIVITY 3.6

Patterning

In Activity 3.6 you will learn when and how to use the patterning method of note taking. You may discover that you are already using patterning to write flowcharts in your biology, math, or computer lab classes. Sometimes concepts are clearer and information is easier to remember when drawn as a picture rather than written as an outline. In addition, when it's time to review, simple diagrams are easy to understand.

On a separate sheet of paper, practice the patterning method of note taking by drawing three generations of your own family tree. Choose either your mother or father's side of the family and list your grandparents' names at the top of your paper. Below their names, list the names of their children (your parents, aunts, and uncles). At the bottom of your family tree, add your own name, as well as the names of your brothers, sisters, and cousins. The basic shape of your three-generation family tree pattern will look like the one following, with variations, of course, based on the number of children in each generation.

———————

——————— ——————— ———————

——————— ——————— ——————— ——————— ——————— ———————

Can you think of any other classes besides the three previously mentioned in which it would be best for you to take notes using the patterning method?

ACTIVITY 3.7

Listing

In Activity 3.7, the focus is on listing, a third method of note taking that is extremely straightforward. Listing is an appropriate form of note taking for such classes as history, when dates and important events must be learned, or classes that involve a lot of vocabulary terms and definitions.

When you use this method in class, listen carefully as your instructor lectures, and then build your list. If your source of information is the text or other printed material rather than your instructor's lecture, read carefully and be guided by signal words and key phrases.

To give you practice, your instructor may read a paragraph in class, asking you to use listing to take notes. If he or she does not do this, set up your own notes by listing the important events coming up for you this week. Begin with a heading such as "Events" and follow with a numbered list.

Events

1.
2.
3.
4.

Were you aware that you really do use three methods for taking notes: outlining, patterning, and listing? Did you realize that different subjects require different note-taking techniques?

Highlighting

A fourth method of note taking is highlighting. A highlighter is a marking pen available where school supplies are sold. It allows you to highlight (draw a line over) any key words or phrases you wish to note or emphasize. The ink of the highlighter is light enough to read through.

As a note-taking technique, highlighting saves you writing time and emphasizes key information to review as you study for a test. The obvious disadvantage, of course, is that you must own your own book or other written material in order to use the method.

To practice highlighting, use the highlighter marking pen to draw a line through (or identify) the most important points in a set of your notes—the points your instructor might include on your next test. You will find it much easier to study from a set of highlighted notes than from notes in which every word seems to be as important as the next one.

Margin Notes

In addition to outlining, patterning, listing, and highlighting, you need to know another time-saving method for note taking. However, you can use this method *only* when you own your text or are allowed to write on the material on which you must take notes. If writing in the book or on the material itself is permitted, you can take margin notes.

When you use margin notes as your form of note taking, you write down key points in the margin of your book as you read. Margin notes are convenient, providing you with a sufficient set of notes for reviewing at test time.

To practice taking margin notes, choose a set of notes from one of your other classes. Notes from a history, geography, or literature class would work well, as would notes from any other class where the information is fairly detailed. Highlight the main ideas. Then in the margin of your notes, beside the major points, write one to four key words that identify those major points. Now try looking at your margin notes as cues and reciting the major points they represent. Do you see what an important review technique taking margin notes can be at exam time?

Streamlining

Now that you have five methods of note taking to draw from, let's look at some methods of making note taking easier for you. Do you feel as if you are writing a book as you try to keep up with your instructor's lecture? If so, you need to learn some shortcuts—some ways to streamline your note taking.

As you read "Streamline Your Note Taking," take notes on each of the streamlining techniques. Then, to help you remember what you have read, illustrate each technique with at least three of your own examples.

Streamline Your Note Taking

When you think of streamlining your note taking, you probably think of taking shortcuts such as writing abbreviations in your notes whenever possible. Here are some abbreviations you may already be using:

subj. for *subject*   *dept.* for *department*

Nov. for *November*   *assn.* for *association*

But there are more ways you can streamline your note taking. Other practical techniques and examples are listed below.

1. Leave periods off abbreviations.

    ex for *example*   *no* for *number*

    st for *street*   *dif* for *different*

2. Use common symbols.

    & for *and*   *+* for *plus* or *positive*

    × for *times (multiplication)*   *#* for *number*

3. Eliminate vowels. If you are unfamiliar with conventional shorthand, the no-vowel system may save you when you have an instructor who has a very rapid speaking style. Try to read the following set of notes taken using the no-vowel technique:

    Ths prgrph ws wrttn n th "n vwl" nd th "bbrvtd" tchnq. Nt ll stdnts lk 2 tk nts ths wy, bt t wrks wll 4 sm. F y cn rd ths, y ndrstnd th mssg.

4. Use word beginnings. Many of you use this technique when you abbreviate.

    intro for *introduction*   *com* for *committee*

    info for *information*   *rep* for *representative*

5. Add *s* to abbreviations to form plurals.

    exs for *examples*   *abbs* for *abbreviations*

    mos for *months*   *yrs* for *years*

6. Use personal shorthand. Make up abbreviations that are meaningful to you. They need not make sense to other people; if you understand them and they save you time, they are valuable. Did you, for example, use *NT* instead of *note taking* anywhere?

    w/ for *with*   *4* for *four* or *for*

    w/o for *without*   *B4* for *before*

Review

Unit 3

On a separate sheet of paper, complete the following to see if you can recall the major points presented in Unit 3.

I. True-False (1–10)

Number your paper from one to ten. Write *true* if the statement is true; write *false* if the statement is false.

1. In order to take good notes, you must concentrate on your instructor's lecture. To do this, you might have to choose a seat away from friends.
2. It is important to review notes soon after taking them.
3. Good notes include all the important points, but they also include some unimportant points.
4. You should choose one system of note taking and stick to that; it is never necessary to use more than one system.
5. In taking notes, you look for the main ideas, which are the points the author is trying to make.
6. The main idea appears in only one position in the paragraph; you will always find it in the first sentence.
7. Note taking is a muscle activity; the muscles you use as you write help you remember the material.
8. Signal words may or may not help you in taking notes.
9. *First, second, third,* and so on are called *half signals.*
10. To use margin notes or highlighting as your note-taking techniques, you have to own your textbook.

II. Five Methods of Note Taking (11–15)

Number from eleven to fifteen. Briefly explain or illustrate with a drawing the five methods of note taking.

11. Outlining
12. Listing
13. Patterning
14. Margin notes
15. Highlighting

III. Listing (16–30)

Number from sixteen to thirty. List five ways to streamline your note taking and give two examples of each.

16–18. First streamlining technique and two examples.
19–21. Second streamlining technique and two examples.

22–24. Third streamlining technique and two examples.

25–27. Fourth streamlining technique and two examples.

28–30. Fifth streamlining technique and two examples.

IV. Short Essay (31–32)

31. Describe the method of note taking you find the most useful and explain why it is your preference.

32. Explain what you found to be the most valuable information in this unit and how knowing it will help you.

Answers for Activities 3.1, 3.3, 3.4, and 3.5

Activity 3.1: Evaluating Your Present System

I.   Develop good NT skills
  A. Concentrate on lecture
  B. Pick out imp. pts. (exclude unimp. pts.)
  C. Develop system
  D. Streamline NT (so imp. pts. not omitted)
  E. Review notes

Activity 3.3: Outlining

1. Main idea: "One of the most important skills to develop early in your school career is that of taking notes in an organized manner."

2. Location: first sentence

3. Main idea: "One of the first steps toward developing an organized note-taking system is being able to recognize the author's main idea."

4. Location: first sentence

5. Main idea: I. Main idea or topic sentence found in a number of positions

6. Major points: A. First sentence
  B. Last sentence
  C. First and last sentence
  D. Between first and last sentences
  E. Split—part in one sentence and part in another
  F. Not stated at all

7. Main idea: I. Most widely used method: the outline
  Major points: A. Format is specific structure
  B. It is concise
  C. Notes well organized
  D. Notes easily remembered

Activity 3.4: More Practice with Outlining

Paragraph One

I.   Three reasons for good notes
  A. helps pay attention
  B. helps remember
  C. helps organize ideas

Paragraph Two

I.   Steps to keep mind from wandering
  A. choose seat carefully
  B. avoid friends
  C. avoid personal matters
  D. stay awake and alert

Activity 3.5: Signal Words

1. Full Signals, Paragraph One: *First; Second; Third*
2. Full Signals, Paragraph Two: *First*
3. Half Signals, Paragraph Two: *Next; In addition; Last*

Taking Tests

What words come into your mind when tests are mentioned? Success or failure? A's or F's? Do you grow numb with panic and dread the thought of a marathon study session late at night? Maybe you feel calm and confident and look forward to doing well. Think about your attitude toward taking tests.

As you already know, tests play an important part in determining your final grades in class. Because of this, it is essential that you know not only how to study for tests, but also how to take tests.

What do you know about preparing for and taking tests? Experts report that you have command of only 20 percent of the material when you cram the night before an exam, and that you will probably experience fatigue, loss of concentration, and test anxiety when you study that way. Do you cram or do you review briefly for several nights prior to the test?

Perhaps your difficulty is not with studying for the test, but with taking it. You become so nervous that your find it hard to concentrate on what you know. In this unit you'll find a list of simple techniques to help you eliminate test anxiety.

Once you study your notes and text and conquer your nervousness, all you have to do is sit down with the test and begin answering the questions, right? Not exactly. When you take a test, you show your instructor how much you know about the subject covered, of course. But you *also* show your instructor what you know about test-taking procedures. You may be surprised to learn that there are specific strategies for taking specific kinds of tests; for example, multiple-choice tests require a different strategy from true-false tests.

Do you want to improve your test scores? Study carefully the information in this unit regarding preparing for tests, reducing test-taking anxiety, and taking tests. Your efforts here will earn you better test scores.

Memory

To learn how to study for tests, you need to learn the basic principles concerning how your memory works and why you cannot always remember material. It is frustrating to study for several hours the night before a test, only to find you don't remember several important things—even though you can sometimes remember the page they were on. Or, worse yet, you manage to remember those elusive things just as you hand in the test and leave the room.

There is a simple explanation for this, and it has to do with how your memory works. Start a section of notes entitled "Test Taking." Then read the selection entitled "How Your Memory Works." As you read, write down what goes on in each layer of memory.

How Your Memory Works

Test! Mention the word, and some people instantly feel fearful and tense. Yet, if you take time to prepare ahead for tests, you don't have to experience such stress.

In order to understand how to prepare for tests, it is helpful to know *how* you remember things. In *How to Study in High School*, Jean Snider describes the four memory layers in your brain. Figure 4.1 shows this concept visually.

Layer One   Layer One is for short-term memory. If an instructor gives you a definition and you can repeat it immediately, Layer One is at work. But if you are asked to give that definition the next day, chances are good that you won't be able to remember it. Short-term memory is exactly that; it is useful for many daily, routine things such as making telephone calls or following directions immediately after they are given, but it is *not* useful for passing tests.

Layer Two   According to Snider, Layer Two is for slightly longer retention. If your instructor announces a test will be given four days from now, and he or she repeats the announcement several times, the message goes from Layer One to Layer Two of memory. It is the *repetition of information* that forces it from Layer One to Layer Two, yet Layer Two is still not very reliable. You will study the test material the night before the test. But during the test, some—if not many—of the answers will escape you.

When you spend the night before a test cramming and then can't remember the answers for the test—even though you can picture the page they were on—the explanation for your memory lapse is simple. The information you studied only went as far as Layer Two.

Layer Three   Layer Three offers good retention, providing you repeat the information several times and write it down. Your writing creates a visual image for your mind to remember.

FIGURE 4.1
The Four Memory
Layers of the Brain

Say, for example, your instructor provides you with terms and their definitions, and you repeat them to yourself several times and then write them down. You will have forced that information into Layer Three, and you should expect fairly good recall for the test.

Now you know why it is necessary to take notes on material you need to remember, why a written sample test that you construct prior to the real test is valuable, and why writing down key words as you review is beneficial. Your muscles help you remember as your write, and your memory sees the material on paper again and takes a picture of it.

Layer Four   Snider says the passage of time is a must for forcing material into the fourth layer of memory. You must *repeat* those definitions each night over a period of time and write them down in order for material to reach Layer Four. But once there, the material is locked in long-term storage.

Smart test takers start reviewing for a test at least three or four days before it will be given. Cramming the night before is not reliable learning. It won't give you the results you want.

> **Summary**
>
> **Layer One:** no repetition—short-term, unreliable memory.
>
> **Layer Two:** some repetition—slightly longer retention, but not reliable.
>
> **Layer Three:** repeating and writing down the information—fairly good retention.
>
> **Layer Four:** repeating and writing down information over a period of three to six days—excellent retention.[1]

ACTIVITY 4.2

How Do You Prepare for Tests?

Now that you know how your memory works, find out how you can organize your study time to suit your memory. In preparing for a test, do you reread the chapter the night before the test? Perhaps you review your notes or answer the questions at the end of the chapter. Have you ever tried to create a sample test for yourself or have someone quiz you?

Using a separate sheet of paper, make a list of the steps you take in preparing for an exam. List everything you do and when you do it. Then, if your instructor allows time, compare your list with your classmates' lists. Brainstorm as many different ways to prepare for tests as you can, and write down each of the methods on your sheet of paper.

If you are doing this exercise as an independent study, interview five successful students you know to find out how they prepare for exams. Or, interview five different instructors for their ideas on studying for tests. Whichever method you choose, be sure to include the results of your interviews in your notes. You will be sharing these results with your instructor.

ACTIVITY 4.3

How Should You Prepare for Tests?

You know how you prepare for tests, and now you know how your classmates go about it. How do your methods compare? Think about some of the new ideas or techniques for preparation that you learned from your peers. Based on what you know about their methods, can you see why one student scores well on tests, while another scores poorly?

The exercise should make this much clear: Rereading the entire chapter the night before is a waste of time. Your memory can't possibly absorb and retain all that material in one night. Instead, anticipate questions you think will be asked and review their answers three to six days in advance of the test date.

Now, compare your list of preparation techniques with the list that follows; add any suggestions your list did not include. When you finish, you will have a list of study techniques that, if used, will enable you to do well on any exam.

---

[1]Figure 4.1 and Summary, Snider, Jean. *How to Study in High School*. Providence, RI: Jamestown Publishers, 1983, p. 36.

Preparing for Tests

1. Ask or anticipate *what material* will be covered on the test and write it down. You can accomplish this by doing the following:
   - Look at tests from other chapters and ask your instructor, or students who have taken the class before, what material might be included.
   - Listen to verbal clues in class. (Verbal clues are like signal words; they flag what your instructor considers to be important and may be included on the test. Verbal clues are phrases such as *be sure to remember that…*; *take notes on this…*; and *you may see this again….*)
   - Pay attention to what your instructor writes on the chalkboard. Write it in your notes and use your highlighter pen to emphasize it; there is a good chance questions relating to that information will be on the test.

2. Find out what *type of questions* will be on the test.
   - Use a different study technique for an essay test than for an objective test. Solving problems involves different preparation than sentence completion does.
   - Look at past tests to discover your instructor's usual test format.
   - Ask your instructor, or students who have had the class before, what types of questions will be included.
   - Listen to lectures and class discussions for clues about the kinds of questions that might be included.
   - Pay attention to the kinds of exercises you do daily in class; the test may parallel these.

3. Discover how much of the test is based on your notes.
   - Consider your instructor's attitude about note taking. Is it required or optional? This is a good clue to whether he or she will include items from the notes on the test.
   - Talk to students who have had the class before, or ask your instructor if you will be tested on the notes.
   - Analyze previous tests to determine the extent of test material drawn from notes.

4. Organize your notes and other study aids to correspond with the material you believe will be covered and the type of test to be given.
   - Gather the material you feel might be on the test (notes, chapter review, problems, etc.)
   - Highlight in your notes the key points that might be covered.
   - Use margin notes (key words written in the margin) to identify main points.
   - Write down any additional information you anticipate will be covered.

5. Avoid cramming. Keep in mind that it takes time to get material into the third and fourth layers of your memory, so begin reviewing the material three to six days prior to the test.
   - First night—skim the material.
   - Second night—skim the material, read margin notes, and recite important points aloud as you read them. (Those of you who learn best by hearing things should study that way, too. Hear yourself *say* the key points to be learned.)
   - Third night—read your margin notes (key words) and, without looking at your notes or the text, recite aloud the important points they represent.

- Fourth night—make up a sample test and answer the questions, or have someone quiz you. If you do well, you do not need to study a fifth night. If you feel you need to do better, look over the material again and repeat this process a fifth, and perhaps a sixth night.

6. Prepare yourself the night before the test.
   - Briefly review the material one more time.
   - Get adequate sleep.

7. Prepare yourself the next day.
   - Briefly review the material one more time when you wake up.
   - Eat a nutritious breakfast.
   - Get your mind and body stimulated with brief exercise (short jog, walk, push-ups) and a shower.
   - Wear something comfortable that makes you feel confident.
   - Get rid of test anxiety (see Activity 4.4).
   - Avoid drugs (drugs make you feel sluggish or nervous and affect your ability to recall and concentrate).
   - Build your self-confidence (tell yourself you have prepared will and so you will do well; a good attitude yields good results).

ACTIVITY 4.4

Test Anxiety

There are just a few minutes to wait before your instructor puts a test in front of you. Are you feeling fidgety and tense, or even sick to your stomach?

If that describes how you feel before you take a test, you probably have test anxiety. Test anxiety is common for almost everyone; even the best students have it. But if you are to do well on a test, your test anxiety must be controlled. Practicing some of the following tips can help you control your anxiety.

Read the suggestions below and, on a separate sheet of paper, write down the tips you feel will be valuable for you. Not all of these suggestions work for everyone because people have different personalities. For some, thumbing through the book prior to an exam builds confidence and reassures them that they know the material. For others, it creates panic because they are afraid they may have forgotten to study something. Those people are better off leaving their textbooks at home. Consider each suggestion, then write down only those that will work for you.

Relieving Test Anxiety

1. Get enough sleep.
2. Eat a good meal prior to the test.
   - Do not eat too much so that you feel groggy, but eat enough to provide your mind and body with the calories they need to function well.
   - Greasy and acidic food and beverages (donuts and coffee) will not provide adequate nutrition and may upset your stomach.

3. Exercise to reduce tension and stimulate thinking.
   - Exercise is a great stress reducer. Jogging, walking, mild aerobics, push-ups, and other forms of exercise not only reduce test anxiety, but stim-

ulate your mind and body to improve your ability to think and concentrate as well.

4. Take a shower.
   - Warm water relaxes some; cold water stimulates others.

5. Allow enough time to arrive at the class without hurrying.
   - Hurrying causes tension; the fear of being late builds anxiety.

6. Provide yourself with time in the classroom to relax and compose yourself.
   - Deep breathing exercises accomplish this. Take a deep breath, then another short breath, and exhale slowly.
   - Close your eyes and imagine a relaxing scene. Allow your muscles to relax. Then think about your test while you are in this relaxed state.

7. Review with your friends *or* don't review with your friends just prior to the test.
   - For some, reviewing with friends before the exam builds confidence; they feel they have command of the material. For others, it incites panic; they feel they don't know the material as well as they should.

8. Thumb through your books and notes *or* don't thumb through your books and notes just prior to the test.
   - Thumb through your notes if it builds confidence; don't look at your notes if doing so creates panic.

9. Develop a positive attitude.
   - Tell yourself you studied as well as you could have for the test and believe it. Convince yourself that others have done well on this test, and you can too.

10. Make sure you can see a clock, plan your time, and pace yourself.
    - Not knowing how much of the test-taking time has elapsed creates anxiety. Budget your time so you can answer all of the questions.

11. Choose your seat carefully.
    - Sitting near friends can be disrupting. If you see them writing furiously, it can make you nervous. If you see them handing in their papers early, you may feel compelled to do the same, and your anxiety will build.
    - Some people may read the test questions softly but audibly as they concentrate. Others may chew gum loudly. These are distractions that may annoy you and cause anxiety. Isolate yourself, if possible.

12. Begin by filling in the answers you know.
    - This builds confidence and relieves anxiety because you see that you do know the answers. Also, it may trigger recall of other answers that you had momentarily forgotten.

13. Don't panic if others are busy writing and you are not.
    - By spending time thinking, you may provide higher quality and better content answers than someone who is writing frantically.

14. Don't panic if you forget an answer.
    - Go on to other questions—the answer will probably occur to you as you continue taking the test.

15. Don't worry if others finish before you do.
    - Finishing first does not guarantee the best grade. Usually the better papers are handed in by the students who spent more time thinking about and checking over their answers before turning in their papers.

16. Don't panic if you run out of time.
   - Ask your instructors if you can stay late; many will let you do this to finish.
   - Outline essay questions you didn't have time to complete. Most instructors will give you points for outlines because they can see you knew the answers but didn't have time to write them in essay form.

ACTIVITY 4.5

Strategies for Taking Tests

Now that you know how to handle the pretest jitters, you need to consider what to do when that test is in your hands. If you are a person who gulps and says "Go for it," you are probably not getting the highest grade you could.

Or maybe you are a person who fails to read the directions on the test carefully *before* you begin writing. If, for example, you miss the words "Choose one of the following three essay questions," and you try to answer all three questions, you will probably run out of time and give incomplete answers. There are fewer unpleasant surprises when you read the directions.

Or perhaps you have been in this unfortunate situation: You are running out of test-taking time, and you still have to complete two essay questions. For the first time, you notice that they are worth twenty points each, and now you don't have enough time to give thorough answers.

Who needs to use test-taking strategies? We all do. Remember, you are not only being tested on the material, you are also being tested on how much you know about taking a test. So, to do the best you can on tests, you have to think about your own test-taking strategies. On a separate sheet of paper, list the steps or strategies you use when taking a test. After you finish, compare your list with your classmates' and, working as a class, develop a more comprehensive list. (If you are in an independent study, interview five successful students to compare your list with their lists of test-taking strategies, adding any new ones to your list.)

Now, compare your comprehensive list of test-taking strategies with the following list and add to your list any techniques that you had not previously included.

Test-Taking Strategies

1. Arrive early.
   - Allow enough time to compose your thoughts, sharpen your concentration, organize your materials, and relax.
2. Bring all materials to class with you.
   - Bring pencils or pens, paper, erasers, calculator (and extra batteries), and any other materials necessary for taking that test.
3. Listen carefully to your instructor's directions and comments.
   - Instructors frequently announce changes in the test or emphasize instructions you may overlook; pay attention to what they have to say.
4. Look over the test, reading the directions carefully.

- If you don't answer the questions as instructed, you may lose points. Even an instruction as simple as "Answer with the complete words *true* or *false*" can cost you points if you don't follow it.

5. Budget your time.
   - You should spend less time on a five-point question than you spend on a twenty-point essay question.
   - Determine the amount of time you have to take the test and the value and difficulty of each section. Then budget your time accordingly.
   - If you have twenty questions and sixty minutes, spend three minutes per question; if you have four questions, each worth twenty-five points, and sixty minutes, spend fifteen minutes on each question.
   - If you don't complete a question in the time you allotted, leave it and come back to complete your answer *only* if you have extra time.

6. Write down key facts or formulas in the margin.
   - This is a safeguard against forgetting key information if you get nervous.

7. Look for qualifying words.
   - Words such as *never, always, rarely, often, seldom, many,* and so on determine the correct answer.

8. Answer easy questions first.
   - Answering the easy questions first will reduce anxiety, build confidence, trigger recall of other answers and the material you studied, and give you points immediately. You will be able to say to yourself, "This isn't so bad after all; I'm going to do well." You will approach the test with more vigor and confidence. Tackling the tough questions first may make you feel unprepared and uninformed, setting you up for failure.

9. Answer objective questions before essay questions.
   - Completing the true-false, multiple-choice, and matching questions may provide you with answers to the essay questions.

10. If you don't know the answer, make a mark next to that question and try to complete it later.
    - Often, answers you can't recall will occur to you as you take the test. If you have provided your memory with enough information, you will think of the answer. If not, don't panic—even the best students face this situation. Neatly write down the most suitable answer you can think of and continue.

11. Guess at answers you don't know, unless there is a penalty for guessing.
    - On true-false questions, you have a 50 percent chance of guessing right; on multiple-choice questions, you often have a 25 percent chance of being correct. Don't pass up potential points by leaving the question blank.
    - The only time you are penalized for guessing is when, in scoring the results, the number wrong is to be subtracted from the number correct. Not very many instructors use this technique, however. Most subtract the number wrong from the total possible.

12. Change answers *only* if you are sure they are wrong.
    - Most sources say first instincts are usually correct; however, sometimes you will recall information that will lead you to believe your first answer was incorrect. If so, make the change.

13. Use all the time allowed.
   - If you finish early, check your paper for errors.
   - Look again at the directions; did you follow them correctly?

Tricks for Taking Tests

Now that you know there are definite techniques for taking tests and have learned the best way to approach tests in general, you are ready for some details. There are specific tricks you can use to take a true-false, multiple-choice, or essay test. If you don't know these tricks, you are at a definite disadvantage, and your grades will reflect it.

To your notes on test taking, add a page labeled "Tricks for Taking Tests." List the following types of tests and, beneath each, write any tricks you already use when taking that kind of test. Leave plenty of space to add additional tricks in each section. The types of tests include true-false, multiple-choice, matching, completion, and essay.

Compare your list of tricks with those of your classmates, add to your list, and then compare your comprehensive list with the one that follows. If you are in an independent study, go directly to the following list and fill in the tricks you are missing.

Test-Taking Tricks

True-False.
1. Beware of qualifying words.
   - Words such as *always, all, none, never,* and so on usually will make a statement false. Very few facts are absolute, and one exception to such a question will make it false.
   - Words such as *usually, sometimes, generally,* and *frequently* will usually make a statement true.
2. Look at the length of the statement.
   - In order for a statement to be true, all parts of it must be true. The longer the statement, the more room there is for a false segment.
3. Be aware of false logic.
   - Two statements that are true may be linked with a word that makes them false. Watch for that connecting word. For example: "The U.S. space shuttle program is famous because there was a shuttle crash." The shuttle program *is* famous and there *was* a shuttle crash, but the crash is not what made the program famous. The *because* makes the statement false.
4. Guess if you don't know the answer.
   - You have a 50 percent change of answering correctly, so take the chance.

Multiple-Choice.
1. Eliminate the answer(s) that is (are) obviously incorrect first.
   - Instructors usually structure a multiple-choice question with one statement that is obviously incorrect. Pick out that statement.

2. Read the question carefully.
   - The question may say "Which is *not* an example of…," "Which is the *incorrect* answer…," or "Choose the *best* answer.…"
3. Read all the choices.
   - You may believe that the first option is the correct one. Read the remaining options anyway. The most correct answer may be further down the list.
4. Pay attention to *all of the above* questions.
   - "All of the above" is frequently the correct answer when it appears as a choice. To determine the extent of the students' knowledge, instructors occasionally like to list several correct answers and conclude with *all of the above*.
   - If two statements appear to be true, you are unsure about the third statement, and the fourth choice is *all of the above*, then the fourth choice is often correct.
5. Look for the longest answer.
   - The longest multiple-choice answer is frequently the correct one. The answer is carefully constructed to be complete.

Matching.
1. Read the list on the right first.
   - First, read the list on the right, which contains the answer choices, so that you are aware of all the possibilities for answers.
   - Your instructor may have written one answer that appears to be correct near the top of the list, but a more correct answer may come lower in the list. If you do not read the entire list first, you will not know all the options.
2. If you are unsure of an answer, mark that questions and return to it later.
   - Solve questions you are unsure of by process of elimination after you have finished using the answers you are sure are correct.

Completion (Fill-in-the-Blank).
1. Reread the question several times.
   - Completion is popular with instructors because they can simply write down a statement and leave out a key word(s).
   - In rereading the question several times, the key word(s) omitted may, because of the repetition, suddenly occur to you.
2. Look for context clues.
   - Often within a completion there are clues to the correct answer. If the blank you are to complete is at the end of the statement, you have more clues to use than if the blank falls at the beginning of the statement.
3. A and *an* are context clues.
   - If *an* appears, the word following must begin with a vowel.
4. Look at the verb in the sentence.
   - If it is singular, the subject or answer must be singular. If it is plural, the subject or answer must be plural.
5. Mark the statements you cannot complete and return to them.
   - Recall of the information you need may be triggered by completing other statements.

Essay.

1. Plan your time carefully.
   - It is easy to lose track of time when writing an essay question response; budget your time and stick to your budget.

2. Know your facts.
   - In objective tests, such as multiple-choice and matching, you have to select the correct answer from other choices given. In answering essay questions, you must frame your own answer, and to do it correctly, you must know the information needed.

3. Organize or outline your answers.
   - In the margin, on the back of the paper, or in the space for the answer, write an outline first. List the facts and number them according to the order in which you wish to discuss them.
   - Outlines enable you to present all the key information in an abbreviated, organized manner. You are less likely to omit important information or ramble if you outline first.
   - If you have the key information in an outline, but run out of time in writing your essay, most instructors will give you partial credit for the outline. They can see you knew the information.
   - Answers presented in a helter-skelter fashion do not represent the logic, reasoning, and organization instructors look for in an essay answer. If your essay is not organized, you will probably lose points.

4. Understand the test terminology.
   - Be certain that you understand what is being asked when the essay question instructs you to compare and/or contrast. *Evaluate* is different from *analyze*, and *interpret* is different from *illustrate*. Activity 4.7 will give you some practice in reviewing these terms.

5. Write neatly, leave suitable margins, and provide space between answers.
   - A good answer is not good at all if it is illegible. Most instructors penalize for sloppy work and look more favorably on work that is neatly done.

6. Write using complete sentences.
   - Essays require complete sentences. Hurried thoughts scribbled in brief do not comply with the more formal essay structure.

7. Restate the question in the first sentence of your essay.
   - Don't stumble around. Get right to the point. If the question is "Discuss the seven ways to improve your study setting," your answer should begin with "The first of the seven ways to improve my study setting involves...."
   - Your instructor will know you are going to be concise and logical and will begin with a favorable attitude toward your answer.

8. Use transition words to emphasize your organization.
   - Tie your thoughts and concepts together with transitions such as the following: *for example, because, for this reason, however, likewise, in summary, ultimately.* There are many transition words you can choose.

9. Keep your answer simple and concise.
   - Avoid flowery language that is meant to pad an answer with words but no information. Instructors can see through that.

10. Identify the favorite concepts of your instructor and use them.
   - If your instructor is sure that TV has ruined the study habits of millions of students, and he or she seems to dwell on that concept, use it in your discussion if it applies.
11. Include a conclusion or summary.
   - Restate your major points in your summary or conclusion. This step will reassure your instructor of your logic, organization, and key points.

Test Terminology

ACTIVITY 4.7

One of the main points mentioned previously involved knowing what type of answer was being asked for on an essay test. *Trace, discuss, justify, review, illustrate*—are you familiar with the subtle differences in test terminology? You can write a lengthy essay answer full of facts and logic, but if you did not address the question, you may score no points at all.

Consider the following terms typically found in essay exams. On a separate sheet of paper, list each term and an explanation of what is required when answering that type of essay question. If you don't know or are not sure what the term means, leave the space next to the term blank and fill in the correct answer later.

A. list	E. summarize	I. compare
B. outline	F. trace	J. contrast
C. define	G. describe	K. discuss
D. criticize	H. diagram	L. justify

How did you do? Sometimes just knowing what answers are suitable for particular terms found on essay tests can add points to your total score. (Compare your list of terms and definitions with those found at the end of this unit in the Appendix.) Correct any errors you made and add those answers you omitted. This list of terms should be added to your section of notes on Test Taking.

Reviewing Your Test

ACTIVITY 4.8

Let's assume you have prepared properly for an upcoming test, reduced the test anxiety successfully, followed the strategies you learned for taking tests, and applied the tricks for taking specific kinds of tests. Now you have the completed, corrected test in your hands.

Do you trash it? File it? Frame it? You should analyze it—not by quickly glancing through it, but by spending time studying it. To complete this unit on test taking successfully, you need to analyze the completed, corrected product and use that information to prepare for future exams.

What kind of questions did your instructor include?

What material did your instructor cover—textbook, lecture notes, exercises from class, or some combination?

What was your instructor looking for in your answers?

What were your strengths in answering the questions?

What were your weak areas?

What test-taking strategies do you need to use again next time?

What changes do you need to make?

Use a test that you have taken recently, either from this class or another, and analyze it. On a separate sheet of paper, using the test you have supplied, answer the questions from the preceding list.

On a separate sheet of paper, answer the following questions. Try to remember the main points and tips given in Unit 4.

I. True-False (1–20)

Number from one to twenty. Write *true* if the statement is true and *false* if the statement is false.

1. When studying, repetition (repeating things several times) is not necessary for remembering things.

2. The passing of time is necessary for forcing material into your memory so that you can remember it for a long period of time.

3. You must repeat material several times *and* write it down in order to remember things well; it is not enough to simply repeat it.

4. It takes approximately three to six nights prior to an essay test for proper review of the material.

5. It takes only one night prior to an objective test for proper review of the material since objective tests are somewhat easier.

6. It is always enough preparation when studying for a test to review your notes and go over chapter headings.

7. Wearing something that makes them feel comfortable and confident helps some people do better on exams.

8. It is helpful when beginning a test to write down important facts or a formula you might otherwise forget as you take the test.

9. Answer the easy questions last and tackle the hard questions first. Hard questions are usually worth more points and you need to be sure you complete them.

10. Answer the essay questions before the objective questions. Essay questions are usually worth more points and you need to be sure you complete them.

11. When answering essay questions, outline your responses first, but do not write the outline down on your test paper.

12. Before beginning a test, budget your time. You should spend about the same amount of time on each question.

13. On true-false questions, you should generally choose the answer that was your first instinct. It is usually correct.

14. On multiple-choice tests you can usually eliminate one answer as being incorrect.

15. When taking a matching test, read the left-hand column first and then choose the correct answer from the right-hand column.

16. You should not guess on fill-in-the-blank questions.

17. You can reduce test-taking stress by doing deep-breathing exercises.

18. Some people reduce test-taking stress by thumbing through their textbooks just prior to exam time.

19. For many people, coffee and a donut are all they need for breakfast, even on the morning of a test day.

20. Exercise not only reduces stress, it also stimulates thinking.

II. Matching (21–30)

Number from twenty-one to thirty. Match the following descriptions with the test terminologies they describe.

21.	Give differences only.	A.	list
22.	Give meanings but no details.	B.	outline
23.	Give details, progress, or history from beginning to end.	C.	define
24.	Prove or give reasons.	D.	criticize
25.	Provide a numbered list.	E.	trace
26.	Give details or a verbal picture.	F.	describe
27.	Give reasons pro and con with details.	G.	compare
28.	Give both similarities and differences.	H.	contrast
29.	Give a series of main ideas supported by secondary ideas.	I.	discuss
		J.	justify
30.	Give your own judgment or opinion based on reasons.	K.	summarize

III. Listing (31–37)

Number from thirty-one to thirty-seven, and list seven steps in preparing for a test.

IV. Essay (38)

38. Choose *one* of the following essay questions and answer it using the essay format discussed in Unit 4.

A. Discuss test anxiety. Begin by defining it and then describe ways that you can control it. (First identify controls that work for you, and then identify additional controls that may work for someone else.)

B. Describe the steps in taking a test. Include as many steps as you can.

C. Discuss the four layers of memory. Include the function of each layer, how you get information into that layer, and which layer you should use for test-taking preparation.

Answers for Activity 4.7

Test Terminology

Term.	Answer Would Include:
A. list	a numbered list of words, sentences, or comments
B. outline	a series of main ideas supported by secondary ideas, etc.
C. define	meanings but no details; this is often a matter of giving a memorized definition
D. criticize	your own judgment or opinion based on reasons; good and bad points should be included
E. summarize	a brief, condensed account of the main ideas; omit details
F. trace	details, progress, or history of the topic from beginning to end
G. describe	details or a verbal picture of the topic
H. diagram	a chart, graph, or geometric drawing with labels and a brief explanation, if needed
I. compare	both the similarities and the differences
J. contrast	the differences only
K. discuss	reasons pro and con with details
L. justify	prove or give reasons

Improving Your Understanding

You have just closed your book after reading an entire assignment that you thought you understood. But already your mind is blank, and you can't remember anything about what you read. Now you will have to spend more time rereading those pages or, worse still, the chapter.

If this situation is all too familiar, you'll be glad to hear that you can improve your comprehension. There are strategies to give you some "mental hooks" on which to hang the information that is vital to your success in school and life. Learning these comprehension survival skills will take effort, practice, and determination, but you cannot overlook them if you want to be a successful student.

To begin improving comprehension, first learn how to recognize main ideas. If you can identify the main ideas—and remember them—in the material you read, you have almost won the comprehension battle.

Finding the main idea may be difficult for two reasons: First, you may not know what a main idea is. The main idea is simply the point the author is trying to get across. It is the gist or substance of a paragraph; the thought that all the other details or pieces of information help support or illustrate. As you read, ask yourself, "What point is the author making in this paragraph?" The answer to your question is the author's main idea.

The second reason recognizing the main idea may be difficult is that you don't know where in the material to look for it. Is it in the first or last sentence, or is it sandwiched somewhere in the middle of the paragraph? Authors can place their paragraph's main idea anywhere. Look for it to come in the first sentence, a middle sentence, or the last sentence. Or, find it in the first sentence and see it restated in the last sentence, in a middle sentence or not stated at all! Think of finding the material's main idea as participating in a scavenger hunt; you know what kind of thing to look for, but not exactly where to find it. You'll have to actively search for it.

This unit will help you develop your ability to recognize main ideas. You will begin by selecting the key words in a sentence, then move on to identifying the main idea in a paragraph. Once you can do that, you will practice recognizing main ideas in longer works. Your goals, then, are:

1. to learn to identify key words in a sentence;
2. to learn to identify the main idea in a paragraph; and
3. to learn to identify the major points of a longer selection.

ACTIVITY 5.1

Recognizing Key Words in a Sentence

To find the main idea in a paragraph, you have to begin by recognizing key words in a sentence. Key words are the important or essential words—the words that determine the meaning of the sentence. Activity 5.1 will give you practice in picking out key words.

On a separate sheet of paper, number from one to ten, skipping every other line. Read the following sentences and list their key words on your paper. The first sentence is done as a sample.

1. You are to report to the principal's office immediately and take your books with you.

    Answer: You report principal's office immediately take books
2. The tryouts for the fall play will be this Thursday evening at 8:00 P.M. in Room 208.
3. The flood destroyed homes, bridges, and roads as it swept furiously through the canyon.
4. The Fourth of July is a special day in the United States because on that date the nation celebrates its independence.
5. Many states experience wide temperature changes during the four seasons.
6. Susan Smith and Joan Vickers ran for president of their class, and Joan won.
7. The football championship was a tie between North and South High Schools.
8. Peer pressure is often a problem for preteens and teens.
9. Regular attendance in school is important if you want to get good grades.
10. Concentration is required as you read these sentences if you wish to identify the key words.

ACTIVITY 5.2

Recognizing Main Ideas in a Paragraph

Once you have developed the ability to identify key words in a sentence, you will find it easier to pick out the main idea in a paragraph. Again, the main idea is the point the author is making; all other sentences in the paragraph work to support or develop this main idea.

On a separate sheet of paper, list the key or main idea in each of the following paragraphs. The first paragraph is done as a sample.

Paragraph One

Young people are faced with many decisions today. They have to choose between drinking or not drinking alcohol. They have to choose between smoking or not smoking. Some of them even choose between chewing tobacco or not chewing tobacco. For many, the decisions are difficult ones.

Answer: Young people are faced with many decisions today.

Paragraph Two

If it is sunny outside, do you feel cheerful? If it is rainy, do you feel depressed? Does the weather affect you? Hot weather makes some people irritable. Others complain that humid weather makes them tired.

Paragraph Three

Most schools are required to offer courses in English, math, science, social studies, and physical education. Schools also offer classes in art, industrial arts, computer science, music, foreign languages, agriculture, business, and auto mechanics. They provide opportunities before, during, and after school for sports, clubs, and other activities. Schools counsel students, reward students, correct students, and even feed students, in addition to educating them. Schools serve a variety of needs.

Paragraph Four

Students have many opportunities to become a part of a group and to acquire a sense of belonging. They can try out for sports teams or become a team manager. They can audition for a play or sing in a choir. They can participate on the speech team or be a member of the chess club. They can join a religious group or become a peer counselor. There are many ways to get involved.

Paragraph Five

We began the day by touring the Museum of Natural History. After we had lunch, we visited the Museum of Fine Arts and had snacks on the top floor terrace. Next, we went to the Planetarium and finished with dinner at a fancy downtown restaurant.

Paragraph Six

By now you know several things about the main idea of a paragraph. You know the main idea summarizes or expresses the major point being made in the paragraph. You know the main idea can be found at the beginning of a paragraph, at the end of a paragraph, within a paragraph, or at the beginning *and* end of a paragraph. You know most paragraphs have a main idea that is stated, but you also know that the main idea can be omitted and only implied. Finally, you know that finding the main idea in the paragraph is one of the first steps toward good comprehension.

ACTIVITY 5.3

Recognizing Main Ideas in an Article

Now work with an article that contains many paragraphs. Read "Use of Credit" and write down on a separate sheet of paper what you consider to be the main ideas of the article. As you read, remember to ask yourself the following: What points are the authors making in this selection?

Next, focus on the supporting details in the article. List the advantages and disadvantages of credit.

Use of Credit

Credit is one money management tool. It is considered a tool because it can be used to realize goals that you have decided to emphasize. Credit can expand buying power and simplify recordkeeping; however, if credit purchases are not related to income and payments are missed, the result is a poor credit history and financial worries. In some cases use of too much credit may lead to bankruptcy.

Credit use can be inexpensive or costly. Many credit grantors do not charge interest for credit card purchases when the balance is paid in full each month. Other types of credit, such as consumer loans, may add interest charges of 36 percent per year. You can decide which type fits your needs.

Consider both the advantages and disadvantages of using credit. As you think about the ways that credit plays a role in your money management program, you may decide to either expand or reduce your use of credit. Credit decisions are very individual and can have beneficial as well as disastrous consequences. This means that you will have to make a conscious decision about how to use credit.

Advantages.   Young people often have greater needs than current income. Credit may be the way to make large purchases such as a home, education, furniture, and appliances.

By borrowing to buy an item, people will have the use of it before they own it. A good example is an automobile—few people can afford to pay cash, and yet most people considered this an essential purchase.

Sometimes the only way to cope with an emergency is to borrow to pay expenses, especially when emergency medical care is needed or unemployment reduces income.

Credit can be used for investments. A house is important for shelter and in recent years has been an excellent investment. Most people usually do not have enough cash to buy a home without credit.

Credit allows people to enjoy conveniences today. Some families find washing clothes at home rather than at a laundromat a real time-saver. A loan may provide an opportunity to add a second bathroom to a home with a growing family.

Using a credit card while traveling can be a great convenience over carrying large amounts of money or trying to cash personal checks.

For people who find it difficult to save for purchases, credit payments may be considered a form of forced savings.

There are also tax advantages for borrowers. Mortgage interest is tax deductible for those who itemize expenses.

Disadvantages.   Consumers may overspend. One-third of all U.S. households have bank credit cards, and 70 percent of those who use cards generally pay only the minimum monthly payment. We have the tendency to spend more money when we charge items compared to paying cash. Researchers concerned with department store purchases found that the average cash sale was $8.25, the average store credit card purchase was $15.93, and the average bank card sale was $20.47. Many people have more than one bank card. When their line of credit on one card is used up, they switch to another card.

Credit has been relatively easy to get, and consumers have found themselves adding credit card to credit card and loan on top of loan to their outstanding debt.

People overlook the fact that when they buy an item they are paying twice for it, first for the item itself and second for the credit they use. Finance charges add to the price of goods and services. For example, we'll assume that a loan is for a travel trailer. The cost of the trailer is $5,000. The credit charges add an additional $902.32 to the price. Credit ties up future income, which means less flexibility for tomorrow's purchases.

Recognizing Sequence by Making Lists

If organization is a strong skill of yours, sequencing (placing things in order) may not seem difficult. If, on the other hand, you often ask yourself "What shall I do first?" or "Why are things so disorganized?" this group of exercises will help you begin thinking sequentially. Remembering becomes much easier when you can arrange the information you read in some sort of order, and catching on to the sequence will improve your comprehension skills as well. Your goal is to read and place things in your mind and memory in logical order.

Making Lists

Determine a heading for each of the following sentences. On a separate sheet of paper, write the heading and list the items in the sentence sequentially as they are presented. The first is done for you.

1. My grocery list included apples, flour, salt, and sugar.
   Answer: Groceries
       1. apples
       2. flour
       3. salt
       4. sugar

2. As he entered the room, he stopped with mouth wide open and eyes rounded in horror.

3. Mr. Smith presented two band awards this year: the Spirit Award and the prestigious John Phillip Sousa Award.

4. The following local scholarships are available to seniors: Columbine Honor Society, Elks, Altrusa, Frank-McKee Memorial, Lions Club, Music Teachers, and Rotary Club International.

5. As she looked forward to a new school year, Sue knew she would need to purchase a backpack, pens, pencils, paper, spiral notebooks, an eraser, and a highlighter.

ACTIVITY 5.5

Recognizing Sequence by Putting Steps in Order

Determining the order in which to do things requires comprehension or understanding. Try your hand at the following passage in which the steps are scrambled. Unscramble the steps and write them in the logical order on your paper.

How to Scramble Eggs

Pour in mixture and reduce heat to low. Heat ½ tablespoon fat for each egg in moderately hot skillet. Break eggs into bowl. When cooked through but still moist (5 to 8 minutes), serve at once. Add 1 tablespoon milk or cream and a dash of salt and pepper for each egg. Cook slowly, turning gently as mixture sets at bottom and sides of pan. Beat well with a fork. Avoid constant stirring.

ACTIVITY 5.6

Recognizing Sequence by Listing Procedures

Now try your skills on a longer selection. This time you will sequence procedures. Read the following questions so you know your purpose for reading the selection and the questions you should be answering as you read. Then read the selection. On a separate sheet of paper:

1. List the three time periods involved in a job interview. Leave space below each time period.

2. Under each time period, list the important points or tips for that portion of the interview.

3. Conclude by writing a brief paragraph summarizing the sequence of procedures in a job interview.

The Job Interview

Once you have an appointment for a job interview, there are certain things that should be done. These can basically be divided into three time periods—before, during, and after the interview.

Dress appropriately as you prepare for the interview. Wear clothes that are commonly worn or accepted in your interviewer's profession. If you are not sure what is appropriate to wear, ask for advice from others, or someone you know in that profession. Dress as if you could go to work at that location immediately.

Go to the interview alone and arrive five to ten minutes early. Being early shows that you are eager and responsible enough to be prompt. You must have done your homework, of course, and know what the company you hope to join makes or the services it provides.

Before leaving for the interview, be sure that you have your Social Security card, several copies of your résumé, and the names, addresses, and phone numbers of at least three people who are not relatives to be used as references or sources of information about you. If the job would include driving as part of the duties, take your driver's license, as well.

During the interview, be polite. Don't smoke or chew gum. Try to look as alert as possible, neither slouching nor sitting ramrod straight. Make frequent eye contact and listen intently to what the interviewer is saying. Answer his or her questions clearly and completely, speaking audibly. *Do not mumble*. Don't hesitate to ask questions of the interviewer as they occur to you, but wait to ask about benefits and vacations until you are actually offered the job. If you are not offered the job but want it, say so to the interviewer. Do not be demanding; simply state confidently that you would like to have the position.

After the interview, be sure to thank the interviewer for spending his or her time to talk with you. After the interview, write a thank you note. This is a polite gesture, often neglected, that may help the interviewer keep you in mind.

If you were told by the interviewer that he or she would contact you, and you do not get a response, call or make a return visit. Perseverance often wins jobs.

Understanding Character Development

ACTIVITY 5.7

You probably remember being asked to read a piece of literature and describe its main character. You were to discuss what the person was like at the beginning of the book and how that person changed. This kind of assignment also involves sequencing. Your purpose in reading required you to trace, in an orderly fashion from the beginning to the conclusion, the development of the main character.

Try that with the following paragraphs. On a separate sheet of paper, first list details that describe the new employee at the beginning of the story, then at the middle of the story, and finally at the end of the story. Then list, in the order they appeared or happened, the people and events that caused the main character to change.

At Last—The Job!

I had passed the test of the interview with flying colors, was given *the* job, and had started to work. Before, my experience had come chiefly from TV, movies, and my imagination. Unfortunately, mind games had not prepared me for the difficult period of adjustment that every inexperienced waitress must face: mixed-up orders, tired feet, spilled Coke, irate customers, crying babies, tired feet, littered tables, sticky plates, and tired feet—and all for small tips.

As you can imagine, I soon became so discouraged with myself and so dissatisfied with my job that I considered quitting. I think my supervisor must have felt the negative vibrations coming from my exhausted self, because she called me into her office and talked to me about both the duties of my new profession and the challenges they presented for sharpening my organizational skills to a fine edge. She also pointed out the direct relationship between my organizational abilities and service and the size of my tip.

That conversation with her helped me change my attitude considerably. I realized then that there was nothing wrong with me or my job that experience and a big smile could not cure. I decided to stay on.

ACTIVITY 5.8

Visualizing Character

As you improve your comprehension skills, you will gain a broader understanding of what you read. You also will remember more if you can train yourself to project mentally beyond the printed, literal meanings.

Think about the new employee in Activity 5.7. What kind of a visual image do you have of that person? Is that person a young girl or a middle-aged woman? How does she look, dress, and act? Through the course of the story, how does she change? Creating a vivid visual image of a character in your mind helps you remember the content of what you read.

Try it. As you read, create a visual image of the characters or scenes being presented in the following five descriptions. Draw from your own experiences and observations. Become that person! It's fun, and you will be surprised at how much longer and more vivid your memory of what you read will be.

On a separate sheet of paper, write a description of the character you "see" in each of the following sentences.

1. Long lashes lowered, she scuffed her patent leather shoes in the dust as she pulled at the ribbon that was her sash.

2. Always shabby in dress and committed to collecting aluminum cans, he never went out to lunch unless I was buying.

3. Massive in stature, his bellowing voice and swooping gestures, combined with his unkempt grey hair and grizzled beard, tended to put people off.

4. His changes of mood and wide-eyed whoops of laughter made his strange predictions very unsettling.

5. As the model pivoted on the runway, teeth flashing, tresses flying, and skirt swirling, I imagined a regal queen, accepting homage from loyal subjects.

Understanding Character Through Background

If you read about a character, visualizing and working to understand him or her based on details of the character's life, you have good comprehension of the character as a whole.

As you read the following paragraphs, try to visualize and then understand the great composer Johannes Brahms. Then, on a separate sheet of paper, answer these questions:

1. Why did Brahms never dare to get married?
2. Form an opinion or make a judgment regarding Brahms' character; justify your own view of it based on your understanding of the man.

Johannes Brahms, 1833–1897

Few great composers had more difficult early years than Brahms. When Brahms was in his teens, he would perform in the waterfront saloons to earn money for his family. Even then, Brahms never used sheet music, for he could play everything from memory.

When he was twenty, Brahms was introduced by letter to the noted composer Robert Schumann. Schumann and his wife, Clara, took Brahms and his music to their hearts. When it became necessary for Schumann to enter an asylum for the insane, Brahms comforted Clara and gradually fell in love with her. Even after Schumann died, two years later, Brahms never spoke of marriage. (He was known for becoming very close to several women, only to bow out of the relationship.) Brahms once said that there were two things he had never dared to try: opera and marriage.

Brahms spent the last half of his life in Vienna, a noted city of music. He was seen as a privately generous, publicly crusty, boorish bachelor. He lived in the simplest of rooms and rose every morning at five o'clock. With his baggy, unimpressive appearance, bulky form, high voice, and his shovel-shaped beard, he was a familiar figure. Those that knew him loved that part of him which was forever young.

This rather disheveled, outwardly eccentric man, who kept his money tied up in bundles and got some of his best ideas while shining his shoes, was one of the supreme architects of complex, orderly musical structure—the symphony.

Sensing Relationships Between Cause and Effect

As your comprehension skills grow sharper, you will soon realize that many of your classes deal, very basically, with what happened first and second and then third to cause an end result. Think of studying the Civil War, for example. You begin by looking at the causes of the war, then the war itself, and finally the effects of the war on the United States and even the world.

Sometimes events are not clearly spelled out in a simple first-second-third sequence, however, and you must dig to uncover information. If you have to make a search, it is helpful to first clearly identify what happened (the cause). Then use your skills at locating key thoughts and proper sequence to uncover the clues necessary to find the target result (or the effect).

Practice identifying reading clues and targets, and your comprehension skills will improve even more because you are alert as you read, actively searching for answers. Your reading rate will improve because you know exactly what you are looking for.

Consider the following example. Jeff has gotten a poor grade on a test because he didn't study, but instead of accepting the grade, he begins arguing with his instructor in an attempt to get more points. After several unsuccessful attempts on Jeff's part, the instructor firmly responds, "Jeff, that's enough!" Jeff is silent.

By following the sequence and reading between the lines, what does this example say to you? The content reveals exactly what Jeff has done and how his instructor responded. But beyond that, what else do you know?"

Jeff was silent. What did Jeff anticipate?

What can you point to as the cause of the instructor's response?

How would you describe the instructor's mood?

What would you anticipate would happen if Jeff continued to argue?

You can see that the answers to these questions are not printed in the paragraph above. To come up with the answers, you have to think beyond what is printed. And to do that, you use higher-level thinking skills.

Concentrate on the sequence of events as you read the following paragraphs. After you finish reading, consider the relationships that are established between the causes and the effects to answer the questions that follow each paragraph. Write your answers on a separate sheet of paper.

Paragraph One

It is a beautiful, sunny summer day, and Tony and Roberto decide to go fishing. Tony grabs he fishing poles and a net, Roberto packs a quick lunch, and they set off. When they reach the lake, they discover they are missing an important item for their fishing excursion.

1. What are Tony and Roberto missing?
2. What will be the effect of fishing without this item?
3. Conversely, if they catch no fish, what is the cause?

Paragraph Two

Yoshimi has gone to the store to buy a birthday present for her mother. She has ten dollars that her father gave her along with specific instructions as to what to purchase. She is to buy a necklace her mother has been hinting about for weeks. As she passes by the store window, Yoshimi sees a purse that she just *has* to have. The purse is on sale for five dollars, and she buys it, She buys her mother a small pair of earrings with the remaining money.

1. What will Yoshimi's father's reaction be?
2. What is the cause of his reaction?
3. What will Yoshimi's mother's reaction be?
4. What is the cause of her reaction?
5. How will her parents' reactions affect Yoshimi?

Paragraph Three

Sean has a part-time job after school at a small grocery store. It is his responsibility to gather the grocery carts from the parking lot and bring them indoors. After the first month of work, he arrives on Tuesday twenty minutes late; his boss comments on it. The following Tuesday he arrives twenty minutes late again; his boss warns him about being late. Again, the next Tuesday, Sean arrives twenty minutes late. His boss is in the parking lot gathering the grocery carts himself.

1. What do you anticipate Sean's boss will do?
2. What are the causes of his boss's actions?
3. Is this result fair for Sean?

Analyzing Causes and Their Effects

ACTIVITY 5.11

Sometimes, causes and their effects are not obvious as you read . To understand the material, you may need to *analyze* it. For example, if you fail a test, you need to analyze the causes of your failing in order to avoid failing again. Once you determine why your test answers were incorrect, you can avoid repeating the same kinds of mistakes on a second test. You analyze the cause of making mistakes to avoid their effect—failure of another test.

Activity 5.11 will give you practice in analyzing causes and their effects. Read "Good Listening Is Difficult" and, on a separate sheet of paper, list seven reasons (or causes) for difficulty in listening. Conclude by explaining what the effect of poor listening skills might be on grades.

Good Listening Is Difficult

Many students would agree that listening is a difficult skill. For most, it is much harder to master new material by listening to a lecturer than by reading a textbook. Since listening, like reading, is a popular method of teaching, both in and out of school, it is important to understand why listening well is so difficult.

When listening, you have to adjust to the speed of speakers. If they speak very rapidly, you may not be able to take in all that they say. On the other hand, if they are very slow and deliberate, you may find it hard to keep your mind on what they are saying. (Your mind's pace is much more rapid than that of *any* speaker.)

You may not be mentally prepared for listening. You may not know anything about the topic and may be confused until you have heard enough to understand and focus on the subject being considered. Perhaps you don't feel well, or you are caught up in a daydream. You cannot choose the time and place for listening.

Unfortunately, there is no "replay button" to push when you are listening. If you miss what was said the first time, it is gone. You have missed it.

It is hard to be a listener and a critical thinker at the same time. When you are reading and you want to stop and consider a particular point, you can put the book aside and do so. However, when you are listening, such lengthy evaluations are not possible.

Distractions are all around you—particularly in the classroom. You may sit by a window and have a tendency to look out and watch the world. Maybe the person behind you has news about something in which you are very interested. Perhaps you would like to date the person seated across the aisle. Once your attention wanders from the speaker, it is hard to concentrate again.

Personal biases or prejudices may make it difficult for you to keep an open mind. Speaking style or physical appearance may influence the way you respond to what you hear. Listening with understanding and reserving judgment until later is difficult for most people.

The reaction of others to a topic or speaker may influence your ability to make a judgment about what the speaker is saying. Weighing the evidence and mentally keeping up with what the speaker is really saying is challenging when others have prejudged and are urging agreement.

Nevertheless, in spite of some of the roadblocks you have just read about, efficient listening in class is a skill that anyone who is committed to becoming a better listener can learn.

ACTIVITY 5.12

Recognizing Inferences and Drawing Conclusions

Are you a good detective? Sometimes you need to be, to understand a situation, make inferences, and draw conclusions from what you read when the results are not clearly stated.

To make inferences, you have to go beyond given words or circumstances to draw conclusions. For example, suppose you just bought a new red pen, and you are certain you left it on your desk. But the pen in missing. You find a note written in red ink by your brother. What do you infer, or what conclusions do you draw, based on your understanding of the situation?

Identifying main ideas, noting the sequence of events, visualizing the material clearly, and targeting the outcome are all skills that you have been acquiring. Now, put them to work and have some fun practicing your sleuthing as you complete the following exercises. Your goals are to understand, to make inferences, and to draw conclusions from what you read.

Begin by reading the following sentences. Then, on a separate sheet of paper, explain what conclusions you have drawn, or predict what might, will, or has happened, based on your understanding of the facts given. The first sentence has been done for you as an example.

1. Take your umbrella, as the clouds look very threatening off to the west.
   Conclusion or prediction: It might rain.
2. Yelling and booing and pointing at the referee followed the final call.
3. It's snowing, blowing, and about two degrees above zero outside.
4. The strange creature was covered with feathers, had a long, sharp bill, and gave shrill, raucous cries when approached by onlookers.
5. The tree was decorated, the stockings were hung, and the smell of pies baking wafted through the house.
6. The three contestants stood in a row, each nervously awaiting the spin of the wheel.
7. In spite of the deafening roar of the fans, the eleven helmeted men lined up, the referee blew the whistle, and the ball was kicked into the air.
8. The student held his breath as his paper was handed back. A quick glance at the top brought a grim expression.
9. A beaker, a few chemicals, and a loud BANG. They had done it again.
10. The hastily drawn posters were hung on the walls, the speeches were nervously given, and the votes were finally tallied. Jana smiled broadly.

Cloze

Another activity that focuses on improving your comprehension is cloze. The word *cloze* comes from the term *closure* and means to bring completion to a sentence. A cloze activity is a puzzle of sorts; you use the clues provided in the context to think of appropriate words to fill the blanks. The purpose of cloze is to teach you to use context clues to figure out the meanings of words you don't know. Cloze improves your reading comprehension, as well.

Read the following selection through first, mentally supplying the words you think belong in the spaces. Then, on a separate sheet of paper, number from one to thirty-two. Read "One Night in the Woods" again, filling in each blank with a word from the list provided. All the words in the list must be used, and some words will be used more than once. Finish by writing the word beside the appropriate number on your paper.

popped	first	five	at	was
fresh	prickles	had	the	imaginations
you	especially	hill	crept	trails
stage	or	moon	tried	a
shadows	feet	imaginary	and	enough
does	I	not	mountainside	

One Night in the Woods

The fresh pine scent in the air made me glad to be out of the stuffy cabin and away from my sleeping companions. I had no flashlight, but it ____1____ just a short way up the ____2____ to the other cabin, and the ____3____ was shining. Confidently I started up ____4____ trail.

Soon I realized that it ____5____ not as bright as I had ____6____ thought. The moon slyly cast only ____7____ light to create eerie shadows. The ____8____ air rattled the aspen leaves. It ____9____ not the chilly air that caused ____10____ to crawl down my spine.

Do ____11____ know Jason? He has retired from ____12____ movie *Friday the 13th* into the ____13____ of many. Now he slithered into my thoughts. Do you know what Jason ____14____ ? He murders people walking up mountain ____15____ in the middle of the night, ____16____ when they're alone.

The moon ____17____ no mercy. It kept the eerie ____18____ set. "Shuuushsh," said something in the ____19____ . Was it the shadow that moved ____20____ something *in* it? I shuddered and ____21____ to control my frightened thoughts.

After ____22____ more careful steps, I plainly heard ____23____ twig snap behind me. *Is* Jason ____24____ ? I instantly felt my heart pounding ____25____ my ribs in panic. Silent horror ____26____ to every part of my body. ____27____ could not look back. With heavy ____28____ I plodded forward.

When another twig ____29____ behind me, I froze. I was ____30____ imagining.

"BOO!" I jumped straight up ____31____ screamed. My terror resounded over the ____32____ . Amy's eyes filled with tears of merriment as she exploded into giggles. After a pause I, too, began to laugh.

On a separate sheet of paper, answer the following questions:

I. Completion

Number from one to five. Fill the blank with the term(s) from this unit that complete the statement.

1. The point the author is trying to get across is called the _____.

2. _____ is understanding the point the author is making.

3. Putting things in order is called _____. You must have a basic understanding in order to do this.

4. Comprehension involves understanding the basic relationship between _____ and effect.

5. _____ comes from the word *closure* and means to complete something. You need comprehension to bring appropriate closure to a sentence.

II. Short Essay

Read the following paragraphs. On a separate sheet of paper, write the number IIA and, below it, write IIB. Beside IIA write the main idea of the paragraphs. Beside IIB, list sequentially six things you can do to develop your skills as a student.

You Can Become a Better Student

There are several things you can do to become a better student. First, you can create a good study setting for yourself; where you study helps improve your concentration and comprehension.

Second, you can budget your time. Decide what subjects you need to study and in what order you should study them. Approximate how long each subject will take to study, time for breaks, and block out that amount of time in your schedule for the day.

Third, work on improving your note-taking abilities. Practice getting the main ideas down in as concise a manner as possible. Use abbreviations, personal shorthand, and a highlighter to mark the important points.

Next, develop and use good test-taking skills. Know the tricks for taking tests in general, as well as those suited to specific types of tests. Know how to handle test anxiety, how to budget your time when taking tests, and how to evaluate your test when it is returned, so that you can do better on the next test.

Fifth, understand the value of reading different material at appropriate and vastly different rates. Know when to speed up and when to slow down; know when to read at 100 words per minute and when to read at 1,000 words per minute. Then use those varying rates.

Finally, develop your listening skills. Sit away from friends, doors, windows, and other distractions. Don't prejudge speakers. Adjust to their speaking speed. And be an active listener; don't put your mind in neutral, but instead participate mentally in what the speaker is saying. Stay with that person—think about what he or she is saying.

Clearly, there are many things you can do to become a better student. Practice these techniques, and watch your grades improve.

III. Application

Choose *one* of the following (a *or* b).

a. Discuss in a brief paragraph some of the *causes* of poor grades and the *effects* poor grades may have on a student's life. Show by your discussion that you understand the cause-effect relationship.

b. Develop four inferences and demonstrate your understanding of the inferences by predicting an outcome or drawing a conclusion.

Example: Hour after hour, day after day, Luis pored over piles of notes, reviewed pages and pages in the text, and created sample test after sample test. He had to pass that final.
Prediction: Luis will pass the test because of all his preparation.

IV. Cloze

Read the entire selection, mentally selecting the appropriate word for the blank *as* you read. Next, number from one to twenty-four. Read "Planning Your Time" again, filling in the blanks with the words from the list provided. All words in the list must be used, and some words will be used more than once. Write the appropriate word in the correct space on your answer sheet.

lower	pays	time	or	your
employer	project	the	search	find
last	sight	should	for	take
in	are	as	of	

Planning Your Time

Even if you are under no economic pressure to find a job quickly, starting your search promptly is a wise policy. Delays may hurt your chances of finding the job you want. If you have just finished school, for example, you __1__ competing for similar positions with other new graduates in __2__ field. Moreover, a long delay between school or your __3__ job and your application for work may give an __4__ the impression that his or her office is one __5__ your last stops in a long fruitless job __6__ .

Once you start your search, you should treat it __7__ a full-time job. Set realistic goals and keep __8__ of them. It is important to remember that looking

___9___ work can be discouraging. Do not let employer rejections ___10___ your self-esteem or serve as an excuse to "___11___ a vacation" from job seeking. Sustained effort usually ___12___ off.

The following suggestions may help you plan your ___13___ for an efficient job search:

1. Plan and start your ___14___ as soon as you know you will need to ___15___ a new job.

2. Make your job hunting a full-time ___16___. You work a 40-hour week for your employer; you ___17___ work no less for yourself.

3. Once you start your ___18___, do not allow yourself little vacations.

4. Apply early enough ___19___ the day to allow time for multiple interviewers, tests, ___20___ other hiring procedures that may be required.

5. Be on ___21___ for appointments.

6. Before approaching a firm, try to learn ___22___ best time and day of the week to apply ___23___ a job.

7. Follow up leads immediately. If you learn ___24___ a job opening late in the day, call the firm to arrange an appointment for the next day. The employer may postpone a hiring decision until then.

Increasing
Speed

Are you reading as well or as fast as you might? If not, don't despair—you are not alone! Most students receive no formal training in the "how to's" of reading after grade school. It is not surprising, then, that you may feel your skills don't meet the demands now being made on them.

Some students read everything at the same slow rate in order the maximize understanding of what they read. But problems come when reading speed is slow enough to allow daydreaming.

Whatever your reading rates, remember that speed and comprehension go hand in hand. Read slowly, and daydreaming sets in; read too fast, and little or nothing stays in your memory.

The information and exercises in Unit 6 will help you improve your reading speed—an area many students find to be a problem, no matter what the subject matter. If you are determined, and if you can exercise self-discipline, you can eliminate some inefficient reading habits that impede your success.

Reading rates are very personal. It is not important to compare your speed with that of another. What is important is that you are reading faster, comprehending more, and remembering longer. The final payoff will be in better understanding of the material and improved grades.

Rapid Discrimination Drills

Reading at a speed that is too slow leads to boredom and daydreaming because your brain is not challenged. If you find yourself daydreaming as you read, perhaps you need to try reading faster. Use the rapid discrimination drills in Activities 6.1 through 6.10 to push yourself to read more quickly.

The drills help you increase your reading speed because they force you to look at words and pick out, at very rapid rates, those that are alike or different. The drills train you to recognize word meanings quickly. In addition, they challenge you to take in longer and longer words at the same rapid rate in which you recognize the shorter words. To use the drills, follow this procedure:

1. Label the upper right-hand corner of a separate sheet of paper as shown:

	Min.	Sec.
Time stopped	_____	_____
Time began	_____	_____
Total time read	_____	_____

2. Number your paper from one to twenty.

If your instructor is timing the drill:

3. Listen carefully to instructions and do not begin working until your instructor gives you the signal.

4. Look up when you finish and record the total time you read based on the time card being held up by your instructor.

5. Correct your paper as your instructor gives the answers, and record the total time you read and your score on the chart you construct. (See the model chart at the end of this introduction.)

If your instructor is not timing the drill, use the following procedure:

3. Using a watch or clock with a second hand, note the time you begin on your sheet of paper.

4. Turn to the proper page, read the instructions at the top of that page, and complete the drill as quickly as possible.

5. Note the time you finish. Subtract the time you began from the time you finish to determine the total time you read. Grade your paper using the answer key in the appendix at the end of this unit. Then, compute your score by giving yourself five points for each correct answer; record your score on a chart such as the one shown below.

Remember, your goal is to improve or maintain your reading time and score while increasing the length of the words you are reading. To benefit more from these drills, practice them on four consecutive days, using three sequential exercises each day.

RAPID DISCRIMINATION DRILLS

		1	2	3	4	5	6	7	8	9	10
Different Word	*Time*										
	Score										
Same Word	*Time*										
	Score										
Meaning	*Time*										
	Score										

Rapid Discrimination Drill 1

ACTIVITY 6.1

Write the number of the word that is different.

	1	2	3	4	5
1.	site	site	site	side	site
2.	cord	cord	cord	cord	card
3.	nail	mail	nail	nail	nail
4.	maps	maps	naps	maps	maps
5.	pore	pore	pore	pore	bore
6.	raid	paid	paid	paid	paid
7.	look	look	book	look	look
8.	cake	rake	rake	rake	rake
9.	pear	tear	pear	pear	pear
10.	cook	cook	cook	took	cook
11.	felt	felt	felt	felt	melt
12.	cape	cape	tape	cape	cape
13.	jack	rack	rack	rack	rack
14.	veil	veil	veil	veal	veil
15.	hats	rats	hats	hats	hats
16.	jump	jump	jump	jump	pump
17.	pale	pale	dale	pale	pale
18.	pool	pool	pool	poor	pool
19.	tool	took	took	took	took
20.	cart	part	cart	cart	cart

Rapid Discrimination Drill 2

A **key word** is given. Write the column number in which it is repeated.

Key Word	1	2	3	4	5
1. dull	mull	pull	full	dull	cull
2. desk	mask	deck	pest	desk	risk
3. last	mast	last	past	task	fast
4. mask	mope	task	mask	make	made
5. made	raid	fade	paid	jade	made
6. rail	mail	tail	sail	rail	pail
7. hook	hook	took	book	look	cook
8. rule	mule	rule	tool	fool	cool
9. hope	rope	Pope	lope	nope	hope
10. took	took	cook	look	rook	book
11. bone	tone	moan	hone	bone	loan
12. clad	paid	made	fade	glad	clad
13. dirt	curt	tart	dirt	mart	bard
14. feel	meal	zeal	real	feel	peal
15. boat	moat	boat	coat	tote	goat
16. jeer	mere	fear	jeer	tear	leer
17. pony	pony	home	bone	tone	zone
18. real	peal	meal	teal	real	seal
19. pare	bare	mare	tare	fare	pare
20. belt	belt	felt	melt	pelt	welt

Rapid Discrimination Drill 3

List the number of the word(s) that mean(s) the same as the **key word**.

Key Word	1	2	3	4
1. site	hill	scene	place	land
2. spry	old	smart	active	thin
3. rely	ask	depend	expect	balk
4. balk	trip	fall	stop short	frighten
5. bask	play	sun	warm oneself	fry
6. vows	wish	promises	order	command
7. clue	hint	reminder	thought	answer
8. ajar	wide open	unlocked	closed	partly open
9. burr	rough edge	haircut	dig deep	sandy shore
10. hint	answer	slight sign	explanation	essay

11.	vary	shrink	increase	grow	change
12.	feat	foolish	skillful act	trip	flight
13.	chat	speech	easy talk	explanation	lecture
14.	chef	cook	dean	president	policeman
15.	clad	completely	appearing	dressed	working
16.	poll	campaign	question	debate	vote
17.	pant	behave	slight	short breath	enough
18.	odor	neither	smell	danger	taste
19.	rein	rain	reign	bridle strap	razor
20.	heir	session	who inherits	hair	ancestor

Rapid Discrimination Drill 4

Write the number of the word that is different.

	1	**2**	**3**	**4**	**5**
1.	blurt	flirt	flirt	flirt	flirt
2.	power	power	flour	power	power
3.	medal	metal	medal	medal	medal
4.	align	align	align	alien	align
5.	check	check	check	check	cheek
6.	burly	curly	burly	burly	burly
7.	abide	chide	chide	chide	chide
8.	flood	flood	flood	flood	blood
9.	trunk	trunk	trunk	chunk	trunk
10.	plush	plush	blush	plush	plush
11.	glaze	craze	craze	craze	craze
12.	twist	twist	twist	twist	wrist
13.	float	float	floor	float	float
14.	shade	shade	shade	shape	shade
15.	widow	width	widow	widow	widow
16.	hazy	hazy	crazy	hazy	hazy
17.	blush	plush	plush	plush	plush
18.	pedal	pedal	pedal	medal	pedal
19.	chase	chute	chase	chase	chase
20.	shame	shame	shame	shame	share

ACTIVITY 6.5

Rapid Discrimination Drill 5

A **key word** is given. Write the number of the column in which it is repeated.

Key Word	1	2	3	4	5
1. bonus	tones	bonus	cones	hones	phone
2. shame	share	shout	shoot	shore	shame
3. write	trite	sight	write	fight	white
4. weigh	weigh	worry	neigh	wrist	wring
5. glass	glare	globe	glaze	glass	gland
6. blunt	blunt	bloom	bloat	blown	black
7. dingy	diner	dingy	dings	dinky	dingo
8. wield	yield	field	wield	weird	waist
9. gland	gloom	glove	glory	glass	gland
10. wrist	twist	crust	wisps	wrist	grist
11. block	blare	block	blast	blank	blame
12. false	fable	faint	famed	false	fancy
13. boils	boils	toils	foils	coils	bowls
14. aides	maids	raids	aides	paids	fades
15. chase	chaff	chair	chain	chalk	chase
16. legal	legal	leach	leafy	leaky	learn
17. rebel	ready	rebel	realm	recur	reign
18. champ	chalk	chair	champ	chain	chaff
19. agent	again	agaze	agent	agile	aging
20. brief	brick	bribe	bride	brief	briar

ACTIVITY 6.6

Rapid Discrimination Drill 6

List the number of the word(s) that mean(s) the same as the **key word**.

Key Word	1	2	3	4
1. vocal	of voice	simple	harmonizing	loud
2. drawl	slow talk	fast talk	quiet talk	loud talk
3. elude	hide from	void	evade	discover
4. array	table	menu	amount	display
5. scent	choke	odor	sent	mail
6. sheer	very thin	shore	clean	cut
7. adapt	to learn	to modify	to probe	to notify
8. tempt	tame	test	threaten	trust
9. realm	flavor	kingdom	pilot	reality
10. agony	uncertain	pain	acute	scholar

11.	amuse	entertain	harp	ignorance	abuse
12.	alter	additional	graduate	altar	change
13.	prong	sharp edge	blade	pointed end	pin
14.	valet	housekeeper	cook	gardener	servant
15.	abode	dwelling	atmosphere	situation	surrounding
16.	foyer	basement	office	porch	entry hall
17.	horde	swarm	trace	rodent	family
18.	solar	of planets	of stars	of sun	of universe
19.	wield	lift up	accomplish	obtain	hold and use
20.	vivid	empty	cold	alive	dull blue

Rapid Discrimination Drill 7

ACTIVITY 6.7

Write the number of the word that is different.

	1	2	3	4	5
1.	belong	belief	belong	belong	belong
2.	census	census	census	censor	census
3.	facing	facing	facial	facing	facing
4.	agency	agenda	agenda	agenda	agenda
5.	device	device	device	device	devise
6.	tender	hinder	tender	tender	tender
7.	liking	liking	liking	likely	liking
8.	pardon	parent	parent	parent	parent
9.	jacket	jacket	racket	jacket	jacket
10.	triple	triple	triple	triple	ripple
11.	shrewd	shreds	shreds	shreds	shreds
12.	thresh	thresh	thrash	thresh	thresh
13.	reboil	recoil	reboil	reboil	reboil
14.	series	series	serial	series	series
15.	reform	reform	reform	reflex	reform
16.	snatch	snitch	snitch	snitch	snitch
17.	status	status	status	status	static
18.	gratis	gravel	gratis	gratis	gratis
19.	hooded	hooded	hooves	hooded	hooded
20.	tingle	tingle	tingle	mingle	tingle

Rapid Discrimination Drill 8

A **key word** is given. Write the number of the column in which it is repeated.

Key Word	1	2	3	4	5
1. modify	module	modest	modify	modern	models
2. nibble	pebble	treble	nimble	normal	nibble
3. pellet	pellet	mallet	ballet	market	target
4. rescue	resale	resume	resort	rescue	resist
5. sadden	saddle	sadden	sadder	sadism	sacred
6. spider	spinet	spinal	spiral	spider	spirit
7. broken	broken	broach	broker	bronze	brooms
8. change	chance	cancel	change	chapel	charge
9. commit	combat	comely	comets	common	commit
10. damper	damsel	damper	dampen	damask	damage
11. gamble	gander	gamble	gargle	garlic	garret
12. indent	indeed	indebt	indict	indent	indoor
13. jangle	jangle	jingle	jargon	jaunty	jersey
14. misuse	miscue	misery	misuse	misfit	mishap
15. oppose	option	oracle	orbits	orphan	oppose
16. radial	radios	radial	radium	radius	random
17. seaman	season	seater	secede	seaman	second
18. hubbub	hubbub	hugged	humble	humans	hunger
19. limber	linger	lining	limber	liquid	listen
20. memory	method	mental	midget	member	memory

Rapid Discrimination Drill 9

List the number of the word(s) that mean(s) the same as the **key word**.

Key Word	1	2	3	4
1. rustic	rural	rusty	normal	simple
2. hectic	dramatic	dull	very busy	angry
3. deluge	sprinkle	shower	heavy rain	fog
4. relish	care	speed	amusement	enjoy
5. defect	stowaway	noise	fault	repair
6. sultry	hot and humid	sunny	overcast	smelly
7. relent	soften	lend	surrender	hold firm
8. smudge	would	expression	dirt	smear
9. caress	lick	stroke	protect	warm
10. heroic	strong	loyal	friendly	brave

11.	tremor	loud noise	shaking	shock	frighten
12.	stench	stretch	dirty	stingy	bad smell
13.	differ	be like	be unlike	be kind	be common
14.	decree	infant	circular	rejoice	royal law
15.	hatred	flush	great dislike	hurt	sacred
16.	bestow	best one	give	take	put away
17.	offend	kettle	ladder	often	make angry
18.	define	settler	legal	state meaning	defend
19.	emerge	lead on	come out	dispute	image
20.	induce	bring about	enclose	sight	intrude

Rapid Discrimination Drill 10

Write the number of the word that is different.

	1	2	3	4	5
1.	baggage	bagpipe	bagpipe	bagpipe	bagpipe
2.	calcify	calcify	calcium	calcify	calcify
3.	dogwood	dolphin	dogwood	dogwood	dogwood
4.	flatcar	flatcar	flatcar	flatcar	flatten
5.	grating	grating	grating	gratify	grating
6.	hemline	hemlock	hemline	hemline	hemline
7.	illegal	illicit	illicit	illicit	illicit
8.	inverse	inverse	invalid	inverse	inverse
9.	justify	justify	justify	justify	justice
10.	kinetic	kinetic	kinetic	kindred	kinetic
11.	lapsing	larceny	lapsing	lapsing	lapsing
12.	martial	marshal	marshal	marshal	marshal
13.	nitrite	nitrite	nitrate	nitrite	nitrite
14.	offices	offices	offices	offices	officer
15.	plastic	plastic	plastic	plaster	plastic
16.	rampage	rampage	rampage	rampant	rampage
17.	recruit	rectify	recruit	recruit	recruit
18.	secular	section	section	section	section
19.	spastic	spastic	sparkle	spastic	spastic
20.	tipster	tipster	tipster	tipster	timeout

ACTIVITY 6.11   **Timed Readings**

We are creatures of habit, and it is easy to fall into the pattern of reading everything at the most comfortable rate. However, that is not an efficient way to read. Instead, you should vary your rate to suit your purpose, the difficulty of the material, and your background. Sometimes this means reading, without sacrificing comprehension, as quickly as you can. Of course, learning to read more rapidly takes practice, as does anything at which you want to improve.

One easy way to increase reading speed is to read a lot. Choose the type of material that interests you. In order to focus your attention on improving your reading speed, try this method of timed readings two or three times per week over a period of weeks.

1. Write the following on a separate sheet of paper.

number of lines read	(1)
× number of words per line	(2)
total number of words read	(3)
total number of words read	(4)
÷ number of minutes read	(5)
rate in words per minute	(6)

2. Select an article or chapter that interests you.

3. Before starting to read, determine the average number of words per line in the selection you have chosen. To do this, count all the words in 10 lines and divide by 10 for the average number of words per line. Write this number on your sheet of paper in Space 2.

   Number of words in 10 lines ÷ by 10 = average number of words per line

   If your instructor is timing, you will be told when to begin reading and when to stop.
   If your instructor is not timing, you will need a watch with a second hand or a timer.

4. Do two timed readings whenever you practice. Read each time for the same number of minutes. (We suggest three to six minutes per reading.)

5. Set a timer and begin reading at a comfortable rate. When the timer signals that your reading time is finished, note on your paper in Space 5 the number of minutes you read. Then mark your place in the material you read.

6. Count the number of lines you read and write this down in Space 1.

7. Figure the number of words per minute you read by multiplying the total number of lines (Space 1) by the average number of words per line (Space 2).

8. Column Two: Divide the total number of words you read (Space 3 or 4) by the number of minutes you read (Space 5). This figure will be the number of words per minute (wpm) that you read (Space 6).

Example:

1. number of lines read   100
2. number of words per line $\times\,6$
3. total number of words read   600

4. total number of words read   600
5. number of minutes read $\div\,3$
6. rate in words per minute   200

For your second timed reading, continue from where you finished before, pushing yourself to read as quickly as you can without losing comprehension. (This may seem awkward at first.) When you time is up, again compute your words read per minute using the same formula as before.

Record both your comfortable rate and your "push" rate on a chart you make on a separate sheet of paper. Use the following chart as an example.

SPEED-READING CHART

Date	Number of words/line	Number of lines	Number of minutes	Rate in words per minute
9/21	6	100	3	200

As you continue with your timed reading practices during class, you will see progress if you are serious about wanting to read faster. Be sure to compare the differences between your comfortable rates and your push rates, as well as noting your increases in reading speed.

Additional Activities to Increase Reading Speed[1]

There are several other activities you can do to improve your reading speed. You will need light, easy, and enjoyable reading material; choose something you look forward to reading. Make up your mind that you will push yourself beyond your normal reading rate; you will be surprised at how soon the new reading speed becomes comfortable for you.

Decide how much time you can spend on an activity and then select a drill from the suggestions that follow.

---

[1] The activities offered to increase reading speed are from *Improving Reading in Every Class* by Ellen Lamar Thomas and H. Alan Robinson, and *Reading Aids for Every Class* by Ellen Lamar Thomas. Both books were published by Allyn & Bacon, Inc., Boston.

One-Minute Speed Drills

This drill resembles the timed readings discussed previously. Read for one minute, determine your rate in words per minute, and record it on your Speed-Reading Chart. Then read for another minute, trying to beat your previous score. Do this for ten minutes several times a week.

One-Page Speed Drills

In this drill you read one page at a time and work for improvement. Note the time before you begin reading, read the page, and note the time upon ending reading. Try another one-page reading in an attempt to improve your previous time. Repeat this process two or three times a week.

Ten-Page Speed Drills

Count out ten pages and mark the tenth page with a paper clip, Note the time and begin reading. Push yourself. At the end of the tenth page, note the time again and determine how many minutes you spent reading. Record this time; it is this time you want to improve when you repeat the exercise with ten other pages.

One-Hour Speed Drills

Note the time and read for one hour. Count the number of pages you read. Your goal is to read more pages the next time you read for an hour using similar material.

One-Book Speed Drills

This drill is for avid readers. Determine the number of hours it takes you to read a book (approximately). Then divide the number of pages in a book you wish to read by the number of hours it usually takes you to finish reading.

Example: 200 pages in 4 hours = 50 pages per hour

Put a paper clip on the page you should reach after one hour of reading. Set the timer for one hour. Then, at the end of that hour, count how many pages you read and record the results. Repeat the process using the hourly page rate you accomplished in your most recent drill as the rate you want to improve on.

**ACTIVITIES
6.12–6.15**

Speed and Comprehension Drills

Improving your reading speed is of no value if your comprehension doesn't keep up. Comprehension—how well you understand and recognize important points in what you read—is essential to your success as a student.

In Activities 6.12 through 6.15, you will be asked to read several articles at a speed that will ensure 70 percent comprehension or better. As you read, you will learn about reading rates, the process of reading, poor reading habits, and developing a good vocabulary. The ten questions following each article will help you evaluate your comprehension skills.

If your instructor is not timing these exercises, you will need a watch, clock, or timer. Time yourself, and record your time. Your goal is to improve your time—even as the activities get longer. After you read, answer the questions, and check your paper for comprehension errors using the answer key in the appendix at the end of this unit. Score your work by adding a zero to the number correct. Then, on a separate sheet of paper, make a chart entitled "Comprehension Activities" like the one that follows, and record your time and score.

COMPREHENSION ACTIVITIES

	1	2	3	4	5	6	7	8	9	10
Time										
Score										

ACTIVITY 6.12

Speed and Comprehension Drill 1

Read "What Is Your Reading Rate?" and answer the questions that follow the article. Time yourself, or ask your instructor to time you. Record your time on your Comprehension Activities chart.

What Is Your Reading Rate?

If someone asks you "What is your reading rate?" you can be sure that person knows very little about reading. It is incorrect to assume a person has just *one* reading rate. Although research shows the average high school student reads an average of 250 words per minute, the really good reader knows reading rates need to be *flexible*.

Some students think that, if they read everything slowly, they will achieve maximum comprehension. However, they are wrong. In fact, sometimes reading so slowly has the opposite effect because it lulls those people into daydreaming. Their brains are not being challenged. Successful readers learn to read quickly when it is warranted and slowly when it is necessary.

So, what determines the correct reading speed? Three factors determine it. The first is the difficulty of the material. If the material you are reading is complex, you must slow your reading speed. If the material is easy and entertaining, you can speed up your reading. The second factor is purpose. *Why* are you reading the material? If you are reading it to prepare for a quiz the next day, you'd better slow your pace. If you are reading it for pleasure, then you can speed up. Finally, the third factor that determines reading speed is familiarity with the subject matter. If the material and the concepts are new to you, then slow down your reading to take them in. If you are already familiar with the concepts in the material, then speed up. Good readers, learn to vary their speed from 150 to 800 words per minute, choosing their appropriate speed after considering all three factors: difficulty, purpose, and familiarity.

Number from one to ten on a separate sheet of paper. Beside each number write *true* if the statement is true and *false* if the statement is false.

1. Everyone has *one* personal reading rate.
2. High school students read an average of 250 words per minute.
3. Reading slowly assures a student of maximum comprehension.
4. The difficulty of the material is a consideration when choosing a reading rate.
5. A very difficult selection should be read at 250 words per minute.
6. A light, entertaining selection should be read at 250 words per minute.
7. Almost everyone reads material for a quiz at a slower speed than material for relaxation.
8. An astronomy expert can probably read an article on astronomy at a faster rate than someone who knows nothing about the subject.
9. Before selecting your own reading rate, you should consider the average reading rate of others in your class.
10. One of the major points made in this unit is that reading rates must be constantly changing.

ACTIVITY 6.13

Speed and Comprehension Drill 2

Read the article entitled "How Do You Read?" and answer the questions that follow it. Time yourself, or ask your instructor to time you. Then record your time.

How Do You Read?

 Most students probably assume that when they read, their eyes follow in a straight motion across the lines of print, like this:

Eyes follow the print in a straight line.

That is not so. You need only to sit across from someone and carefully observe his or her reading process to discover:

The eyes move in an arc across the lines of print.

Each time the eyes reach the bottom of the arc, they pause, or stop to take in words. These pauses are called *fixations*. It is only at the fixation point that your eyes see words. When the eye is making the arc, the motion is rapid; in fact, it is so rapid the reader is unaware of it. Only your brain "sees" the rapid blur of the arc. It is fortunate that as you read you do not see the arc—it would cause a terrible headache! As your eyes go through the motions of reading, they are in the arc 6 percent of the time; 94 percent is spent at the points of fixation.

Slow readers move their eyes in the word-by-word arc illustrated above. It is easy to see why slow readers tire easily and become discouraged. Reading is a difficult process for them.

Fast readers, on the other hand, read more fluently.

Fast readers take in 2.5 to 3 words per fixation, making the task of reading a much simpler one. Our goal in this unit is to use the rapid discrimination exercises as beginning drills to expand the amount of letters, and then words, you can take in per fixation. You begin with as few as four *letters* per fixation. With practice, you can work up to 2.5 to 3 *words* per fixation. This skill will help you be a better reader and will save you time, as well.

Number from one to ten on a separate sheet of paper. Beside each number write *true* if the statement is true and *false* if the statement is false.

1. A fixation is a pause or stop of the eyes to take in words.
2. A reader's eyes do not move in a straight line when reading.
3. Fifty percent of a reader's time is spent in motion between words, and 50 percent is spent fixating.
4. An inefficient or slow reader takes in one word per fixation.
5. An efficient reader takes in four to five words per fixation.
6. The eyes of a slow reader make an arc every 2.5 to 3 words.
7. The eyes of an efficient reader make an arc covering one word at a time.
8. Readers are aware of the blur made when their eyes make the arc motion from one fixation to the next.
9. The blur made by the arc motion causes some people to get frequent headaches when reading.
10. There is no difference between the amount of effort a slow reader puts forth while reading and the amount of effort a fast reader puts forth.

Speed and Comprehension Drill 3

ACTIVITY 6.14

Read the following article and answer the questions. Time yourself, or ask your instructor to time you. Then record your time; are you improving?

Reading Habits That Slow You Down

As you work to build your speed in reading, be alert to four common reading habits that may slow you down.

The first, *vocalizing*, is mouthing or saying the words aloud as you read them. It is easy to spot someone who has this problem. And vocalizing *is* a problem, because the act of mouthing or speaking slows you down; it takes too much time to say the words with your lips. There are several ways to help yourself stop vocalizing. Try chewing gum or holding a pencil clenched between your teeth as you read. Or, put your hand over your mouth or keep it at your throat to feel for vibrations of vocalizing.

Unfortunately, the second problem reading habit is much harder to detect. It is called *subvocalizing,* and it is characterized by a reader's forming the words in his or her larynx. In order to avoid pronouncing internally the words you read, practice reading rapidly under timed conditions, or talk about the material to yourself.

The third problem reading habit is *pointing.* When you point with your finger or a pencil or a ruler, you add another mechanical step to the reading process. This can only slow you down. The solution is to make pointing impossible by folding your hands in your lap.

The last problem reading habit is *head movement.* Following the lines of print with your head does not increase reading speed. Like pointing, it adds another mechanical step to the reading process. To avoid it, hold your chin in your hand, or place your hand against the side of your head.

Once you are aware that these reading habits can slow you down, you can begin improving your reading speed on a daily basis. Be aware that an exception to the total elimination of these habits might be when you are reading difficult materials. Vocalization, subvocalization, and following along with a finger may help some people remember complex information.

Number from one to ten on a separate sheet of paper, Beside each number write *true* if the statement is true and *false* if the statement is false.

1. *Vocalizing* is mouthing the words when reading.
2. Vocalizing does not slow a reader's speed; it just distracts others.
3. Chewing gum while reading is a cure for vocalizing.
4. Subvocalizing is like vocalizing; the words are said aloud for everyone to hear.
5. Reading rapidly under timed conditions is a cure for subvocalizing.
6. Pointing with your finger helps you keep your place and improves your reading speed.
7. Pointing with a pencil or ruler is preferred to pointing with a finger.
8. Moving your head to follow the lines of print slows your reading speed.
9. A cure for head movement is to hold your hand against the side of your head as you read, so that you can feel any head movement.
10. There are only four reading problems people need to consider.

ACTIVITY 6.15   ## Speed and Comprehension Drill 4

Read the article entitled "Vocabulary Affects Speed and Comprehension" and answer the questions that follow. Time yourself, or ask your instructor to time you. Record your time, then compare it to your time on the first drill.

Vocabulary Affects Speed and Comprehension

The previous comprehension activity focused on four common reading problems that affect reading speed. A fifth problem is a poor vocabulary. If you stumble over words, or you have to stop and think about them, your reading speed is slowed. Developing a good vocabulary will help you improve both your reading speed and your comprehension.

One way to improve your vocabulary is to read a lot. The more you read, the more words you will encounter, and the more your vocabulary will grow.

You can also improve your vocabulary by paying attention to new words. Instead of skipping over it, stop and figure out what a new word means. Use context clues from the sentence, if possible.

If context clues don't help, look up the meaning of the word in your dictionary. Then make a special effort to learn it. Using the new word in your writing or conversations will help you remember it.

Keeping a vocabulary notebook will also help. Although writing down the new words and their meanings takes more time, the benefits to you will make your efforts well worthwhile.

If possible, get involved in an organized vocabulary program in class. Use a vocabulary workbook and complete at least one lesson per week. Your vocabulary will grow if you make a genuine effort to learn and use the words in each lesson.

Finally, become aware of root words, prefixes, and suffixes. In *Speedreading for Better Grades*, Ward Cramer states it is possible to double your vocabulary by learning no more than a couple dozen prefixes.

Of course, the key to developing your vocabulary is by *being aware* of new words, by *discovering* their meanings, by *committing* them to memory, and by *using* them in your conversations.

Number from one to ten on a separate sheet of paper. Beside each number write *true* if the statement is true and *false* if the statement is false.

1. Developing a good vocabulary will help your reading speed but not your comprehension.
2. The more you read, the more your vocabulary will grow.
3. Using clues within a sentence to determine the meaning of a word will help increase your vocabulary.
4. Context clues are the clues to a word's meaning given by the sentence or paragraph in which the word appears.
5. The process of looking up a word's definition in the dictionary is sufficient for learning that word.
6. Using a new word in your conversation with others does not help you learn the word.
7. Keeping a vocabulary notebook takes too much time, and the payoffs aren't worth it.
8. Completing lessons in a vocabulary workbook pays off in an increased vocabulary.
9. Learning a couple dozen prefixes will double your vocabulary.
10. Learning root words is a waste of time for vocabulary building.

Review

Unit 6

Answer the following on a separate sheet of paper.

I. True-False (1–10)

Number your paper from one to ten. Read the following statements. Write *true* if the statement is true or *false* if the statement is false.

1. A knowledgeable and efficient reader reads all materials at the same rate.
2. Reading rate is not affected by having a good vocabulary or a poor one.
3. One way to build a good vocabulary is to read a lot.
4. You can build a good vocabulary by using the dictionary to look up meanings of words you don't know.
5. One way to build a good vocabulary is to use new words frequently in writing and conversations.
6. To build a vocabulary, you should skip over a word you do not know, unless it appears more than once in your reading.
7. To build a good vocabulary, keep a vocabulary notebook.
8. Learning common prefixes, suffixes, and roots of words can help you build your vocabulary.
9. Your eyes move in a straight line across the lines of print as you read.
10. Reading rates are much the same from one person to the next.

II. Multiple Choice (11–14)

Number your paper from eleven to fourteen. Place the letter of the correct answer beside the corresponding number on your paper.

11. Reading speed is determined by which of the following:
    A. your purpose.
    B. your background.
    C. the level of difficulty.
    D. A, B, and C

12. A *fixation* is a pause or stop of the eyes to take in words as you read. How many words does a slow reader take in at one fixation?
    A. one
    B. two
    C. three
    D. none of these

13. How many words does a fast reader take in at one fixation?

    A. one

    B. one to two

    C. two or more

    D. none of these

14. How many words does an efficient reader take in at one fixation?

    A. 1.0 to 1.5

    B. 2.0 to 2.5

    C. 2.5 to 3.0

    D. none of these

III. Matching (15–21)

Four common reading faults are listed in the left column, and cures for each are listed in the right column below. Number your paper from fifteen to twenty-one. Choose the cure(s) for each fault and write the answer(s) beside the correct number on your paper.

15.–16. Vocalization (pronouncing each word)—Two cures	A. Fold your hands and let your eyes do the work.
17.–18. Subvocalization (nothing visible; words are formed in the larynx)—Two cures	B. Place your hand against the side of your head.
19.–20. Head movement—Two cures	C. Chew gum as you read.
21. Pointing with finger, pencil, or pen—one cure	D. Talk about the problem to yourself.
	E. Hold a pencil clenched between your teeth.
	F. Read rapidly under timed conditions.
	G. Hold your chin firmly in your hand.
	H. None of the above.

IV. Short Essay (22–23)

22. Discuss the value of the rapid discrimination drills and whether they have helped you. If they have helped, explain how; if they haven't, explain why not.

23. Discuss what you learned in Unit 6 about reading speed (and comprehension). How can you apply this knowledge to your own reading skills?

Answers to Rapid Discrimination Drills 1–10

Activity	1	2	3	4	5	6	7	8	9	10
Question: 1	4	4	2	1	2	1	2	3	4	1
2	5	4	3	3	5	1	4	5	3	3
3	2	2	2	2	3	3	3	1	3	2
4	3	3	3	4	1	4	1	4	4	5
5	5	5	3	5	4	2	5	2	3	4
6	1	4	2	2	1	1	2	4	1	2
7	3	1	1	1	2	2	4	1	1	1
8	1	2	4	5	3	2	1	3	4	3
9	2	5	1	4	5	2	3	5	2	5
10	4	1	2	3	4	2	5	2	4	4
11	5	4	4	1	2	1	1	2	2	2
12	3	5	2	5	4	4	3	4	4	1
13	1	3	2	3	1	3	2	1	2	3
14	4	4	1	4	3	4	3	3	4	5
15	2	2	3	2	5	1	4	5	2	4
16	5	3	2	3	1	4	1	2	2	4
17	3	1	3	1	2	1	5	4	4	2
18	4	4	2	4	3	3	2	1	3	1
19	1	5	3	2	3	4	3	3	2	3
20	2	1	2	5	4	3	4	5	1	5

Answers to Comprehension Questions 1–4

Activity	6.12	6.13	6.14	6.15
Question: 1	false	true	true	false
2	true	true	false	true
3	false	false	true	true
4	true	true	false	true
5	false	false	true	false
6	false	false	false	false
7	true	false	false	false
8	true	false	true	true
9	false	false	true	true
10	true	false	false	false

Skimming and Scanning

You already have been introduced to the idea that you read different materials at different rates of speed. For example, you would not read *Mad* Magazine at the same speed that you would read a letter from a lawyer about an inheritance from a distant aunt. Different speeds should be used for different purposes when reading. If you are reading everything at the same rate, you are wasting your time!

Unit 7 focuses on the range of your reading rates. Do you read at speeds of 100 to 200 words per minute (wpm)? Do you think you can read at speeds of close to 1,000 wpm? You are about to discover the answers to these questions.

You will begin with a slow and careful rate and advance through the rapid and very rapid rates achieved in skimming and scanning. The range of your reading rates may surprise you.

Flexible Reading Rates

ACTIVITY 7.1

First you need to be aware that there *are* different reading rates. You may be surprised at just how flexible your current rates are. For instance, without realizing it, you probably use different rates to skim the newspaper and scan the phone book than you use to read this textbook.

On a separate sheet of paper, begin a section of notes entitled "Skimming and Scanning." Read the selection "Reading Rates Should Be Flexible," and answer the following questions. Remember, for better memory retention and re-call, be sure to write both the questions and the answers.

Skimming and Scanning

1. What three things determine your reading rate?
2. What is *scanning*? When should you use it?
3. What is *skimming*? When should you use it?
4. When should you use a rate that is rapid? Very rapid? Average? Slow and careful?
5. What two factors influence reading rates?

Reading Rates Should Be Flexible

If someone asks you "What is your reading speed?" you can assume that he or she doesn't know much about reading. Reading everything fast or slow is the sign of a poor reader. If you are a good reader, you have several different reading rates.

A good reader shifts from one rate to another according to the following considerations:

1. What is the *purpose* of your reading? Are you studying or reading for pleasure? Are you getting a general overview, or are you looking for specific facts?
2. How *difficult* is the material to comprehend? Is it hard or easy for you to read the selection?
3. How *familiar* is the subject matter to you? Is this all new material or do you have some background in the subject?

Good readers use many different rates. If you have never thought about this, you will be surprised to learn that good readers switch from one rate to another as they need to. No conscious thought process is used; they just switch automatically.

Let's consider the rates involved in skimming and scanning. In *skimming*, you get an overview or hit only the major points of the material. You read the first few paragraphs, then glance over the remaining material, noting the chapter headings and words in bold type. Skimming is useful for getting acquainted with a new text, for choosing suitable reference material for a report, or for selecting a book from the library. Your skimming rates might range from 800 to 1,000 words per minute (wpm).

In *scanning*, you glance at material until you find a particular piece of infor-mation. When you look for a telephone number, or you find a particular date in a history book chapter full of dates, you scan. Your scanning rate might be 1,000 to 1,500 wpm or more.

Clearly, skimming and scanning are valuable skills for you to acquire. They have many practical uses.

You range of reading rates will include the following:

1. Very rapid—perhaps 400 wpm. Used for light, entertaining reading, such as fast-moving fiction.

2. Rapid—perhaps 350 wpm. Used for fairly easy material from which you need only the more important facts.

3. Average—perhaps 250 wpm. Used for most of the material read in daily life and for some school work.

4. Slow and careful—perhaps 200 down to 50 wpm. Used for thorough reading, to remember details, difficult concepts, and vocabulary.

You may need to shift from one reading rate to another within the same article or chapter. Good readers can do it without even thinking about it. For example, you might read the beginning of an article at an average rate, as you are being introduced to its contents. But as you proceed, a step-by-step technique is outlined, and you would switch to a slow and careful rate to increase your memory retention. At the end of the article, the author might restate the major points covered. Again you would shift gears, returning to an average of fairly rapid reading rate, depending on your familiarity with the material.

Remember that your reading rates are extremely personal. Although you may have a variety of rates that you have learned to use easily, the speeds you can attain are not the same as those of another person. Temperament and intelligence also influence reading rates. With practice, you will learn what reading rates work best for you.

Skimming and Scanning

ACTIVITY 7.2

In Activity 7.1 you were introduced to the concepts of skimming and scanning. You may have been surprised to find that you already use these techniques in your everyday life without even thinking about it. But you do use these same tools in your academic pursuits? If you do not, you are wasting valuable study time. Skimming and scanning are reading techniques you should use when you study.

For example, do you reread the entire chapter the night before a test? Instead of wasting your study time doing that, use the skimming technique to review the chapter. Skimming has another practical academic use: If you were not able to read the chapter in time for class discussion, try previewing or overviewing as an emergency measure.

In Activity 7.2, you will learn about three specific techniques: previewing, overviewing, and reviewing. They will increase your ability to read only the parts that you need to know for a particular situation.

Begin by reading the selection entitled "Skimming and Scanning." On a separate sheet of paper, add to your notes on this topic. Then define the following new terms: *preview*; *review*; *overview*. Be sure to include examples of their uses.

Skimming and Scanning

You have already done a number of activities that focused on the skill of reading materials at different rates. Learning how to vary the rate at which you read is invaluable. It will not only save you time, it will also increase your comprehension.

You have already been introduced to two types of very rapid reading.

- **Skimming:** passing quickly over an entire selection to get a general idea or "gist" of its contents. For example, you skim a chapter in your history book to review your knowledge of the Civil War.

- **Scanning:** glancing at a selection for a specific piece of information and stopping when you find it. For example, you scan the S column in the telephone book looking for Joe Santiago's number.

The major difference, then, between skimming and scanning is that, when you finish skimming, you have covered the entire selection briefly; in scanning, you glance only until you find what you are looking for, and then you stop.

Skimming and scanning both involve reading selectively. In other words, you read only those parts that will serve your purpose. Skimming, however, involves three basic forms of selective reading—previewing, overviewing, and reviewing.

- **Previewing:** The prefix *pre* means before; to preview is to view the material *before* you actually begin reading it. Previewing is usually followed by a more thorough reading. You can use previewing to select a book, survey a chapter, or search for appropriate research material.

- **Overviewing:** Overviewing is getting a "big picture" view of the material. Overviewing usually is *not* followed by another reading. You use overviewing to get an overall sense of the content of an article or book.

- **Reviewing:** The prefix *re* means *again*. When you review, you view the material again. Reviewing follows a previous reading. You can use reviewing to go back over material to refresh your memory, especially before a test or important discussion.

Skimming and scanning are both done rapidly. Remember, though, that they differ in purpose and length.

ACTIVITIES
7.3–7.7

Your Personal Reading Rates

Now that you understand about flexible rates and varying purposes for reading, you will have an opportunity to see just how greatly your reading rates can vary. Intellectually, you know that you don't read everything at the same speed. As you follow the instructions for the reading rate samples, you will see just how different the rates really are.

You will begin by examining and recording your *slow and careful* rate—the rate you use when you study or when you want to remember specific details. Next, you will have an opportunity to use and record your *average* rate. This rate is used when you want to recall main ideas. A faster rate may be used when you are reading for pleasure. Recording your skimming speed will tell you how fast your *rapid* or "once over lightly" rate is. Your scanning rate will be *very rapid*, since you race along looking for a specific item when you scan. As you compare the different speeds, you will realize how variable your reading rates are.

Reading Rate Chart

You will need a chart for recording your reading rates. Divide a sheet of paper into two columns. Label the columns with the headings shown in the illustration. Be sure to leave plenty of room to record times and answer questions. You will use this chart for Activities 7.4 through 7.8.

First you will record the time you begin reading; then the time you stop reading. Next, answer the comprehension questions.

After you have answered the questions, subtract the time you began from the time you stopped to find your total reading time.

Example: Time stopped   2:30
Time began   <u>2:22</u>
Total time   :08

Next, turn to page 106 to find the number of words per minute you read.

READING RATE CHART

Time	Minutes	Seconds
Activity 7.4 **Slow and Careful**		
Time stopped	_____	_____
Time began	_____	_____
Total time read	_____	_____
Words per minute	_____	
Score	_____	
Activity 7.5 **Average**		
Time stopped	_____	_____
Time began	_____	_____
Total time read	_____	_____
Words per minute	_____	
Score	_____	
Activity 7.6 **Rapid**		
Time stopped	_____	_____
Time began	_____	_____
Total time read	_____	_____
Words per minute	_____	
Gist of article:		
Activity 7.7 **Very Rapid**		
Time stopped	_____	_____
Time began	_____	_____
Total time read	_____	_____
Words per minute	_____	
What does it mean to "learn your boss's management style"?		

Slow and Careful Reading Rate

Before you begin reading the article "Creating Successful Study Habits," note the time and write it on your paper. (For greater accuracy, if your instructor is not timing you, use a watch or clock with a second hand.)

Read this article as a *slow* and *careful* rate for maximum comprehension. The material you will be reading is similar to that in a textbook, and you will be given a test over specific details from the article.

When you finish reading, again note and record the time. In order to compute the total amount of time you spent in reading the selection, subtract the time you began reading from the time you stopped. Next, consult the conversion chart on page 106 in order to record your reading rate in words per minute.

To measure your comprehension, without looking back at the article, answer on a separate sheet of paper the ten true-false questions in the Comprehension Test section. Check your answers; then compare your score by multiplying your number correct by ten.

Creating Successful Study Habits

Webster's Dictionary states that a habit is something done often and easily. The word *often* should be emphasized whenever speaking about developing study habits. The habits that will help you be most successful in your studies are the ones that you repeat daily both at school and at home.

You should practice the following study habits daily.

1. Use an assignment sheet in every class.
2. Write down all assignments in full detail.
3. Read the assignment sheets after the end of your class, but *before* leaving school.
4. Bring home all the books, worksheets, folders, and notebooks needed to complete the homework.

If you want to study and complete assignments successfully at home, you must develop these study habits *at school.* After all, the most common excuses for not finishing or doing homework are that the book was left at school or that the assignment was forgotten. You won't forget if you develop the study habits that help you remember these important items.

The study habits that will help you at home include the following.

1. Begin your homework at the same time every night.
2. Do your work in the same place each night.
3. Ask your parents or guardians to help you maintain a positive work environment.

Once again, you must repeat this routine every night in order to make these successful study habits. Common homework hassles such as difficulty getting started or failing to allow enough time to finish the work are avoided by starting the work at the same time each night. Your starting time should allow at least one and one-half hours for completing the assigned work.

Where you do your work should also become a habit. Always doing the work at the same location breeds success in several ways. First, it helps you get started on your work at the same time each evening. Supplies you use often, such as paper, pen, pencil, ruler, and eraser, can all be stored at or near your study area. Thus, you avoid a time-consuming and distracting hunt for these items each night.

Your work area should be well lit and should include a large flat surface. It should also be as free of noisy distractions as possible. The most common distractions are televisions, radios, stereos, ringing telephones, and younger brothers and sisters. Every distraction makes it harder to complete the work and do it well.

In addition, the encouragement and support of a parent or guardian constitutes an important aspect of creating good study habits. Ask a parent to get in the routine of not only asking if you have homework, but also asking to see your day's assignment sheet. You parent might help by quizzing you, or by assisting with any problems you encounter with an assignment. He or she might also review your completed work.

You'll finish your homework more quickly and efficiently if you adopt and practice the study habits discussed here. With self-discipline and dedication, you, too, can be a good student.

Below are ten questions. Read each one carefully. Then, on a separate sheet of paper, write the correct answer beside the appropriate number. Do not look back at the article. When you finish, check your answers and multiply your number correct by ten. Record your comprehension score on your paper.

1. You should use an assignment sheet in:
   A. every class.
   B. some classes.
   C. important classes.

2. You should use the assignment sheet:
   A. often.
   B. daily.
   C. occasionally.

3. You should read the assignment sheet:
   A. at the end of each class period.
   B. after your last class ends, but before you leave school.
   C. before you start your homework at night.

4. Beginning homework at the same time each night:
   A. helps you get started more easily.
   B. provides you with enough time to finish everything.
   C. both of the above

5. Your starting time should allow you:
   A. a half hour of study time each night.
   B. one hour of study time each night.
   C. one and one-half hours of study time each night.

6. Doing your work in the same place each night:

    A. helps you get started at the same time each night.

    B. avoids delay because all your supplies are there.

    C. both of the above

7. According to the author, distractions should be avoided because:

    A. they slow you down.

    B. they make it harder for you to complete the work and do it well.

    C. both of the above

8. A parent might help by:

    A. asking if you have assignments.

    B. asking to see your assignment sheet.

    C. both of the above

9. A parent can also help by:

    A. quizzing you on your work.

    B. reviewing your completed work.

    C. both of the above

10. You will benefit from the study habits discussed in this article if you practice them:

    A. the evening before a test.

    B. at least three evenings each week.

    C. every evening.

ACTIVITY 7.5

Average Reading Rate

Let's go on to consider average reading to determine your rate in words per minute. You will be using a light, entertaining selection that you can read at a faster rate than the previous article. However, do not read so fast that you lose comprehension.

Note the time and write it on your paper. Then begin reading. When you finish reading, again note the time and record it. Subtract the time you began from the time you stopped to determine the total time read. Turn to the Conversion Chart on page 106 to compute your words read per minute, and record this figure. Then take the comprehension test for this story.

Mary Had a Little Lamb

It's a little-known fact of nature that sharks are not the only animals which have feeding frenzies. The slightest hint of a milk bottle will send orphan (bum) lambs wild. They will stampede, trampling any hapless bystanders in the dust. Anyone brave enough to try feeding two bottles to more than two lambs will have fingers chewed, ears nibbled, and noses bitten. The mere presence of a known food supplier will turn a field of angelic bum lambs into a frenzied mob. Yet, there are some compensations to owning bums if you can solve the feeding problem. Pincushion is an example.

Pincushion and his sister Giraffe entered the world on a chilly, blustery March day. Preemies, they were too weak to stand, too small to have reached their mother if they could have stood. Only my timely arrival saved them being put out of their misery by my husband, Chris, who thought they would never survive. I took them home to see if I could save them, while my husband gave the grieving ewe a new lamb who needed a mother.

Giraffe we named immediately. She had a long delicate face and looked for all the world like a miniature giraffe. Pincushion' s name came later.

Once home I began the process of warming the half-frozen lambs. They were immersed in comfortably hot water and fed a small amount of brandy to warm their insides. After they were briskly rubbed dry, I gently forced colostrum milk down their throats with a needleless syringe. They were too weak to suck from a bottle.

Within two hours they could raise their heads and were placed in their new home—our bathtub with a rug in the bottom. Within four hours they had developed pneumonia, and the fight for their lives began. They were each given three shots—two antibiotics and a stimulant. Feeding continued every three to four hours. Shots were administered daily.

By the third day we seemed to have conquered the pneumonia. It looked as though we were going to save them. Then scours (diarrhea) hit them. The needles came out again. More medicine was administered, and Pincushion earned his name. None of our other bums had ever been given this many shots in this few days.

When the crisis passed, the lambs gained enough strength to stand and take faltering steps. We cheered their progress around the house. They began to suck a bottle of milk and rapidly became family pets.

These lambs weighed perhaps a pound a piece when they were born. Their legs resembled matchsticks. Their heads were as fine as a fawn's, and their emaciated bodies were painful to see. By the time they were two weeks old, their bodies had begun to fill out. My husband wanted his tub back. It was time to move the lambs to our lamb nursery.

In an old house we owned, we had set up a straw-lined pen for newborn bums. Pincushion and Giraffe were installed in this pen. Tragically, Giraffe's delicate constitution could not withstand the transition. Soon we were fighting a losing battle with pneumonia.

While Giraffe struggled to keep a spark of life, Pincushion grabbed hold of life. His small size allowed him to slip through the sides of his pen. Once outside he mingled with lambs six to ten times his size. Mealtimes were trample time for Pincushion. He was always on the bottom of the pile but always fighting his way toward the top.

Time and time again we placed him back in the nursery, plugging more holes each time. Time and time again we picked him up from the bottom of the heap when we returned to feed the bums. Finally, we left him with his friends.

When Pincushion was about a month old we put a self-feeder in with the lambs. we were tired of having our fingers gnawed at feeding time. As soon as we saw that the bums had the hang of things, we left to complete our other chores. When we returned, Pincushion lay on the floor moaning and writhing in agony.

His belly was distended to three times its normal size. He was a victim of his own gluttony.

With tears in my eyes I moved Pincushion back to his old bathtub to die in peace. I closed the shower curtains and left him there while I went to town for an appointment. I knew nothing I could do to ease his agony, and I could not stand to see the end.

When I returned and threw back the shower curtains, Pincushion was gone. "Well," I thought, "he died, and Chris has taken the body away." Some need to say "good-bye" drove me to search the trash can—no Pincushion. "Chris probably took him somewhere so that I didn't have to see him"—my thoughts were interrupted by a faint bleating. I hurried to a small outdoor pen, and there Pincushion stood demanding to be fed.

The rest of the story I heard from Chris. He had stopped at the house to pick up the body a few hours after I left. He was sure that the lamb would have died by then. Instead he was greeted at the door by a vigorous Pincushion, wanting food. He replaced Pincushion in the tub and closed the curtains, but before he could leave the bathroom, Pincushion was out of the tub and at his heels. That is when Pincushion was transferred to the outdoor pen.

When Pincushion could be trusted to digest all he could eat at the self-feeder, we transferred him back to the bum pen. Although the tiniest of all the lambs, once he grabbed a nipple at the feeder no lamb could ever dislodge him. He sucked until the last drop of milk was gone, oblivious of the other lambs who pushed, shoved, crawled over and under him. He thrived, grew, and finally became the leader of the bums.

Pincushion outgrew many of the bums and lived a long, pleasant summer with us. We never lacked for companionship when Pincushion was near. He followed at our heels, nudged us to be petted, and nuzzled us with affection.

We sold Pincushion in the fall. There is no room on a modern farm for a nonproducing animal. We turned our heads and could not look at this gentle friend and companion. We were ashamed that scarce dollars dictated the fate of Pincushion.

In his short time with us, he was a model of bravery, indomitable courage, perseverance and friendship. Tucked away with all my memories of good and fine things is the memory of Pincushion.

To measure your comprehension, without looking back at the article, answer the following ten questions. On a separate sheet of paper, write the letter of the correct answer beside the appropriate number. When you finish, check your answers and multiply your number correct by ten. Record your comprehension score on your paper.

1. A bum lamb is a lamb that is:

    A. deformed.   B. sick.   C. an orphan.

2. The sight of _____ will send angelic lambs into a frenzied mob.

    A. their mother   B. a milk bottle   C. hay

3. Pincushion and Giraffe were sick because they were:

    A. cold.   B. preemies.   C. ignored.

4. In order to save the lambs, the author:
   A. immersed them in comfortably hot water and rubbed them dry.
   B. fed them a small amount of brandy and colostrum milk.
   C. both A and B

5. The first new home for the lambs was:
   A. a bathtub.   B. a playpen.   C. an old house.

6. The lambs had to battle:
   A. pneumonia.   B. scours.   C. both A and B

7. The lamb that showed the greatest will to survive was:
   A. Pincushion.   B. Giraffe.   C. neither A nor B

8. Pincushion battled for survival a fourth time because of:
   A. the cold.   B. greed for food.   C. the other lambs.

9. Pincushion survived because of:
   A. loving care.   B. a strong spirit.   C. both A and B

10. The author:
    A. cared very much for the lambs.
    B. was happy to sell the lambs and take a profit.
    C. wondered why she spent so much time with the lambs.

Rapid Reading Rate

The next reading rate we will focus on is skimming. There is a technique to skimming efficiently. Try it on the article entitled "Guidelines for Succeeding with Your Boss."

A. Read the title.
B. Read the introduction (first four paragraphs).
C. Read the ten rules (headings only).
D. Read the conclusion (last two paragraphs).

Begin by noting the time and writing it on your chart. Then skim "Guidelines for Succeeding with Your Boss," using the method outlined above.

When you finish, record the time you stopped; then subtract the time you began from the time you stopped to determine the total time read. Turn to the Conversion Chart on page 106 to compute your words read per minute.

Next, to check your comprehension, write a brief paragraph explaining the gist of the article.

Guidelines for Succeeding with Your Boss

All the books and articles on how to make good at work usually ignore one very basic premise in "how to get ahead." This practical bit of wisdom never seems to come up in polite conversation, although every employee from the office assistant to the vice president is well aware of it.

Figure Out What the Boss Wants   There is no mystery to this; it is really only common sense. Find out how your boss likes to be dealt with and learn how to do it. You will both benefit.

Here are ten guidelines for getting along with your boss that surveyors of management methods have gleaned from their work with bosses of all types.

1. *Be professional.* Bosses set the tone for the degree of formality or informality that they are most comfortable with in the workplace. Also, as a general rule, to avoid embarrassment for one or both of you, personal problems are usually best left at home.

2. *Respect them and their authority.* Remember that the buck stops with them. They are ultimately responsible for every success or failure. Don't challenge their right to tell you what to do or to judge what you have done. They are paid to do just that. It is their job.

3. *They are in touch with the whole picture.* You deal with only one aspect of the company's business. Their scope of responsibility is much greater than yours. They may, in turn, report to several bosses instead of one, as you do.

4. *Is your timing appropriate?* At what time of the day is your boss most receptive to new ideas? When is he or she most likely to be irritable? Be aware of your boss's schedule. Think about what might be happening in the company that will demand his or her undivided attention. Then plan your time with your boss accordingly.

5. *Learn their management style.* Some bosses delegate a lot of authority. Others do not. Some bosses expect to be consulted about everything. Others expect you to do your job on your own, once you have instructions. Some bosses are very formal in their manner, while others are more relaxed and friendly. Learn all you can about your boss's style.

6. *Find out how they prefer to be contacted.* Can you drop by anytime, or do you need an appointment? Can you do your business over the phone, or does your boss prefer that you sit down across the desk from him or her?

7. *They are only human.* Many people expect their bosses to be perfect and then complain when they are not. Remember, bosses make mistakes and say things without thinking just as you do. They also may have other things on their minds when you approach them. Recognize that they, too, are human, and you will avoid much anxiety and misunderstanding when some days do not go as smoothly as you would like.

8. *Keep them aware of what goes on.* This is the highest priority for many bosses surveyed. They want to know who, what, why, when, and where. They need to know these five Ws in order to plan ahead, make decisions, and report to their own bosses. When you are reporting to them about something, be sure to learn whether they like to know all the details or want

only general information. Also remember that bosses like to learn good news as well as the bad. It may be a pleasant change.

9. *Don't try too hard to please the boss.* To constantly try to please makes you less than a favorite among your co-workers, and you probably spend more time with them than with your boss, anyway. There's an old saying that "cream always rises to the top." Your path will be smoother if, on the way up, you get along with others.

10. *Bosses are individuals.* Keep this in mind when trying to understand them. They are not a company—they are real and unique people. Management techniques are helpful only if they relate to your particular boss.

You will benefit by learning about your bosses' management styles. Of course, the best way to succeed with your boss is to do your job well, but the extra effort it takes to learn more about his or her style of operating pays dividends for both of you.

Remember, if you look good, your boss looks good. Your ability to help your boss do his or her job better will lead you to even more success in the future.

Very Rapid Reading Rate

ACTIVITY 7.7

To conclude this survey of your reading rates, focus now on scanning, the fastest reading rate of all. Note the time you begin and write it on your chart; then turn back to page 104 and scan the article "Guidelines for Succeeding with Your Boss" to answer this question: What does it mean to "learn your boss's management style"?

As you finish, record the time you stopped; subtract your starting time from your stopping time and convert the result to words per minute using the chart on page 106. Answer the question briefly.

Now take a look back at the range of your personal reading rates. You may read at speeds of 100 to 200 words per minute or at speeds approaching or exceeding 1,000 words per minute. Whatever your rates, no doubt you'll agree: Your reading rate is flexible.

Conversion Chart for Reading Rates

COMPUTING READING RATES IN WORDS PER MINUTE

Slow and Careful

"Creating Successful Study Habits"

550 words total

2 minutes = 276 words per minute
2:10 = 254 words per minute
2:20 = 236 words per minute
2:30 = 219 words per minute
2:40 = 206 words per minute
2:50 = 194 words per minute
3:00 = 183 words per minute
3:10 = 174 words per minute
3:20 = 165 words per minute
3:30 = 157 words per minute
3:40 = 150 words per minute
3:50 = 144 words per minute
4:00 = 138 words per minute
4:10 = 132 words per minute
4:20 = 127 words per minute
4:30 = 122 words per minute
4:40 = 118 words per minute
4:50 = 114 words per minute
5:00 = 110 words per minute

Average

"Mary Had a Little Lamb"

1,120 words total

3 minutes = 373 words per minute

3:10 = 358 words per minute	5:10 = 218 words per minute
3:20 = 343 words per minute	5:20 = 212 words per minute
3:30 = 328 words per minute	5:30 = 206 words per minute
3:40 = 313 words per minute	5:40 = 200 words per minute
3:50 = 298 words per minute	5:50 = 194 words per minute
4:00 = 280 words per minute	6:00 = 186 words per minute
4:10 = 271 words per minute	6:10 = 182 words per minute
4:20 = 262 words per minute	6:20 = 178 words per minute
4:30 = 253 words per minute	6:30 = 174 words per minute
4:40 = 244 words per minute	6:40 = 170 words per minute
4:50 = 235 words per minute	6:50 = 166 words per minute
5:00 = 224 words per minute	7:00 = 160 words per minute

Rapid Skimming

"Guidelines for Succeeding with Your Boss"

692 words total

:30 = 1,384 words per minute
:40 = 1,308 words per minute
:50 = 830 words per minute
1:00 = 692 words per minute
1:10 = 593 words per minute
1:20 = 519 words per minute
1:30 = 461 words per minute
1:40 = 415 words per minute
1:50 = 377 words per minute

Very Rapid Scanning

"Guidelines for Succeeding with Your Boss"

:10 = 2,400 words per minute
:20 = 1,200 words per minute
:30 = 800 words per minute
:40 = 600 words per minute
:50 = 480 words per minute
1:00 = 400 words per minute
1:10 = 343 words per minute
1:20 = 300 words per minute
1:30 = 266 words per minute

Skimming a Book

Any skills that save you time and make you a better reader are skills worth learning. Skimming and scanning will do just that. Try the following exercise using skimming to improve your rapid reading techniques.

Periodically, you will need to select a book for a project, report, or research paper, and you will have to look at several books before choosing the best one for the assignment. Knowing how to skim a book quickly will be a valuable skill. To give you practice in skimming for this purpose, select a book that pertains to a current research assignment. Or, choose a book from those provided for you by your instructor. Then use the following techniques to skim it.

1. Look at the title, author, and publication date. Has the book been reprinted? If so, how many times? Is the publication date recent enough to be appropriate for your research topic?
2. Read the publisher's comments on the cover or dust jacket.
3. Look at the preface or other introductory material.
4. Look at the table of contents (if there is one).
5. Look at the first chapter, using a skimming (previewing) technique.
6. Leaf through the rest of the book, looking at major headings, charts, pictures, graphs, and so on.

Now, on a separate sheet of paper, write a brief paragraph summarizing the contents of the book, and conclude with a statement of whether the book will be of value to you.

More Skimming and Scanning

The next four activities will give you practice in scanning. The activities are similar to those you might do in everyday situations at school or at work. Without scanning, these would become very time-consuming tasks. Imagine how long it would take to use the dictionary, telephone book, or encyclopedia if you had to start at the beginning and look at every entry until you came to the information you were seeking. Clearly, scanning is an essential reading technique.

Use a separate sheet of paper and a watch or clock with a second hand to time yourself if your instructor is not timing you. Be sure to note and record the time you begin and the time you finish each exercise. When you finish, subtract the time you started from the time you finished to compute the total time it took you to do the exercise.

Next, check your answers for accuracy and write a brief sentence explaining why this was an exercise in scanning. Can you see improvement as you compare your reading rates and the accuracy you achieved?

ACTIVITY 7.10

Listing Dates

Number a separate sheet of paper from one to fifteen, note and record the time, and begin. Arrange the following list of dates in order, starting with the least recent and ending with the most recent.

10/5/85	4/25/95	8–08–90
June 1, 1976	August 12, 1980	1/12/93
6–21–86	Nov. 4, 1990	2/14/94
January 25, 1989	12–25–94	March 17, 1987
May 1, 1992	7–02–82	September 5, 1991

Did you use skimming or scanning to do this exercise?

ACTIVITY 7.11

Commuter Train Schedule

For Activity 7.11, pay close attention to the column headings in the excerpt from a commuter train schedule in Figure 7.1. To read the timetables first note that the direction of the train (Harvard, Illinois, to Chicago, Illinois) and that the effective days of the week are indicated in the shaded areas of the schedule. Next, note that the train numbers are listed at the top of the timetables in this excerpt. Note where the various stations are listed. Follow across to the right to determine the departure time of each train. Note that you move down the schedule to determine the arrival time for each train at each station.

FIGURE 7.1   Commuter train schedule

Harvard to Chicago – Monday through Friday

CONNECTING SERVICES	PARKING	ZONES	STATIONS		602	604	606	608	610	612	614	616	618	620	622	624	626
					AM	AM	AM	AM	AM	AM	AM	AM	AM	AM	AM	AM	AM
Pace	b	M	HARVARD	LV:	—	—	—	—	5:48	—	—	—	—	6:22	—	—	—
Pace	b	K	McHENRY	LV:	—	—	—	5:53	—	—	—	—	—	—	6:54	—	—
Pace	b*	K	Woodstock		—	—	—	6:02	—	—	—	—	—	6:38		—	—
Pace	e*	I	Crystal Lake		4:50	5:20	5:40		6:14	—	6:18	6:35	—	6:50	↓	7:00	—
	c*	H	Cary		4:56	5:26	5:46		6:22	—	6:27		—	6:58	7:12	↓	—
	b*	H	Fox River Grove		4:59	5:29	5:49	↓	6:25	—	6:30		—	7:01	7:15	↓	—
Pace	e*	G	Barrington		5:07	5:37	5:57	6:18	6:34	6:27	6:38	↓	—	7:11	7:24	7:15	7:27
Pace	e*	F	Palatine		5:14	5:44	6:04	6:27	—	6:36	x6:47	6:56	—	x7:20		7:24	—
Pace	e*	E	Arlington Park		5:19	5:49	6:09	6:32	x6:43	6:41	x6:52	—	x7:11			7:29	x7:40
Pace	e*	E	Arlington Heights		5:23	5:53	6:13	6:37		6:46	x6:56	7:04	x7:16			7:33	x7:45
Pace	e*˙	D	Mount Prospect		5:28	5:58	6:18	6:42		6:51	x7:01		x7:22	↓		7:38	x7:50
Pace	c*	D	Cumberland		5:31	6:01	6:22	6:46	↓	—	x7:05	↓		x7:31	↓	7:42	x7:53
Pace	d*	D	Des Plaines		5:35	6:05	6:26		x6:54	6:56	x7:10	7:13			x7:41	7:45	x7:57
Pace	b	C	Dee Road		5:38	6:08	6:30			6:59	—	7:17			x7:45	↓	x8:02
Pace, CTA Bus	d*	C	Park Ridge		5:41	6:11	6:33			7:02	x7:16	7:21			x7:50	↓	x8:06
CTA Bus	c	C	Edison Park		5:44	6:14	6:36			7:05		7:23				7:54	
CTA Bus	a	C	Norwood Park		5:47	6:17	6:39			7:08		7:26				7:58	
CTA Bus	a	B	Gladstone Park		5:50	6:20	6:42			7:11		—				8:01	
CTA Rail & Bus, Pace	b	B	Jefferson Park		5:53	6:23	6:45			7:14		7:32				8:04	
CTA Rail & Bus	b	B	Irving Park		5:57	6:27	6:49	↓	↓	7:19	↓	7:36	↓	↓	↓	8:08	↓
Metra CTA Bus	a	A	Clybourn		6:03	6:33	6:54	7:05	x7:11	7:26	x7:31	7:41	x7:46	x7:51	x8:05	8:14	x8:21
Metra CTA, Rail & Bus Amtrak, Wendella		A	CHICAGO Passenger Terminal	AR:	6:12	6:42	7:03	7:14	7:19	7:35	7:40	7:50	7:55	8:00	8:15	8:24	8:30

PARKING: Number of spaces available at "a" is 50-99; "b",100-249; "c",250-499; "d",500-749; "e",750 or more.
Wendella Commuter Boat Service operates from late April through early October. For more information call (312) 337-1446.
X: Train stops on center track.   * Bicycle racks available.

FIGURE 7.1 Commuter train schedule (continued)

Harvard to Chicago – Monday through Friday cont'd

STATIONS		628	630	632	634	636	638	640	642	644	646	648	650	652	654	656	658	660	662
		AM	AM	AM	AM	AM	AM	AM	AM	PM	PM	PM	PM	PM	PM	PM	PM	PM	PM
HARVARD	LV:	—	7:08	—	—	7:35	—	9:35	—	—	1:35	—	—	4:35	—	5:35	—	8:35	—
McHENRY	LV:	—	—	7:36	—	—	—	—	—	—	—	—	—	—	—	—	—	—	—
Woodstock		—	7:23	▽	—	7:48	—	9:48	—	—	1:48	—	—	4:48	—	5:48	—	8:48	—
Crystal Lake		—	7:36		—	8:00	9:00	10:00	11:00	12:00	2:00	3:00	4:10	5:00	—	6:00	8:00	9:00	11:59
Cary		—	7:43		—	8:06	9:06	10:06	11:06	12:06	2:06	3:06	4:16	5:06	—	6:06	8:06	9:06	12:05
Fox River Grove		—	7:46	▽	—	8:09	9:09	10:09	11:09	12:09	2:09	3:09	4:19	5:09	—	6:09	8:09	9:09	—
Barrington		7:42	7:54	8:04	7:47	8:16	9:16	10:16	11:16	12:16	2:16	3:16	4:26	5:16	6:05	6:16	8:16	9:16	12:12
Palatine		x7:51	▽	▽	7:56	8:23	9:23	10:23	11:23	12:23	2:23	3:23	4:33	5:23	—	6:23	8:23	9:23	12:19
Arlington Park		x7:56			8:01	8:28	9:28	10:28	11:28	12:28	2:28	3:28	4:38	5:28	6:16	6:28	8:28	9:28	12:24
Arlington Heights		x8:01			8:05	8:32	9:32	10:32	11:32	12:32	2:32	3:32	4:42	5:32		6:32	8:32	9:32	12:28
Mount Prospect				x8:18	▽	8:37	9:37	10:37	11:37	12:37	2:37	3:37	4:47	5:37		6:37	8:37	9:37	12:33
Cumberland			▽		8:11	8:40	9:40	10:40	11:40	12:40	2:40	3:40	4:50	5:40	▽	6:40	8:40	9:40	—
Des Plaines				x8:12	8:14	8:44	9:44	10:44	11:44	12:44	2:44	3:44	4:54	5:44	6:24	6:44	8:44	9:44	12:38
Dee Road			▽		8:17	8:47	9:47	10:47	11:47	12:47	2:47	3:47	4:57	5:47	—	6:47	8:47	9:47	
Park Ridge					8:21	8:50	9:50	10:50	11:50	12:50	2:50	3:50	5:00	5:50	6:29	6:50	8:50	9:50	
Edison Park				x8:28		8:53	9:53	10:53	11:53	12:53	2:53	3:53	5:03	5:53		6:53	8:53	9:53	
Norwood Park					8:25	8:56	9:56	10:56	11:56	12:56	2:56	3:56	5:06	5:56		6:56	8:56	9:56	
Gladstone Park					8:28	—	—	—	—	—	—	—	—	—	▽	—	—	—	▽
Jefferson Park					8:31	9:00	10:00	11:00	12:00	1:00	3:00	4:00	5:10	6:00	6:36	7:00	9:00	10:00	12:49
Irving Park		▽	▽	▽	8:35	9:04	10:04	11:04	12:04	1:04	3:04	4:04	5:14	6:04	6:40	7:04	9:04	10:04	▽
Clybourn		x8:26	x8:31	x8:42	8:44	9:11	10:11	11:11	12:11	1:11	3:11	4:11	5:21	6:11	6:47	7:11	9:11	10:11	▽
CHICAGO Passenger Terminal AR:		8:35	8:40	8:51	8:53	9:20	10:20	11:20	12:20	1:20	3:20	4:20	5:30	6:20	6:57	7:20	9:20	10:20	1:08

Wendella Commuter Boat Service operates from late April through early October. For more information call (312) 337-1446.
X: Train stops on center track.

From the Metra (Union Pacific/Northwest Line) timetable, effective as of 1996.

For this activity, your speed in not important as your accuracy. You will use this type of information (transportation timetables) in everyday life as a commuter and as you plan to travel for yourself or for others.

Write your responses to the following questions on a separate sheet of paper. Use the train schedule provided in Figure 7.1 to answer the questions.

1. If you were going to Chicago, Illinois, from McHenry, Illinois, what is the earliest time you could leave in the morning?

2. How many stops are scheduled between McHenry and Chicago leaving at that time?

3. Which stations have between 250–499 parking spaces available?

4. How many stations have bicycle racks available?

5. If you are meeting a friend in the Chicago passenger terminal at noon, what time must you leave the Des Plaines station? What is the number of the train you need to take?

6. How many connecting service providers are listed? Which one provides limited service?

7. How long does it take to travel between Fox River Grove and Chicago if you take train number 638? Number 630?

8. At what time do the trains begin running each day during the week? When do they stop?

9. How many stops are scheduled at Gladstone Park? What is the number of the train that would allow you to arrive in Chicago before 8:30 A.M.?

10. What are the numbers of the last two trains you could board in Barrington in order to arrive in Chicago before 8:30 A.M.?

Skimming, to review, means reading through an entire selection quickly to get a general idea of its content. Many students find skimming to be one of the most useful techniques they have learned; it will be valuable to you as well. Besides saving you time, skimming also improves your comprehension. In fact, skimming followed by actual reading can double comprehension.

How much information can you get just by skimming something? You will get an opportunity to compare test scores on information you skim with test scores on information you read completely. Both tests will use the same material.

Remember, when you master skimming, you will be able to preview, review, or overview material quickly and easily. This technique will be invaluable for both school and work situations.

In order to skim efficiently, use the following method.

1. Read the title of the selection.
2. Read the first paragraph.
3. Read the first sentence of each of the other paragraphs.
4. Read the final paragraph.

Use a separate sheet of paper. Label it as shown below.

Skimming		**Actual Reading**	
Time stopped	_____	Time stopped	_____
Time began	_____	Time began	_____
Total time	_____	Total time	_____
Words per minute	_____	Words per minute	_____
Score	_____	Score	_____

ACTIVITY 7.12

Skimming

If your instructor is not timing you, use a watch or a clock with a second hand to note the times you start and finish each exercise. Record these times on your paper. When you ar ready, or when your instructor gives the signal, begin reading "Cycling's Risks" using the skimming technique described previously in Steps 1 to 4. When you finish with the exercise, subtract the time you started from the time you stopped to determine the total time used. Then turn to the Conversion Chart (page 114) to figure the number of words per minute. Next, number a separate sheet of paper from one to ten and answer the Comprehension Test questions.

ACTIVITY 7.13

Actual Reading

Now read the entire article entitled "Cycling's Risks." Record the times you begin and finish. Subtract your beginning time from your finishing time to find total time read; again, turn to the Conversion Chart on page 114 to convert the results to words per minute. Take the Comprehension Test again, writing your answers on a separate sheet of paper. Also, now that you have read all of the article, make any changes you want to in your answers to the first Comprehension Test you took after using skimming.

For *each* test (after skimming and then after actual reading), multiply your number correct by ten to get your percentage scores. Record these scores in the appropriate blanks. Now compare them. How many answers did you change? (If you scored 70 percent or better on the skimming test, you are using skimming very effectively.) Notice how much information you got simply by skimming. Did you notice skimming helped you improve your comprehension when you did the actual reading of the article? You will find skimming beneficial with many kinds of reading materials.

Cycling's Risks

My noncycling friends think bike racers are crazy. They can't believe how long road races are. If they get on a bike and try to sustain 20 mph they become exhausted. As a result they are flatly incredulous when I tell them that races go at 25 to 28 mph for several hours. Sprinters' hills loom like mountains in their minds and the Mt. Evans Hill Climb is simply unimaginable. When I assert that the training which brings such performances within reach is enjoyable rather than agonizing, they nod knowingly to one another.

But these doubters reserve their most vehement attacks on my sanity for what they perceive as the unacceptable dangers of cycling. Recently a friend picked up an old copy of a racing publication and read about Alan Kingsbery's near-fatal collision with a truck crossing a time trial course. When he finished he looked at me searchingly. "How can you justify your sport," he said, "when you have a wife and son?"

I did not consider the question idle, presumptuous, or even rhetorical. I have asked it of myself at times, especially after crashes or close calls. Certainly there are safer activities for a person in his thirties who has heavy responsibilities in life. But because I enjoy cycling so much, I find it easy to justify—what dangers there are seem eminently worth the risk. Yet part of me realizes that my justifications are not the real reason I ride in spite of the hazards. Consider how easily I can find excuses to ignore the danger:

> Given the state of automobile accident statistics, I am probably at least as safe when racing, commuting, and training as I would be in a car.
>
> Wearing a hardshell cycling helmet cuts down on the risk of serious injury and fatality. And I wear one at all times, not just when racing.
>
> We have to take some calculated risks in life. Man is by nature a risk-taker, a challenger of limits, or he would not have evolved. In fact, the whole evolutionary history of life is a history of the risks that nature takes when minute individual differences are introduced into the species. Many of these fail, but some are successful and lead to improved adaptation to the challenges of life. In the same way, an individual human life without risk would

result in a stagnant personality. Thoreau was right: When it comes time for me to die, I do not want to look back on my life and find that I have not lived.

Racing helps me to stay fit. The alternative, a sedentary lifestyle, is more deadly than any danger faced while cycling. Of course, I could get fit by swimming, but I have no talent for it—I would probably drown (that really is an unjustifiable risk). Serious running, for me, is unhealthy. My knees can rarely handle runs over twenty miles and my hips get sore at random, apparently just to be contrary. Although it may be argued that I could maintain my fitness by recreational cycling and avoid the sport's dangers, I see commuting, training, and racing as part of the whole experience. Each reinforces and gives meaning to the others until the composite attitude toward transportation, health, enjoyment, and competition merges into a lifestyle.

I am safer in cycling than in other sports I could choose. I played football enthusiastically and with abandon for ten years, but the major injury and death statistics from that sport continue to appall me. After college I got involved in mountaineering. I still have recurring visions of a basketball-size boulder bounding at me down a couloir on Crestone Needle. It missed; my knees shook for an hour. When I downhill ski it is either me or the mountain and I've never won yet. I could become a motorcycle racer, a cliff diver, a Pipeline surfer or an Indy driver. In comparison to many sports, not to mention wars to everyday household accidents, cycling is outrageously safe.

Even though all these arguments roll glibly off my tongue, responsibility to family remains a disturbing and pertinent point. However, I would rather take a small and calculated risk to be a fit, alive, interesting, and exuberant cyclist than come ponderously home each evening to the TV and snack tray. The risks of such a lifestyle may be less obvious than those of racing, but they are more insidious, more deadly and, to my mind, far less acceptable. In the end I can easily justify my cycling: We cannot choose the time and manner of our deaths, but we can have a say in the style and quality of our lives.

But to list reasons why I can accept the dangers of cycling is merely to eliminate the negative. Trying to justify cycling by checking off the debits ignores the positive reasons for racing and training that overwhelm the drawbacks.

My reasons for racing do not arise out of a simplistic view of competition. I rarely taste the thrill of victory; as for the agony of defeat, I try to keep my performances in proper perspective. Racing is certainly not my whole life, nor do I wish it to be. When I am honest with myself I realize that I race for three reasons, all compelling, but none noble or unselfish.

I race because I hate pain. I know that such an admission, besides sounding like a paradox, is inconsistent with the cliché of the macho cyclist picking gravel out of grisly abrasions while gritting his teeth on a spare crankset bolt, but it is true. The longer I have been involved in sports, the more fascinated I have been by my reaction to pain. I have become addicted to the process of facing that pain and trying to beat my fear and loathing. The result is now a post-race euphoria that is only slowly replaced by accelerating anxiety about the next contest. Aristotle may not have been a bike racer, but he knew about fear and pain. He called it catharsis: a combination of pity, terror, and relief. He was talking about the audience's reaction to tragedy, but it is applicable to us moderns as we experience self-inflicted "sports pain"—pity for ourselves at the specter of approaching pain, terror that it will hurt so much we'll quit or slow down and get dropped, and finally relief that the demon has been met face to face and conquered, or at least confronted honestly. In the weekly cycle of quiescence, anxiety, competition, and catharsis, my fear and hatred of pain is purged.

I also race because I like to ride with other people—sometimes. Since I live far from the area where most of Colorado's races and riders are located, I usually train alone. I prefer it that way because I can ride when it fits my schedule. But part of the thrill of cycling is how bikes handle around other bikes: the vacuum, suction, lightening sensation of a big pack, the psychedelic patterns of alloys and jerseys, the sense of shared enterprise and momentary alliances, the way the pack develops a mind and will of its own, independent of, and yet connected to, each rider's perceptions and personality. Nowhere is this better experienced than in a race where individuals merge into one sinuous group while still maintaining their separate wills and motivations and personalities. When I train alone, I clear my head of all the trivia of the day. But when I am in a pack of riders, I feel a part of the race sharing the hopes, dreams, and honest fears of everyone else.

Finally, I simply like to ride a bicycle and racing gives me an excuse to do it often. I don't need to justify my riding to other people, but when daily tasks press hard on the time I set aside for me, it helps to be able to justify it to myself.

On a separate sheet of paper, write *true* if the statement is true or *false* if the statement is false.

1. Noncyclists think bike racers are to be admired for their bravery.
2. Noncyclists think cycling is dangerous.
3. Fred Matheny, the author of this article, feels he is as safe when cycle racing as when riding in a car.
4. Matheny feels wearing a helmet offers very little protection from serious injury.
5. The author believes in taking risks to some degree.
6. He feels he is safer in cycling than in playing football or in downhill skiing, but not as safe as when swimming.
7. Matheny prefers to ride with others all the time.
8. Matheny uses racing as an excuse to ride his bike simply because he loves to ride it.
9. The author periodically considers giving up bicycle racing because of the dangers involved and because he hates pain.
10. Matheny thinks about bike racing's dangers versus his responsibility to his family.

CONVERSION CHART: SKIMMING AND ACTUAL READING

"Cycling's Risks"

1,110 words total

30 sec = 2,220 words per minute
40 sec = 1,666 words per minute
50 sec = 1,325 words per minute
1:00 min = 1,110 words per minute
1:10 min = 943 words per minute
1:20 min = 827 words per minute
1:30 min = 733 words per minute
1:40 min = 662 words per minute
1:50 min = 601 words per minute
2:00 min = 550 words per minute
2:10 min = 507 words per minute
2:20 min = 472 words per minute
2:30 min = 440 words per minute
2:40 min = 413 words per minute
2:50 min = 388 words per minute
3:00 min = 366 words per minute
3:10 min = 347 words per minute
3:20 min = 330 words per minute
3:30 min = 314 words per minute
3:40 min = 300 words per minute

3:50 min = 287 words per minute
4:00 min = 275 words per minute
4:10 min = 264 words per minute
4:20 min = 254 words per minute
4:30 min = 244 words per minute
4:40 min = 236 words per minute
4:50 min = 227 words per minute
5:00 min = 220 words per minute
5:10 min = 212 words per minute
5:20 min = 206 words per minute
5:30 min = 200 words per minute
5:40 min = 194 words per minute
5:50 min = 188 words per minute
6:00 min = 183 words per minute
6:10 min = 179 words per minute
6:20 min = 175 words per minute
6:30 min = 171 words per minute
6:40 min = 167 words per minute
6:50 min = 163 words per minute
7:00 min = 159 words per minute

On a separate sheet of paper, number from one to twenty-five. Follow the directions for each section of the review and write your answers beside the corresponding numbers on your answer sheet.

I. Vocabulary Terms (1–9)

Use the following terms to identify the type of reading described below:

skimming	review	overview
scanning	very rapid reading	slow and careful reading
preview	rapid reading	average reading

1. This follows a previous reading and is used when you go back over material to study for a test or to prepare a report.

2. Moving quickly over an entire selection to get the gist of it is _____.

3. This is most often followed by a second reading; it is used in selecting a book, surveying a chapter before reading it, and so on.

4. This rate is used when covering difficult concepts and vocabulary, when reading technical material, and when it is necessary to retain every detail.

5. This rate is used for light, easy, and entertaining reading.

6. When you glance over material very quickly until you find a desired piece of information, and then you stop reading, you are using _____.

7. A reading to get a general impression of the material is a(n) _____; it is not followed by another reading.

8. This rate is used for magazine articles or some chapters in social studies and is about 250 words per minute.

9. This rate is for fairly easy material and when you want only the more important facts.

II. Completion (10–18)

Write the correct answer in the corresponding space on your answer sheet.

10–12. Your reading rate is determined by three factors. They are __10__ , __11__ , and __12__ .

13–14. Two other factors that influence your own ability to read rapidly are __13__ and __14__ .

15–18. The four steps in skimming an essay, a chapter, or a book are __15__ , __16__ , __17__ , and __18__ .

III. Application (19–25)

The following are descriptions of material you might encounter and the purposes you might have for reading it. Read the description and the purpose. Then select the appropriate reading rate from the list provided. Write the rate you have chosen beside the corresponding number on your answer sheet.

scanning	very rapid	average
skimming	rapid	slow and careful

Type of Material	Your Purpose	Rate
19. The chapter in a social studies textbook on Reconstruction after the Civil War	You need to understand completely. A test on details is coming up.	?
20. A light, fast-moving Louis L'Amour story, *Buck, the Cowboy Renegade*	You are reading for pleasure.	?
21. An encyclopedia article on the life of Herbert Hoover	You want to know what college President Hoover attended.	?
22. Your English teacher has made the following assignment: List the characteristics of a good writer.	You need to research several articles to locate the parts that list the characteristics. You will read them more carefully later.	?
23. An interesting adventure story in a magazine	You are reading in the dentist's waiting room to pass the time.	?
24. You bought a new car. You are considering what type of insurance to buy.	You want to understand fully the extent of the coverage you need.	?
25. Local news in your paper	You want to know what's going on in your town.	?

Using the Dictionary

Dictionaries contain a lot of information. You may know that a dictionary can help you spell and find the meanings of unfamiliar words. But what you may not know is that a dictionary can also help you find words that have similar meanings, give you the population of Mankato, Minnesota, and tell you when the expression *last straw* was first used to refer to something other than the one that broke the camel's back. Information that you may have felt you needed to use an encyclopedia to find might instead be found in your dictionary.

Knowing how to use a dictionary is a valuable study skill. Once you learn how to find the information you need quickly, you can improve both your reading and writing skills.

ACTIVITY 8.1

Alphabetical Order

Not all dictionaries are alike. The dictionary you use at school may be different from the one you use at home or in the library. But one thing all dictionaries have in common is their basic organization; words are arranged in alphabetical order. So, to find a work in a dictionary—*any* dictionary—you need to know the order of letters in the alphabet.

Why should you improve your alphabetizing skills? Alphabetizing skills are especially useful when you are using a dictionary; however, they are also helpful when you want to find a section in the Sunday paper, locate a book in a library card catalog, or find a file in an office drawer.

Follow the instructions for each step of Activity 8.1. Try to increase your speed as you work though each section.

Section One

Using a separate sheet of paper, number from one to ten. Next to the corresponding number write the letters that come right before and right after the letter that is shown. For instance, in the first example using the letter *w*, *v* comes before *w* in the alphabet, and *x* comes after *w*.

1. ___v___ w ___x___   6. _____ s _____
2. _____ b _____   7. _____ g _____
3. _____ x _____   8. _____ c _____
4. _____ m _____   9. _____ l _____
5. _____ j _____   10. _____ q _____

Section Two

Using a separate sheet of paper, number from one to twelve. This time supply the missing letter in each group of letters. The first has been done as an example.

1. b ___c___ d   7. w _____ y
2. v _____ x   8. e _____ g
3. j _____ l   9. t _____ v
4. q _____ s   10. m _____ o
5. a _____ c   11. f _____ h
6. i _____ k   12. g _____ i

Section Three

Using a separate sheet of paper, number from one to ten. In the groups of letters below, the letters are scrambled. Write the one letter that should come *first* in each group beside the number.

1. b f g ⓐ   6. l f s k
2. m p z l   7. t s r x
3. r x c g   8. l p d q
4. q s v y   9. h e k i
5. w t m p   10. i m k q

More Alphabetical Order

Using a separate sheet of paper, number from one to ten. Write the words in each group below as they would appear in alphabetical order. Note that each set of words begins with the same letter. You will have to look to the second or third letter to arrange these words. Use the first set as an example.

1. easy
   easement
   east

   Answer:
   easement, east, easy

2. grand
   garage
   garbage

3. locomotive
   locomotion
   location

4. shield
   shelter
   sheet

5. clank
   clangor
   clang

6. twilight
   twinkle
   twist

7. wood
   waste
   wonder

8. indent
   incident
   indicator

9. atomic
   atrocious
   attach

10. upstairs
    upstart
    upstage

Dictionary Terms and Definitions

Most people think of a dictionary only as a source of word meanings or spellings. Activity 8.3 gives you an opportunity to find other kinds of information in each dictionary entry. For example, do you know where the inflected form of a word is found? Or its variant spelling? What about the word's etymology? Are these all new terms to you?

Figure 8.1 shows where in a typical dictionary entry to find such information. Remember that a page from your own dictionary may look slightly different from the page shown here; just check the beginning of your version of a section explaining how your dictionary is organized.

In Figure 8.1 you will notice various vocabulary terms, each serving as a label to identify some part of a dictionary entry. As you read on, you will learn more about the meaning of these vocabulary terms and how your knowing and using them can sharpen your study skills.

On a separate sheet of paper, take notes on the following dictionary terms and their definitions. Keep your notes brief.

Main Entry

The *main entry* is the word or phrase that you look up. It is usually printed in bold type in a position slightly to the left of the body of the entry.

Syllabication

The *syllabication* shows how a word is divided. The divisions are usually indicated by small dots. You can use syllabication when you write to determine how to divide a word at the end of a line. **Example:** goal•keep•er.

FIGURE 8.1   Dictionary Entries

Main entry — Guide words
Inflected form(s) — Syllabication
Diacritical marks — Part of speech
Variant(s) — Etymology
Pronunciation key

augment | autograph

aug·ment (ŏg-mĕnt′) *v.* To make or become greater; enlarge; increase. [< LLat. *augmentare*.] —**aug′men·ta′tion** *n.*
au gra·tin (ō grät′n, grăt′n) *adj.* Covered with bread crumbs and often grated cheese and browned. [Fr.]
au·gur (ô′gər) *n.* A seer; soothsayer. —*v.* 1. To prognosticate; foretell. 2. To serve as an omen of; betoken. [Lat.]
au·gu·ry (ô′gyə-rē) *n., pl.* **-ries.** 1. The practice of divination. 2. An omen.
au·gust (ô-gŭst′) *adj.* Inspiring awe or reverence; majestic. [Lat. *augustus*, venerable.] —**au·gust′ly** *adv.*
Au·gust (ô′gəst) *n.* The 8th month of the year, having 31 days. See table at **calendar.** [< Lat. *(mensis) Augustus,* (month) of Augustus.]
auk (ôk) *n.* A chunky, short-winged sea bird of northern regions. [< ON *alka.*]
auld lang syne (ōld′ lăng zīn′, sīn′) *n.* The good old days long past. [Sc., old long since.]
aunt (ănt, änt) *n.* 1. The sister of one's father or mother. 2. The wife of one's uncle. [< Lat. *amita,* paternal aunt.]
au·ra (ôr′ə) *n.* 1. An invisible breath or emanation. 2. A distinctive quality that characterizes a person or thing. [< Gk., breeze.]
au·ral (ôr′əl) *adj.* Of, pertaining to, or received through the ear. [< Lat. *auris,* ear.]
au·re·ole (ôr′ē-ōl′) *n.* Also **au·re·o·la** (ô-rē′ə-lə). A halo. [< Lat. *aureolus,* golden.]
au re·voir (ō′ rə-vwär′) *interj.* Good-by. [Fr.]

aus·tral (ô′strəl) *adj.* Southern. [< Lat. *auster,* south.]
Aus·tra·lian (ô-strāl′yən) *n.* 1. A native or citizen of Australia. 2. An aborigine of Australia. 3. Any of the languages of the Australian aborigines. —**Aus·tra′lian** *adj.*
Aus·tro-A·si·at·ic (ôs′trō-ā′zhē-ăt′ĭk) *n.* A family of languages of southeastern Asia once dominant in northeastern India and Indochina. —**Aus′tro-A′si·at′ic** *adj.*
aut- *pref.* Var. of **auto-.**
au·then·tic (ô-thĕn′tĭk) *adj.* 1. Worthy of trust, reliance, or belief 2. Genuine; real. [< Gk. *authentikos < authentēs,* author.] —**au·then′ti·cal·ly** *adv.* —**au′then·tic′i·ty** (-tĭs′ĭ-tē) *n.*
au·then·ti·cate (ô-thĕn′tĭ-kāt′) *v.* **-cat·ed, -cat·ing.** 1. To prove. 2. To establish as being genuine. —**au·then′ti·ca′tion** *n.* —**au·then′ti·ca′tor** *n.*
au·thor (ô′thər) *n.* 1. The writer of a literary work. 2. The beginner, originator, or creator of anything. [< Lat. *auctor,* creator.] —**au′thor** *v.*
au·thor·i·tar·i·an (ə-thôr′ĭ-târ′ē-ən, ə-thŏr′-, ô-) *adj.* Characterized by or favoring absolute obedience to authority. —*n.* One who believes in authoritarian policies. —**au·thor′i·tar′i·an·ism** *n.*
au·thor·i·ta·tive (ə-thôr′ĭ-tā′tĭv, ə-thŏr′-, ô-) *adj.* 1. Having or arising from proper authority. 2. Having or showing expert knowledge. —**au·thor′i·ta′tive·ly** *adv.* —**au·thor′i·ta′tive·ness** *n.*

ă pat ā pay â care ä father ĕ pet ē be ĭ pit ī tie î pier ŏ pot ō toe ô paw, for oi noise oo took
oo boot ou out th thin th this ŭ cut û urge yoo abuse zh vision ə about, item, edible, gallop, circus

When you have to divide a word at the end of a line, you should follow the syllabication shown in your dictionary. However, also keep in mind these three rules.

1. Do not divide one-syllable words (house).

2. Do not divide a word so that only one letter is left on a line (able).

3. Try to divide hyphenated words only at the hyphen (self-control).

Variants

Variants are two or more correct spellings of a single word. They are usually in bold type and may be treated in two ways.

1. If a variant spelling is separated from the main entry by the word *or* (or a comma in some dictionaries), that variant spelling is used as frequently as the spelling of the main entry. **Example:** *ax* or *axe* (*ax, axe*). Both spellings, *ax* and *axe*, are used equally frequently.

2. If a variant spelling is separated from the main entry by *also*, the main entry spelling is preferred. **Example:** *medieval* also *mediaeval*. *Medieval* is the preferred spelling.

Etymology

A word's *etymology* indicates its origin (where it came from) and the etymological meaning of the word in that language. Etymologies usually appear in brackets or in parentheses. **Example:** the origin of the word retract is [<Lat. *retractare,* to

handle again]. Etymologies may come directly after the main entry or, as in the sample dictionary page shown, at the end of the dictionary entry. A question mark in the etymology means that the origin of the word is unknown.

Inflected Forms

Inflections are changes in the form of a word due to a tense change or a plural form. To save space, dictionaries list only irregular inflected forms, such as the plural *oxen* for *ox* or the past tenses *swam* and *swum*. (If *ox* were regular, its plural would be *oxs*, and it would not be listed in the dictionary; if *swim* were regular, its past tense would be *swimmed*, and it would not be listed.)

Inflected forms usually appear in bold type following the label specifying part of speech. If inflected forms are not listed for a word, you can assume that these forms are regular.

You may want to look up inflected forms when you need to know any of the following information: the plural form of a word or how to spell it, or the past tense of a word or how to spell it. **Example:** *think* v. *thought, thinking*.

Parts of Speech

A word's *part of speech* is usually indicated by italic type (letters that slant) and often follows the main entry. It is important to check a word's part of speech to make sure that you do not use a word incorrectly. For example, when you see in the dictionary that a particular word in a noun, you won't try to use it as a verb. The part of speech is usually abbreviated. Some common abbreviations include the following:

n.—noun   *pron.*—pronoun
v.—verb   *conj.*—conjunction
adj.—adjective   *interj.*—interjection
adv.—adverb

Homographs

Homographs are words that have the same spelling, but different meanings and origins. **Example:** *bark*—the noise a dog makes; *bark*—the outer covering of a tree; *bark*—a three-masted sailing ship.

Diacritical Marks

Diacritical marks are the dots, dashes, and other signs that show how to pronounce a word. The system for using these signs is usually explained in a *Pronunciation Key* at the top or bottom of the page. **Example:** potato (pə-tā′tō).

Guide Words

Guide words are the words at the top of the dictionary page. The guide words indicate the first and last main entry words found on that page. They help you locate the word you want more quickly. **Example: broadcast/broth.**

ACTIVITY 8.4

Recognizing Dictionary Components

On a separate sheet of paper, number from one to nine. Use the illustration in Figure 8.2 to identify the numbered components of the dictionary entry. Choose the correct term from the list provided, and use each of the terms one time. Write the term beside the appropriate number on your paper.

main entry	pronunciation key	diacritical marks
etymology	part of speech	syllabication
guide words	variant	inflected forms

FIGURE 8.2
Recognizing
Dictionary
Components

bugbear | bum —— 1

bug·bear (bŭg′bâr′) *n.* An object of excessive concern or fear. [ME *bugge*, hobgoblin + BEAR.]
bug·eyed (bŭg′īd′) *adj. Slang.* Agog.
bug·gy (bŭg′ē) *n., pl.* **-gies.** A small, light, four-wheeled carriage. [Orig. unknown.]
bu·gle (byōō′gəl) *n.* A trumpetlike instrument without keys or valves. [< OFr.] —**bu′gle** *v.* —**bu′gler** *n.*
build (bĭld) *v.* **built** (bĭlt), **build·ing.** **1.** To erect; construct. **2.** To fashion; create. **3.** To add to; develop. **4.** To establish a basis for. —*phrasal verb.* **build up.** To construct in stages or by degrees. —*n.* The physical make-up of a person or thing. [< OE *bold*, a dwelling.] —**build′er** *n.*
build·ing (bĭl′dĭng) *n.* **1.** A structure; edifice. **2.** The act, process, art, or occupation of constructing. —— 6
build-up (bĭld′ŭp′) *n.* Also **build-up.** **1.** The act of amassing or increasing. **2.** Widely favorable publicity, esp. by a systematic campaign
built-in (bĭlt′ĭn′) *adj.* **1.** Constructed as a nondetachable part of a larger unit. **2.** Natural; inherent.
bulb (bŭlb) *n.* **1.** A rounded, modified underground stem, such as that of the onion or tulip, from which a new plant develops. **2.** A rounded object, projection, or part. **3.** An incandescent lamp or its glass housing. [< Gk. *bolbos*, bulbous plant.] —**bulb′ar** *adj.*
bul·bous (bŭl′bəs) *adj.* **1.** Shaped like a bulb. **2.** Growing from bulbs.
Bul·gar·i·an (bŭl-gâr′ē-ən, bŏŏl-) *n.* **1.** Also **Bul·gar** (bŭl′gər, bŏŏl′gär′). A native of Bulgaria. **2.** The Slavic language of the Bulgarians. —**Bul·gar′i·an** *adj.* —— 7
bulge (bŭlj) *n.* A protruding part; a swelling. —*v.* **bulged, bulg·ing.** To swell or cause to swell out. [< Lat. *bulga*, bag, of Celt. orig.] —**bulg′y** *adj.*
bulk (bŭlk) *n.* **1.** Great size, mass, or volume. **2.** The major portion of something. —*v.* To be or appear to be great in size or importance; loom. —*idiom.* **in bulk.** Unpackaged; loose. [< ON *bulki*, cargo.] —**bulk′i·ly** *adv.* —**bulk′i·ness** *n.* —**bulk′y** *adj.* —— 8
Syns: *bulk, amplitude, magnitude, mass, size, volume n.*
bulk·head (bŭlk′hĕd′) *n.* **1.** An upright partition that divides the inside of a ship into compartments. **2.** A wall or embankment constructed in a mine or tunnel. [Orig. unknown.]

1. To dig up or move with a bulldozer. **2.** *Slang.* To bully. [Poss. < obs. *bulldose*, severe beating.]
bull·doz·er (bŏŏl′dō′zər) *n.* A large, powerful tractor having a vertical metal scoop in front for moving earth and rocks.
bul·let (bŏŏl′ĭt) *n.* A cylindrical usu. metal projectile that is fired from a firearm. [< Lat. *bulla*, ball.] —**bul′let·proof** *adj.*
bul·le·tin (bŏŏl′ĭ-tn, -tĭn) *n.* **1.** A printed or broadcast statement on a matter of public interest. **2.** A periodical issued by an organization. [Fr.] —— 2
bulletin board *n.* A board mounted on a wall, on which notices are posted.
bull·fight (bŏŏl′fīt′) *n.* A public spectacle, esp. in Spain and Mexico, in which a matador engages and usu. kills a fighting bull. —**bull′fight·er** *n.* —**bull′fight·ing** *n.*

bullfight

bull·finch (bŏŏl′fĭnch′) *n.* A European songbird with a short, thick bill and a red breast. —— 4
bull·frog (bŏŏl′frôg′, -frŏg′) *n.* A large frog with a deep, resonant croak.
bull·head (bŏŏl′hĕd′) *n.* A North American freshwater catfish.
bull·head·ed (bŏŏl′hĕd′ĭd) *adj.* Very stubborn; headstrong. —**bull′head′ed·ly** *adv.* —**bull′head′ed·ness** *n.* —— 5
bul·lion (bŏŏl′yən) *n.* Gold or silver bars or ingots. [OFr. *bille*, stick, and < OFr. *boillon*, molten metal.]
bull·ish (bŏŏl′ĭsh) *adj.* **1.** Like a bull. **2.** Stubborn. **3. a.** Expecting a rise in stock-market prices. **b.** Optimistic. —**bull′ish·ly** *adv.* —**bull′ish·ness** *n.*
bul·lock (bŏŏl′ək) *n.* A steer or young bull. [< OE *bulluc*.]
bull·pen (bŏŏl′pĕn′) *n. Baseball.* An area where relief pitchers warm up during a game.
bull session *n. Informal.* An informal group discussion.

—— 3

—— 9
ă pat ā pay â care ä father ĕ pet ē be ĭ pit ī tie î pier ŏ pot ō toe ô paw, for oi noise ŏŏ took
ŏŏ boot ou out th thin th this ŭ cut û urge yŏŏ abuse zh vision ə about, item, edible, gallop, circus

Discovering Etymologies

English is a language that has borrowed words and phrases from many languages. Sometimes the etymology of a word can help you determine its meaning, as when the word comes from a common Latin or Greek root. Other times, the meaning of the word has changed so much that it has little relation to the foreign word it developed from. For these reasons, discovering a word's etymology and etymological meaning can be very interesting.

The following activity will give you practice in reading etymologies in dictionary entries. Be sure to follow the instructions for each step. Begin by numbering a separate sheet of paper from one to seventeen. Using the dictionary entries provided in Figure 8.3, find the etymology for each of the words listed.

FIGURE 8.3
Etymologies

emporium | encumber

employing. 2. The state of being employed. 3. An activity or occupation.

em·po·ri·um (ĕm-pôr'ē-əm, -pōr'-) n., pl. **-ums** or **-po·ri·a** (-pôr'ē-ə, -pōr'-). A store carrying a wide variety of merchandise. [< Gk. *empo·rion*, market.]

em·pow·er (ĕm-pou'ər) v. To invest with legal power; authorize.

em·press (ĕm'prĭs) n. 1. The female sovereign of an empire. 2. The wife or widow of an emperor. [< OFr. *emperesse*.]

emp·ty (ĕmp'tē) adj. **-ti·er, -ti·est.** 1. Containing nothing. 2. Having no occupants or inhabitants; unoccupied. 3. Lacking purpose, substance, value, or effect. —v. **-tied, -ty·ing.** 1. To make or become empty. 2. To discharge or flow: *a river that empties into a bay.* —n., pl. **-ties.** An empty container, esp. a bottle. [< OE *ǣmtig*.] —**emp'ti·ness** n.

emp·ty-hand·ed (ĕmp'tē-hăn'dĭd) adj. 1. Bearing nothing in the hands. 2. Having gained or accomplished nothing.

em·py·re·an (ĕm'pī-rē'ən) n. 1. The highest reaches of heaven. 2. The sky or firmament. [< Gk. *empurios*, fiery.]

e·mu (ē'myōō) n. A large, flightless Australian bird related to and resembling the ostrich. [Port. *ema*, flightless bird of South America.]

em·u·late (ĕm'yə-lāt') v. **-lat·ed, -lat·ing.** To strive to equal or excel, esp. through imitation. [Lat. *aemulari*.] —**em'u·la'tion** n.

e·mul·si·fy (ĭ-mŭl'sə-fī') v. **-fied, -fy·ing.** To make into or become an emulsion. —**e·mul'si·fi·ca'tion** n. —**e·mul'si·fi'er** n.

e·mul·sion (ĭ-mŭl'shən) n. 1. A suspension of small globules of one liquid in a second liquid with which the first does not mix. 2. A light-sensitive coating, usu. of silver halide grains in a thin gelatin layer, on photographic film, paper, or glass. [< Lat. *emulgēre*, to drain out.] —**e·mul'sive** adj.

en (ĕn) n. *Printing.* A unit of measure equal to half the width of an em.

en-¹ or **em-** pref. 1. **a.** To put into or on: *enthrone.* **b.** To go into or on: *entrain.* 2. To cover or provide with: *enrobe.* 3. To cause to be: *endear.* 4. Thoroughly. Used often as an intensive: *entangle.* [< Lat. *in, in.*]

en-² or **em-** pref. In; into; within: *empathy.* [< Gk.]

-en¹ suff. 1. **a.** To cause to be: *cheapen.* **b.** To become: *redden.* 2. **a.** To cause to have: *hearten.* **b.** To come to have: *lengthen.* [< OE -*nian.*]

-en² suff. Made of or resembling: *wooden.* [< OE.]

en·a·ble (ĕn-ā'bəl) v. **-bled, -bling.** 1. To provide with the means, knowledge, or opportunity; make possible. 2. To give legal power, capacity, or sanction to.

en·act (ĕn-ăkt') v. 1. To make (a bill) into a law. 2. To act out, as on a stage. —**en·act'ment** n.

e·nam·el (ĭ-năm'əl) n. 1. A vitreous, usu. opaque coating baked on metal, glass, or ceramic ware. 2. A paint that dries to a hard, glossy surface. 3. The hard substance that covers the exposed portion of a tooth. —v. **-eled** or **-elled, -el·ing** or **-el·ling.** To coat or decorate with enamel. [< AN *enamailler*, to put on enamel.] —**e·nam'el·ware'** n.

e·nam·or (ĭ-năm'ər) v. Also chiefly Brit. **en·am·our.** To inspire with love; captivate. [< OFr. *enamourer.*]

en bloc (äʀ blŏk') adv. All together; as a whole. [Fr.]

en·camp (ĕn-kămp') v. To set up or live in a camp. —**en·camp'ment** n.

en·cap·su·late (ĕn-kăp'sə-lāt') v. **-lat·ed, -lat·ing.** To encase or become encased in a capsule. —**en·cap'su·la'tion** n.

en·case (ĕn-kās') v. **-cased, -cas·ing.** To enclose in or as if in a case. —**en·case'ment** n.

-ence or **-ency** suff. Action, state, quality, or condition: *reference.* [< Lat. -*entia.*]

en·ceph·a·li·tis (ĕn-sĕf'ə-lī'tĭs) n. Inflammation of the brain. —**en·ceph'a·lit'ic** (-lĭt'ĭk) adj.

encephalo- or **encephal-** pref. The brain: *encephalitis.* [< Gk. *enkephalos*, in the head.]

en·ceph·a·lon (ĕn-sĕf'ə-lŏn') n., pl. **-la** (-lə). The brain of a vertebrate. [Gk. *enkephalon.*]

en·chain (ĕn-chān') v. To bind with or as if with chains; fetter.

en·chant (ĕn-chănt') v. 1. To cast under a spell; bewitch. 2. To delight completely; enrapture. [< Lat. *incantare.*] —**en·chant'er** n. —**en·chant'ment** n.

en·chi·la·da (ĕn'chə-lä'də) n. A rolled tortilla with a meat or cheese filling, served with a sauce spiced with chili. [Mex. Sp.]

en·ci·pher (ĕn-sī'fər) v. To put (a message) into cipher. —**en·ci'pher·ment** n.

en·cir·cle (ĕn-sûr'kəl) v. **-cled, -cling.** 1. To form a circle around; surround. 2. To move or go around; make a circuit of. —**en·cir'cle·ment** n.

en·clave (ĕn'klāv', ŏn'-) n. A country or part of a country lying entirely within the boundaries of another. [< OFr. *enclaver*, to enclose.]

en·close (ĕn-klōz') v. **-closed, -clos·ing.** Also **in·close** (ĭn-). 1. To surround on all sides; fence in. 2. To include in the same container with a package or letter. [< Lat. *includere*, to include.] —**en·clo'sure** (-klō'zhər) n.

en·code (ĕn-kōd') v. **-cod·ed, -cod·ing.** To put (a message) into code. —**en·cod'er** n.

en·co·mi·um (ĕn-kō'mē-əm) n., pl. **-ums** or **-mi·a** (-mē-ə). Lofty praise; eulogy. [< Gk. *enkōmios*, of the victory procession.]

en·com·pass (ĕn-kŭm'pəs, -kŏm'-) v. 1. To surround. 2. To comprise or contain; include.

en·core (ŏn'kôr', -kōr') n. 1. A demand by an audience for an additional performance. 2. An additional performance in response to an audience's demand. —v. **-cored, -cor·ing.** To demand an encore of or from. [< Fr., again.]

en·coun·ter (ĕn-koun'tər) n. 1. A casual or unexpected meeting. 2. A hostile confrontation, as between enemies; clash. —v. 1. To meet, esp. unexpectedly. 2. To confront in battle. [< OFr. *encountre.*]

en·cour·age (ĕn-kûr'ĭj, -kŭr'-) v. **-aged, -ag·ing.** 1. To inspire with courage or confidence. 2. To help bring about; foster. [< OFr. *encoragier.*] —**en·cour'age·ment** n. —**en·cour'ag·ing·ly** adv.

en·croach (ĕn-krōch') v. To intrude or infringe gradually upon the property or rights of another; trespass. [< OFr. *encrochier*, to seize.] —**en·croach'ment** n.

en·crust (ĕn-krŭst') v. Also **in·crust** (ĭn-). To cover or become covered with or as if with a crust. —**en'crus·ta'tion** (ĕn'krŭ-stā'shən) n.

en·cum·ber (ĕn-kŭm'bər) v. 1. To weigh down excessively; burden. 2. To hinder; impede. [< OFr. *encombrer*, to block up.] —**en·cum'brance** (-brəns) n.

Write the etymology out in full (do not use abbreviations), and, if it is given, write the etymological meaning for each word. (Etymological meanings are found with the etymologies in the square brackets.)

You will need to know these abbreviations:

Gk—Greek	*Port*—Portuguese	*Fr*—French
OFr—Old French	*Lat*—Latin	*Mex Sp*—Mexican Spanish
OE—Old English	*AN*—Anglo-Norman	

1. enchilada
2. emporium
3. enclave
4. encroach
5. emu

6. enclose
7. encore
8. enamel
9. empty
10. encumber

11.–17. Now write all the words from Figure 8.2 shown that have Old French as their etymology.

ACTIVITY 8.6

Using Other Information in a Dictionary Entry

This activity gives you practice in using some of the other information that is given in a dictionary entry. This time, you will check word division and find in-flected forms of words. These skills are worth practicing because, in order to spell and write words correctly, you must know how they are divided and how their forms vary.

On a separate sheet of paper, number one to ten. Refer to the dictionary entry in Figure 8.4 as you answer the questions listed in Section One and Section Two.

Section One: Syllabication

Using the dictionary entries from Figure 8.4, look up the words listed, determine their proper division into syllables, and write the syllabicated words beside the correct number on your paper.

1. glacial
2. gladiator
3. glamour

4. gladiolus
5. glaciate

Section Two: Inflected Forms

Using the same group of dictionary entries from Figure 8.4, look up the following words and write their inflected forms beside the correct number on your answer sheet.

6. give
7. glaciate
8. glamorize

9. glad
10. gird

FIGURE 8.4
Syllabication and
Inflected Forms

gird (gûrd) v. gird-ed or girt (gûrt), gird-ing.
1. To encircle with or as if with a belt or
band. 2. To fasten with a belt. 3. To equip or
prepare for action. [< OE gyrdan.]
gird-er (gûr'dər) n. A strong horizontal beam
used as a main support in building.
gir-dle (gûr'dl) n. 1. A belt, sash, or band
worn around the waist. 2. A supporting undergarment worn over the waist and hips.
—v. -dled, -dling. To encircle with or as if
with a belt. [< OE gyrdel.] —gir'dler n.
girl (gûrl) n. 1. A female child or young un-
married woman. 2. Informal. A woman. 3. A
sweetheart. 4. A female servant. [ME girle.]
—girl'hood n. —girl'ish adj. —girl'ish-ly adv.
—girl'ish-ness n.
girl Friday n. A female assistant with a great
variety of duties.
girl-friend (gûrl'frênd') n. Also girl friend.
1. A female friend. 2. Informal. A sweetheart
or favored female companion of a man.
Girl Scout n. A member of the Girl Scouts,
an organization for girls between 7 and 17
that stresses physical fitness, good character,
and homemaking ability.
girt (gûrt) v. A p.t. & p.p. of gird.
girth (gûrth) n. 1. Size measured by encircling
something; circumference. 2. A strap encircling an animal's body to secure a load or
saddle. [< ON györdh.]
gist (jîst) n. The central idea; essence. [<
OFr., it lies.]
give (gîv) v. gave (gāv), giv-en (gîv'ən), giving. 1. a. To make a present of: give flowers.
b. To make gifts. c. To deliver in exchange or
in recompense: give five dollars for the book.
2. To entrust to or place in the hands of: Give
me the scissors. 3. To convey: Give him my

gla-cial (glā'shəl) adj. 1. Of, relating to, or
derived from glaciers. 2. Often Glacial. Characterized or dominated by the existence of
glaciers. 3. Extremely cold. [Lat. glacialis,
icy.] —gla'cial-ly adv.
gla-ci-ate (glā'shē-āt', -sē-) v. -at-ed, -at-ing.
1. To subject to glacial action. 2. To freeze.
[Lat. glaciare, to freeze.] —gla'ci-a'tion n.
gla-cier (glā'shər) n. A large mass of slowly
moving ice, formed from compacted snow. [<
Lat. glacies, ice.]
glad (glăd) adj. glad-der, glad-dest. 1. Feeling,
showing, or giving joy and pleasure; happy.
2. Pleased; willing: glad to help. [< OE glæd.]
—glad'ly adv. —glad'ness n.
Syns: glad, cheerful, cheery, festive, gay, joyful, joyous adj.
glad-den (glăd'n) v. To make or become glad.
glade (glăd) n. An open space in a forest.
[Perh. < GLAD, shining (obs.)]
glad hand n. A hearty, effusive greeting.
—glad'-hand' v.
glad-i-a-tor (glăd'ē-ā'tər) n. 1. A man trained
to entertain the public by engaging in fights
to the death in ancient Roman arenas. 2. A
person who engages in a sensational struggle.
[Lat.] —glad'i-a-to'ri-al (-ə-tôr'ē-əl, -tōr'-) adj.
glad-i-o-lus (glăd'ē-ō'ləs) n., pl. -li (-lī', -lē') or
-lus-es. A widely cultivated plant with
sword-shaped leaves and a spike of showy,
variously colored flowers. [< Lat. gladius,
sword.]
glad-some (glăd'səm) adj. Glad; joyful.
—glad'some-ly adv. —glad'some-ness n.
glam-or-ize (glăm'ə-rīz') v. -ized, -iz-ing. Also
glam-our-ize. To make glamorous. —glam'-
or-i-za'tion n. —glam'or-iz'er n.
glam-our (glăm'ər) n. Also glam-or. An air of

Using Diacritical Marks

You have come across a new word in your reading. Looking up the meaning of
that new word is not enough to learn it. You must also know how to pronounce
the word, so you can say it as well as write it. Diacritical marks help you learn a
word's pronunciation. They are the focus of this activity.

Section One

On a separate sheet of paper, number from one to ten. Using the following pronunciation key as a guide, determine the pronunciation of the words in the left-
hand column. Then match the words with their correct definitions by placing the
letter of the definition beside the corresponding number on your answer sheet.

1. glā$' sh@r
2. ô-thĕn' tĭk
3. o' th@r
4. ĕn-ăkt'
5. ĕn-klōz'
6. bro͞o-nĕt'
7. brou
8. ĕn-kûr' ĭj
9. jīst
10. ô-g@st'

A. to act out, as on a stage
B. having dark or brown hair
C. the writer of a literary work
D. to inspire with courage
E. to surround on all sides
F. the forehead
G. genuine, real
H. the central idea
I. the eighth month of the year
J. a large mass of slowly moving ice

Section Two

The joke written below belongs to the oldies but goodies category. Use the dictionary pronunciation key to decipher it. Then, on a separate sheet of paper, write the answers to the questions that follow it.

> Door'ing @ foot'bol gam, wun uv th@ pla'@ers had @ kup'@l uv fing'g@rs bad'le smash'd. Th@ tem dok't@r igzamin'd and dres'd th@ hand.
>
> "Dok't@r," ask'd th@ pla'@r angk'sh@s-le, "wil i be ab@l too pla th@ pe-an'o?"
>
> "Surtn'le yoo wil," promis'd th@ dok't@r.
>
> "Yoo'r wun'd@r-f@l, dok't@r," sed th@ hap'e pla@r. "I kood nev'@r pla th@ pe-an'o bi-for'!"

1. What happened to the football player?
2. What did the doctor promise him?
3. Why was the football player so pleased?

ACTIVITY 8.8

Other Kinds of Information in a Dictionary

Besides information about words and their meanings, many dictionaries provide information about geographical places and famous people. In addition, some dictionaries give information about grammar, punctuation, correct form for writing letters, and how to footnote information. Dictionaries may also include illustrations, so you can see what different alphabets look like or how a disc brake is constructed.

Dictionaries present these "extra" kinds of information in one of two ways. Usually, some of the special information is given in sections at the front or the back of the dictionary. Lists of grammar rules usually will appear in a special section separate from the word entries.

A second way of presenting such information is to include it in the body of the dictionary, among the word entries. For example, names of famous people or geographical places may be mixed in among word entries in the body of one dictionary, or they may fall in separate sections at the back of another dictionary.

To find out where you can find various kinds of information in your own dictionary, you should preview it, just as you would preview a textbook. Look at the table of contents and the introductory material. Then leaf through the pages, from front to back. If your dictionary has cut-out alphabet guides, you may also find guides for biographical (people) and geographical (places) lists.

Activity 8.8 gives you a chance to explore your dictionary for different kinds of information. On a separate sheet of paper, number from one to ten. Use the dictionary entries provided in Figure 8.5 to answer the questions that follow.

1. Who was James Buchanan?
2. What is the capital of Brazil?
3. Draw a picture of the configuration of a benzene ring.
4. What is the pattern of sound for an *I* in Morse Code?

FIGURE 8.5   Extra Dictionary Information

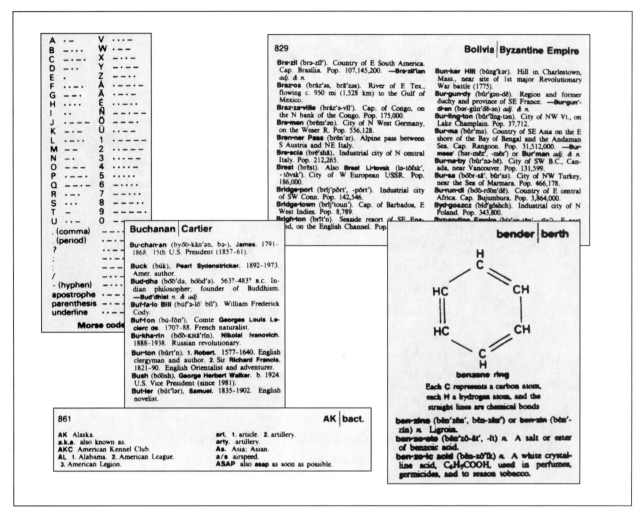

5. What does the abbreviation *a.k.a.* stand for?

6. What does the abbreviation *ASAP* stand for?

7. What is the formula for benzoic acid?

8. What was Buffalo Bill's real name?

9. What does the dictionary say about Bunker Hill?

10. When was George Bush born?

Homographs

The words in bold letters in the sentences below are homographs. On a separate sheet of paper, number from one to eleven. Beside each number write the letter of the dictionary entry that correctly identifies the homograph as it is used in the sentence. The first has been done as an example.

1. Early settlers in America arrived in a **bark**.
2. The **bark** was stripped from the aspen by a deer.
    A. bark—the sound a dog makes
    B. bark—the outer covering of a tree
    C. bark—a sailing ship with three to five masts
    Answer: 1. C

3. The wall acted as a **buffer** and protected her from the oncoming car.
    A. buffer—an implement used to shine or polish
    B. buffer—something that lessens or absorbs the shock of impact

4. The baby was wrapped in a **bunting**.
5. Betsy Ross may have used **bunting** in her first sewing project.
    A. bunting—a light cloth used for making flags
    B. bunting—a bird with a short, cone-shaped bill
    C. bunting—a hooded sleeping bag for infants

6. The detective solved the **case** after discovering one more clue.
    A. case—a specified instance
    B. case—a container or receptacle

7. Unfamiliar with the land, he fell into the **pit**.
    A. pit—a relatively deep hole in the ground
    B. pit—the single, hard-shelled seed of certain fruits

8. She used her crutch as a **prop** to hold the door open.
9. The director said the **prop** for Scene Two was inappropriate.
    A. prop—a support or stay
    B. prop—a stage property
    C. prop—a propeller

10. He angrily accused his neighbor of trying to **pry**.
    A. pry—to look closely; to snoop
    B. pry—to raise, move, or force open with a lever

11. The gale-force winds left a gaping **rent** in the curtain.
    A. rent—periodic payment in return for the right to use the property of another
    B. rent—an opening made by a rip

In Unit 8 you have practiced using dictionary entries to find information about words, people, and places. You might have been surprised to learn just how much information your dictionary contains. Using what you now know and the dictionary entries provided in this unit, answer the following questions. On a separate sheet of paper, number from one to fifteen and begin.

1. Define *main entry*.
2. Define *syllabication*.
3. Syllabicate the word *dependent*.
4. Define *variant spellings*.
5. Give the variant spelling of the word *dependent*.
6. Define *etymology*.
7. Give the etymology of the word *deplete*.
8. What is the etymological meaning of the word *deplete*?
9. Define *inflected form*.
10. Give the inflected form of the word *deplane*.
11. Define *guide words*.
12. List the guide words for the dictionary entry on page 123.
13. Define *homograph*.
14. List three parts of speech.
15. List all the parts of speech for the word *dependent*.

Exploring the Library/ Media Center

What is it that you want to know? Maybe you have a term paper assignment and you need material on the life of Ernest Hemingway. Perhaps you are interested in collared lizards and don't know where to begin looking for information about them. To settle a bet with a friend, you may need to know the greatest number of home runs ever hit by one player in a World Series. No matter what kind of information you seek, the library/media center is the place to begin looking.

Library/media centers are designed with your needs as a student in mind. Why, then is the card catalog a mystery? Why is searching a periodical index so confusing? And, what about using the Internet? If the thought of having to go to your local library to do any of these makes you want to run, relax. This unit is designed to quickly and painlessly acquaint you with library services and materials.

Though libraries vary in arrangements, each has a collection that includes books, periodicals, microforms, and pamphlet materials. Some collections also include records, tapes, videos, and electronic references as well.

Your librarian can also help. Librarians and their assistants are there to make sure that the information you need is available to you. Of course, if you don't ask them questions, librarians can't know your needs. Don't be shy! There is no such thing as a dumb question.

ACTIVITY 9.1

Classification of Fiction

In most school and public libraries, books are classified and arranged on the shelves under the categories of fiction or nonfiction. Activity 9.1 deals with fiction books; Activity 9.2 discusses nonfiction books.

Writing that is based on imagination—that is not true—is called *fiction*. Fiction includes novels and short stories. In a library, fiction books are arranged alphabetically by the author's last name. For example, a book by James Michener will be found under the letter M. Collections of short stories written by several authors are arranged alphabetically by the collection editor's name.

Number a separate sheet of paper from one to five and arrange the following fiction books in the order they would appear on the library shelves.

1. *Siege of Silence* by A. J. Quinell
2. *The Land That Time Forgot* by E. R. Burroughs
3. *Follow the River* by J. A. Thom
4. *The Monkey Wrench Gang* by E. Abbey
5. *The Warrior's Path* by L. L'Amour

ACTIVITY 9.2

Classification of Nonfiction

A second major category of books on the shelves in library/media centers is the nonfiction category. All books that are not novels or short stories—that are factual—are labeled *nonfiction*. Nonfiction materials are organized by two main classification systems: the Dewey decimal system, which uses numbers for identifying ten major subject categories, and the Library of Congress system, which uses extra letters for identifying twenty-one major categories. (See example below.)

You need not to memorize either classification system. Just be aware that both systems are used, and that the LOC (Library of Congress) system is usually used in larger city and university libraries.

ABBREVIATED DEWEY DECIMAL CLASSIFICATION SCHEME

000–099	General Works
100–199	Philosophy and Psychology
200–299	Religion
300–399	Social Sciences
400–499	Language
500–599	Pure Sciences
600–699	Technology
700–799	The Arts
800–899	Literature
900–999	History

ABBREVIATED LIBRARY OF CONGRESS CLASSIFICATION SCHEME

A   General Works

B   Philosophy, Psychology, Religion

C   History: Auxiliary Sciences (Archaeology, Numismatics, Genealogy, etc.)

D   History: General and Old World

E   History: American and U.S., general

F   History: American and U.S., local

G   Geography, Anthropology, Folklore, Dance, Sports

H   Social Sciences: Sociology, Business, and Economics

J   Political Science

K   Law

L   Education

M   Music

N   Fine Arts: Art and Architecture

P   Literature

Q   Science

R   Medicine

S   Agriculture

T   Technology

U   Military Science

V   Naval Science

Z   Bibliography and Library Science

Continuing on a separate sheet of paper, number from one to five again. List the identifying codes for the major categories in which books on the following topics would be found. Use the classification schemes for the Dewey decimal system to help you decide.

1. Buddhism

2. Civil War (U.S.)

3. Mental disorders

4. Conversational Dutch

5. Modern music

Reading Call Numbers

ACTIVITY 9.3

In all libraries, nonfiction books are arranged on the shelves, or stacks by their call numbers. Each book has its own call number made up of its classification code (either Dewey decimal or Library of Congress), as well as its own letter-number combinations, which indicate the book's author.

Dewey decimal call numbers should be read one line at a time.
Example:
  Complete call number 527.6 . . . . Line One (classification)
           JEN . . . . Line Two (author)

The books are first arranged numerically, according to the numbers in Line One.
Example:

Line One is arranged alphabetically by the first three letters of the author's last name. In the case of a collection where there is no one author, the book is arranged by the first three letters of the title.
Example:

The following numbers are call numbers of books classified under the Dewey decimal system. On a separate sheet of paper, arrange them in the correct order by call number, as if they were actual books. Then, using the ten main divisions of the Dewey decimal system, name the category to which each book would belong.

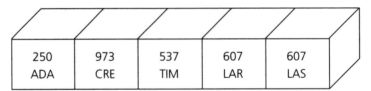

Determining Classification Groups Using Titles

The following titles clearly reveal their subject matter. List the authors and titles on the separate sheet of paper you are using. Opposite each, write the Dewey decimal classification group to which it belongs.

1. John Carroll, *The Study of Language*
2. J. Newton Friend, *Man and the Chemical Element*

3. Harry Emerson Fosdick, *The Man from Nazareth*

4. John Gunther, *Inside Latin America*

5. Ivor Brown, *Shakespeare in His Time*

Determining Classification Groups Using Dewey Numbers

ACTIVITY 9.5

The titles in the following list do not clearly indicate the subjects of the books. Determine the subject matter of each book by comparing the Dewey classification number after each title with the Dewey classification list. Number from one to five on a separate sheet of paper and write the letter of the correct answer beside the appropriate number.

1. *I Can Jump Puddles* (616)

   A. a novel

   B. a biography

   C. a book telling how a polio victim overcame hardships

2. *The Wild Duck* (808.8)

   A. a scientific book for biology class

   B. a book on hunting wild game

   C. a play

3. *The Crack in the Picture Window* (711)

   A. the history of glass

   B. an inquiry into the architecture of American housing developments

   C. a history of government foreclosures of mortgages

4. *Journey Into Light* (617.7)

   A. a biography

   B. the story of medical help for the blind

   C. a travel book

5. *Horsefeathers* (422)

   A. a book dealing with word origins

   B. a book of party games

   C. a book of veterinary medicine

Understanding the Card Catalog

ACTIVITY 9.6

The easiest way to find the books you want in the library is by using the card catalog, which will probably be on the library's computer. The card catalog contains alphabetically arranged cards or references listing the call numbers of each book in the library's collection. There are usually three cards or references for each book: an author listing, a title listing, and a subject listing. You may also find a cross-reference listing, referring you to another related topic.

SUBJECT LISTING

```
Raptors

598.91     Weidensel, Scott
   Raptors: the birds of prey by Scott Weidensal.
New York: Lyons & Burford, 1995
   382 p. Includes biographical references and
index.
```

TITLE LISTING

```
   Raptors: the birds of prey.
598.91 By Scott Weidensal. New York: Lyons & Bur-
ford, 1995
   382 p. Includes bibliographical references and
index.
```

AUTHOR LISTING

```
   Weidensal, Scott
   Raptors: birds of prey. By Scott Weidensal. New
York: Lyons & Burford, 1995
   382 p. Includes bibliographical references and
index.
   1. Raptors    2. Birds, predator    3. Birds of
prey
```

SEARCH LISTING

```
   RAPTORS
   BIRDS, PREDATOR
   BIRDS OF PREY
```

Refer to the previous examples of listings for the books on raptors. Number a separate sheet of paper from one to ten and try to answer the following questions.

1. What three ways are books usually listed in the card catalog?
2. What is the title of the book?
3. Who wrote the book?
4. Who is the publisher?
5. When was the book published?
6. What kind of a book does the Dewey decimal call number indicate it is?
7. How many pages does this book have?

8. Does the book contain a bibliography?

9. What other reference is included?

10. What are the other cross references that might apply to raptors?

Using the Card Catalog

ACTIVITY 9.7

On a separate sheet of paper number from one to five. Using the card catalog in your library/media center, find the author, title, and call number for each of the following.

1. A book written *by* Samuel Clemens (Mark Twain)

2. A book written *about* Samuel Clemens

3. A nonfiction book written about Africa

4. A collection of American poetry

5. A book about space travel

Using Reference Materials

ACTIVITY 9.8

Reference books are valuable information sources usually kept together in the reference section of the library. They must be used in the library; they cannot be checked out.

Before attempting to use any reference book for the first time, skim its introductory pages to learn how to use it and how to decode the symbols and other abbreviations used in that particular volume. Reference books include the following.

- **Dictionaries**
  In addition to the familiar collection of words and definitions, there are dictionaries on languages, medicine, math, and music, to name only a few.

- **Encyclopedias**
  Encyclopedias are some of the best places to begin looking for research materials. Here you will find articles on a variety of subjects written by experts. Topics are arranged alphabetically; the letters on the spine of each volume indicate the portion of the alphabet that volume covers.

- **Almanacs and Yearbooks**
  These volumes, published annually, summarize the previous year's events. They contain factual and statistical information on current developments in such areas as government, sports, economics, careers, and so on.

- **Biographical Reference Books**
  These books offer brief biographical sketches of notable people in all fields, worldwide. Some list living, currently prominent persons, while others refer to specific groups, such as actors or presidents.

- **Literary Reference Books and Books About Authors**
  Anything you need to know concerning literature can be found under this category. Find who wrote it or said it or where it came from by consulting

such volumes as *Twentieth Century Authors, Bartlett's Familiar Quotations, Granger's Index to Poetry,* and *The Oxford Companion to American Literature.*

- **Periodicals**

  When doing research, you'll often find newspapers, magazines, and digests quite useful. They may be used to supplement information you find in books, or, for certain topics, they may be the only information source available. Some libraries keep back issues of periodicals on microforms (microfilm and microfiche) and CD ROMs for convenient storage. Current events digests such as *Facts on File, A Matter of Fact,* and *Social Issues Resources Series, Inc. (SIRS)* are available in some libraries.

- **Maps and Atlases**

  Most libraries have a selection of atlases containing a variety of interesting data and maps. Where do Kudus roam when they are not in a zoo? Check the *Atlas of World Wildlife.* What is the highest mountain peak on each continent? Look in the *Rand McNally World Atlas.*

- **Vertical File**

  Usually found in filing cabinets accessible to library users, the vertical file contains the "et cetera" category in most libraries. This is the place you will find small pamphlets, booklets, catalogs, and clippings on a variety of topics. Depending on the rules at your library, information from the vertical file may sometimes be checked out.

Because you will use them often, it is important to know where in your library the reference area is and what particular reference volumes are available there. To help you find out, take a trip to the reference area of your library and, on a separate sheet of paper, write the answers to the following questions. Be sure to note both the titles and page numbers of the reference books you use, as well as the answer to each question.

1. What is the height of the Statue of Liberty?

2. When is Tom Cruise's birthday?

3. What is the difference in elevation between the highest and lowest points in the United States?

4. What is the language spoken in Jordan?

5. From what language do we get the word *recipe*?

6. Who is the author and what is the title of a poem in which these lines appear:

   "And what is so rare as a day in June?
   Then, if ever, came perfect days...."

7. List the title of a catalog found in the vertical file.

8. What type of sporting events are featured in the latest issue of a newspaper kept in your library?

9. List the titles of two magazines that include information on health and nutrition.

10. What was the year women were first allowed to vote for the president of the United States? Who was elected that year?

Periodical Indexes

When you need to locate articles on a specific subject, you can sit down and browse through piles of magazines and stacks of newspapers. Or, you can save time and consult a periodical index. Periodical indexes enable you to find material on a given topic or by a specific author quickly.

At your local library, you may need have access to the *Readers' Guide to Periodical Literature* in bound volumes, or probably, you will be able to use an electronic magazine index consisting of a computer and a compact disk or a computer and the Internet. Either way, if you could compare the indexes, you would find that they use basically the same form of entry.

An entry in the *Readers' Guide* or in an electronic magazine index is called a *citation*. A citation looks something like the following.

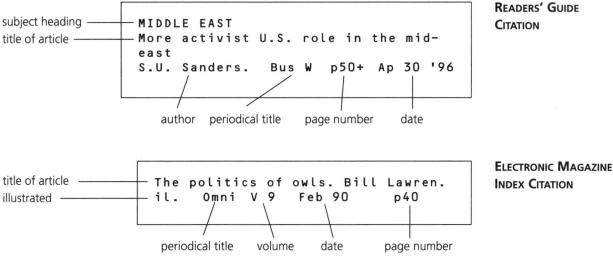

READERS' GUIDE CITATION

subject heading ——→ MIDDLE EAST
title of article ——→ More activist U.S. role in the mideast
S.U. Sanders.   Bus W   p50+ Ap 30 '96

author   periodical title   page number   date

ELECTRONIC MAGAZINE INDEX CITATION

title of article ——— The politics of owls. Bill Lawren.
illustrated ——— il.   Omni V 9   Feb 90   p40

periodical title   volume   date   page number

Notice that each citation includes abbreviations. Some, like the examples given, are very easy to decipher. Others, however, are more difficult, so always check the list of abbreviations given at the beginning of the index for a complete translation.

As you do research, get in the habit of writing down the entire citation, along with the title of the index in which you found it. This will simplify your task when you have to list the sources of your information.

As you can imagine, storage is becoming an ever-increasing problem in this age of mass communication. Many libraries use microforms to solve storage problems. The term *microform* describes information that has been photographed and reduced in size. Libraries often store newspapers and magazines on microfiche or microfilm—two types of microforms frequently used. Special machines called *readers*, some equipped with printers, are required in order for you to use the microforms. Ask your librarian to help you learn to use the reader machine.

The names of the publications found in the microfilm collection are sometimes listed in the card catalog. Other libraries list microforms in a special catalog. CD-ROM disks, used with computers, also store large amounts of text in small amounts of space. No matter where you find the cards in your library, they will look something like this:

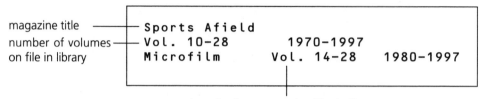

magazine title
number of volumes
on file in library

```
Sports Afield
Vol. 10-28        1970-1997
Microfilm         Vol. 14-28    1980-1997
```

number of volumes on microfilm in library

Now that you are more familiar with periodical indexes, number a separate sheet of paper from one to ten and list two complete citations for each of the following topics. Use the *Readers' Guide to Periodical Literature* or an electronic index to find the magazine articles.

A. TV advertising
B. environmental control
C. photography
D. baseball
E. elections

ACTIVITY 9.10

Using Electronic Magazine Indexes

Using the sample pages from Infotrac, list the names of the magazines that include articles on the following topics. If there is more than one article for the topic, list only the first magazine.

A. sports cars—design
B. sports medicine
C. stage fright
D. Olympic athletes
E. List the complete citation for an article on sports medicine that includes illustrations.

```
InfoTrac*
Heading: SPORTS MEDICINE
        -Innovations
1.   Scalpel, krazy glue, Gore-tex, . . . (FDA
     approves Gore-tex artificial knee ligaments and
     testing of butyl cyanoacrylates as surgical
     adhesive) (column) by Craig Neff v65 Sports
     Illustrated Dec 8 '86 p18(1)
        37E1939
     HEADINGS
2.   Sports massage muscles in. by David Levine il
     v77 Sports April '86 p105(2)
     HEADINGS
3.   Out of the lab and into the stadium of ultra
     sports. (technology and athletic training) by
     Mark Teich and Pamela Weintraub il v7 Omni Aug
     '85 p38(10)
     HEADINGS
```

```
Heading: STAGE FRIGHT
1.   Stage Fright. (book reviews) by Gillian
     Linscott rev by Mary T. Gerrity
     A v40 School Library Journal July '94 p129(1)
     74H1508
     HEADINGS
2.   Stage Fright. (book reviews) by Gillian
     Linscott rev by Emily Melton
     A v90 Booklist Dec 1 '93 p678(1)
     HEADINGS
3.   Stage Fright. (book reviews) by Ellen Hart
     rev by Gail Pool
     D v67  1. Stage Fright. (book reviews) by
     Gillian Linscott rev by Mary T. Gerrity
     A v40 School Library Journal July '94 p129(1)
     74H1508
     HEADINGS
```

```
Heading: Olympic Athletes
        -Health aspects
 1.    Little girls in pretty boxes: the quest for
       Olympic gold can be brutal, often taking a
       tragic toll on gifted teen gymnasts. (excerpt
       from book, 'Little Girls in Pretty Boxes') by
       Joan Ryan il v219 Cosmopolitan Sept '95
       p246(6)
          ABSTRACT
 2.    A message worth repeating. (Greg Louganis)
       (Column) by E.M. Swift il v82 Sports
       Illustrated March 6 '95 p100(1)
          ABSTRACT/TEXT
 3.    Pregnancy doping. (Soviet female Olympic
       athletes were reportedly ordered to become
       pregnant and then have abortions in late
       1960's so their bodies would produce more male
       hormones) (Scorecard) (Brief Article) v81
       Sports Illustrated Dec 5 '94 p16(2)
          TEXT
 4.    A gift greater than gold: Olympian Kristen
       Talbot medals in sisterly love. by Michael
       Neill il v41 People Weekly Feb 14 '94 p69(2)
          ABSTRACT/TEXT
 5.    Flying on a miracle's wings/ (sprinter Gail
       Devers) (Column) by Dave Kindred il v214 The
       Sporting News August 10 '92 p5(1)
          ABSTRACT
 6.    Cold comfort. (health dangers in cold
       weather) (includes related articles) by
       Richard Chevat il v48 Science World Jan 24 '92
       p9(5)
          63C0032
          ABSTRACT
 7.    Uphill climb. (cyclist Mo Manley battles
       multiple sclerosis) (Scorecard) (Brief
       Article) by James Rodewald il v76 Sports
       Illustrated Jan 20 '92 p7(2)
 8.    Orlando, Si, Barcelona...? (Magic Johnson's
       desire to play again) (Inside The NBA) by Jack
       McCallum il v76 Sports Illustrated Jan 20 '92
       p56(2)
          ABSTRACT
 9.    Olga Korbut's deadly foe. (gymnast fighting
       to save herself from Chernobyl's radiation) il
       v35 People Weekly March 4 '91 p34(6)
          58M0479
10.    Sprinter Ben Johnson says getting caught
       saved his life. (lost Olympic medal for using
       steroids) il v79 Jet Jan 7 '91 p50(1)
          58C0119
```

```
InfoTrac*  TOM Index ~ 1985 - Oct 1995
Heading: SPORTS CARS
        -Design and construction
  1.    '95 Geneva motor show. (automobile exhibi-
     tion) by Michael Cotton il v47 Motor Trend
     June '95 p18(3)
          79F1093
          ABSTRACT/HEADINGS
  2.    Sportech. (automobile) by John Lamm il v45
     Road & Track May '94 p61(2)
          ABSTRACT/HEADINGS
  3.    Toyota breeds a mighty Celica. (automobile)
     by Jack Yamaguchi il v45 Road & Track May '94
     p67(2)
          ABSTRACT/HEADINGS
  4.    1963 Lamborghini 350 GTV. (automobile) by
     John Lamm il v45 Road & Track May '94 p120(7)
          ABSTRACT/HEADINGS
  5.    Jiotto Caspita, at long last. (Letter from
     Japan) (Column) by Jack Yamaguchi il v45 Road
     & Track Nov '93 p46(1)
          ABSTRACT/HEADINGS
  6.    Words to live by: 'It's only metal.' (auto-
     mobile design) (Column) by Brock Yates v39 Car
     and Driver Nov '93 p16(1)
          70M1813
          ABSTRACT/HEADINGS
  7.    Hard-core Camaro. (1994 Chevrolet Camaro Z28
     1LE) by Mac DeMere il v45 Motor Trend Nov '93
     p26(1)
          70M0707
          ABSTRACT/HEADINGS
  8.    Tighten your belts: first rides in the
     McLaren F1 Supercar. by Phillip Bingham il v45
     Motor Trend Sept '93 p18(2)
          70E0665
          ABSTRACT/HEADINGS
  9.    '61 Jaguar XK-E. (includes an excerpt from
     an April 1961 evaluation article) by Dean
     Batchelor and C. Van Tune il v45 Motor Trend
     April '93 p98(3)
          68F0747
          ABSTRACT/HEADINGS
 10.    Future Corvettes. by C. Van Tune il v44
     Motor Trend Dec '92 p52(4)
          67L1003
          ABSTRACT/HEADINGS
```

What is the Internet?

The Internet is a collection of computer networks that supply information on a variety of topics to people around the world. This new communication medium was established in the 1970s by the U.S. Department of Defense as a support for military research. Since then, computers, networks, and the World Wide Web have become familiar terms to all of us. They are now a part of education, business, and leisure time activities. The Internet is a gateway into the future!

In order to be prepared for the twenty-first century we need to learn how to use the Internet efficiently. In a way, it is similar to having your own personal library at your fingertips. It's instant communication. It's also a gigantic bulletin board with messages of all kinds waiting to be read. It's worldwide sharing of information. It's mind boggling! With a computer and access to the Internet you can research a term paper, send your Connecticut grandmother birthday wishes, contact other jazz fans around the world, and make travel reservations for your next trip.

The whole thing can seem overwhelming at first, but once you understand the basic tools and how to use them, the confusion will turn to excitement. You may soon become an Internaut, one of the people who regularly explores the Internet!

Basic tools for understanding the Internet:

- *telnet*—This tool allows the user to access remote computers. The use of telnet can also help you find a book in the public library or register for a college class.

- *ftp* (File Transfer Protocol)—This is the tool that helps retrieve information you find on the Internet. Ftp allows you to download your own copy of what you need for a term paper or the directions for a model plane you want to build.

- *e-mail*—This tool lets you send messages across the room or around the world. It is more than just a faster letter because your message can be delivered anywhere, at any time, to any number of people, and there are no long-distance charges. It is electronic, person-to-person communication.

- *mailing lists*—These are special kinds of electronic mail addresses that automatically send topic specific material to your e-mail address. This is like having a subscription to a magazine that deals with one topic only, like race cars or fashion modeling.

- *Usenet newsgroup*—This is a public access bulletin board that allows sharing of information on topics of interest. Newsgroups are different from mailing lists because the messages are sent to the bulletin board for all interested parties to read instead of to your individual mail box.

- *IRC* (Internet Relay Chat)—Real time "talk" is similar to a global conference call. Many people from hundreds of locations can instantly respond to the thoughts of others as they sit at their keyboards.

- *WWW* (World Wide Web)—This exciting feature of the Internet allows the user to access huge databases of information and thousands of retrievable files. These web sites, or pages, often feature pictures, sound, and graphics. There are many Internet searching tools called *search engines* to help navigate this exciting new territory. These tools are where you might begin your journey!

As you can see, using the Internet allows you to exchange ideas with people all over the world. Through the wonders of electronic communication, you can instantaneously reach almost anyone from the president of the United States to a rock star. Interaction is possible by way of *net-talk*. Because net-talk is conversation, there are several rules of etiquette that experienced users practice:

- Anything that you say on e-mail becomes public knowledge. Think before you upload.

- Inappropriate language is inappropriate language both off and on the net. Forgetting this fact could make you an unwelcome visitor.

- Because there is no body language accompanying your conversation, be careful with sarcasm. If people can't see the shrug or wink that accompanies something you've said that is totally outrageous, they may think you're rude.

- Flaming, or angry outbursts, should be resisted on your part and ignored when they come from others.

- ALL CAPITAL LETTERS ARE CONSIDERED TO BE SCREAMING !!

There are special ways of expressing yourself on the Internet, though:

- IMHO—In my humble opinion.
- CUL—See you later.
- BTW—By the way.
- FYI—For your information.
- IOW—In other words.
- FAQ—Frequently asked questions.
- OTOH—On the other hand.
- FYA—For your amusement.
- ROTFL—Rolling on the floor, laughing.
- LOL—Laughing out loud.
- <grin> or :-)
- <frown> or :-(
- [[ ]]—a hug.

Becoming familiar with the Internet is fascinating and exciting. With some practice you can make contacts around the world and keep current with what's happening in the world, not to mention looking like a super student because the papers you hand in are so dynamic and interesting.

Using the Internet

ACTIVITY 9.11

Have a separate sheet of paper ready to write down the steps as you begin your internet search. Start at the menu and follow this route as you browse the World Wide Web (WWW).

1. Click on the "search" title that you find on the menu.
2. List a specific topic or query of interest to you.
3. Scroll down the list under that topic. Click on one.
4. List five of the sites listed under the query you selected.
5. Search one site further and summarize your findings.

Mini Research Project

Now you can practice your newly acquired library skills by completing the following project. We have carefully divided the project into manageable steps. You will need to allow several hours to complete this project, and you must have access to a library or media center as you work. Follow these steps.

1. Choose a topic that interests you. You may know very little or a lot about the topic, but you should definitely choose a topic you want to know more about. Be specific rather than broad in your choice of topics.

2. Do the research.
   - Look up the topic in the *Readers' Guide* or in an electronic magazine index using the computer.
   - If you are using magazines, list three or four complete citations for your topic. If you limit yourself to one article, that periodical might not be available, and you will have to begin again. If you are using the Internet, browse the available documents and decide which three or four files you will download using ftp.
   - If you are using magazines, check the periodicals listed in your citations against the "Magazine Holding Directory" (a list of magazines in your library) to be sure that your library has that particular periodical available. (No library has funds or room for all the periodicals published.)
   - For each citation, you will be asked to fill out a periodical request slip that looks something like this:

```
PERIODICAL REQUEST SLIP

Name of Magazine _____
Date of Issue: Month _____ Day _____ Year _____
Volume _____      Page _____
Your name _____
```

   If the periodicals are not kept in open stacks, your librarian will get them for you.
   - *Save* the periodical request slips when you have the magazines or newspapers. You will need the slips to list your sources.
   - Read the articles carefully, taking notes on their contents.

3. Write the summary.
   - Write your name in the upper right-hand corner of a separate sheet of paper. Below that, list the name of this class and the date.
   - On the first line, in the center, write the title of your summary.
   - Using your notes, summarize what you have read. Make it interesting to your reader. Use your own words, not the author's.
   - On a separate sheet of paper entitled "Bibliography," list the complete citations for all of the articles you read to make your summary. Arrange the citations alphabetically according to magazine title.
   - Your instructor will want to see the periodical request slips or the Internet search route you filled out, in addition to your summary and bibliography.

Number a separate sheet of paper from one to thirty. After reading the question and referring to the typed entry, select the correct multiple-choice answer or the appropriate answer to fill in the blank. Write your answer beside the corresponding number on your paper.

```
332.6092
Lo       Author    Lowenstein, Roger
         Title     Buffett: The Making of An American
                   Capitalist / Roger Lowenstein
         Pub.      New York: Random House, 1995
         Bibliog.  473p, Includes bibliographical
                   references and indexes.
         Subjects  1. Buffett, Warren
                   2. Capitalists and financiers--
                      U.S., Biography
                   3. Stockbrokers--U.S., Biography
```

1. The card shown would be found in the catalog under:

   A. Lo.

   B. 332.6092.

   C. Roger.

   D. The.

2. The card shown is called a(n):

   A. title card.

   B. author card.

   C. subject card.

   D. all of the above.

3. The author of the book is:

   A. Lowenstein, Scott.

   B. Scott Lowenstein.

   C. Random House.

   D. none of the above.

4. The title of the book is:

   A. The Making of an American Capitalist / Roger Lowenstein.

   B. Buffett: The Making of an American Capitalist.

   C. Making of an American Capitalist.

   D. none of the above.

5. The subject of this book is:
    A. Buffett, Warren.
    B. Capitalists and financiers—U.S., Biography.
    C. Stockbrokers—U.S., Biography.
    D. all of the above.

6. The call number of this book is:
    A. 332.6092
    B. 332.6092
        Lo
    C. 473
    D. none of the above.

7. The book is:
    A. nonfiction.
    B. fiction.
    C. reference.
    D. none of the above.

8. The book was published by _____.

9. It was published in _____.

10. The abbreviation *Bibliog* means _____.

```
YUGOSLAVIA - FOREIGN RELATIONS
949.742
Ow      Author  Owen, David
        Title   Balkan Odyssey / David Owen
        Ed.     1st U.S. ed.
        Pub.    New York: Harcourt Brace, 1996
        Sub     1) Owen, David Charles
                2) Yugoslav War, 1991--Diplomatic
                   History
                3) Yugoslav War, 1991--Personal
                   Narratives, British
                4) Diplomats--Great Britain--
                   Biography
                5) Yugoslavia--Foreign Relations--
                   Great Britain
                6) Great Britain--Foreign
                   Relations--Yugoslavia
```

11. The card shown is a(n):
    A. title card.
    B. author card.
    C. subject card.
    D. all of the above.

12. The author of this book is:
    A. Owen Charles David.
    B. David Charles Owen.
    C. Owen David Charles.
    D. Charles David Owen.

13. The call number of this book is:
    A. 949.702.
    B. 949.702
       Ow.
    C. Owen.
    D. none of the above.

14. The title of the book is _____ .

15. The publisher is _____ .

16. The publication date is _____ .

17. 1st U.S. ed means _____ .

18. The book's primary topic is _____ .

```
SPACE Flight
                  Manned flights
Charts may guide return from moon. H. Taylor.
Time 89:51 Je 25 '97
```

19. The title of the magazine article is:
    A. SPACE Flight.
    B. Manned Flights.
    C. Charts may guide return from moon.
    D. none of the above.

20. The subject of the article is:
    A. Manned flights.
    B. SPACE Flight.
    C. both of the above.
    D. Charts may guide return from moon.

21.   The author of the article is _____.

22.   The name of the magazine is _____.

23.   The volume number of the magazine is _____.

24.   The page(s) the article is found on is (are) _____.

25.   The date the magazine was published is _____.

```
New way of living; excerpt from a new kind of
country. il McCalls 105:193-200 My 19 '97
```

26.   The title of the article is _____.

27.   The article is taken from what larger work?

28.   The article appears in what magazine? _____

29.   Which volume? _____

30.   What is the date of the magazine? _____

Reading for Enjoyment

How long has it been since you read something for relaxation or fun? For many people, reading for pleasure is a rare treat—a chance to catch up on sports news, to learn how to do a weekend project, or to get caught up in a mystery or science-fiction fantasy.

As you read and complete the activities in this unit, you will have opportunities to read your local newspaper, browse through a magazine, or get lost in a good book. The most important goal is to rekindle your enthusiasm for reading for pleasure.

Begin your reading for pleasure by sitting down with a copy of your local newspaper. Some of you will read metropolitan papers; others will read papers from small towns. As you read, notice the unique style of your local newspaper. Compare its format to that of one of your classmate's newspapers. Notice how the writing style varies from reporter to reporter. You'll find that newspapers contain a wealth of information beyond advice columns, the comics, and the sports section. Avid reader or not, you will learn from and enjoy reading your local newspaper.

Newspaper Survey

ACTIVITY 10.1

This activity will help you evaluate your reading habits regarding the daily newspaper. Using a separate sheet of paper, write your responses to the Newspaper

Survey that follows. Your instructor may ask you to share your responses so you can compare your reading habits with those of your classmates.

Newspaper Survey

1. What newspaper(s) do you read?
2. How frequently do you read a newspaper?
3. What time of the day do you read the newspaper?
4. Indicate which newspaper sections you read and how often you read them by writing the name of the section and *always, usually, sometimes,* or *never* after each section you list.

front page	features
sports	classified ads
editorials	general ads
business	weather
comics	obituaries

5. If you didn't have the opportunity, would you miss reading the newspaper? If so, why?

ACTIVITY 10.2

Newspaper Jargon

There are some common terms used frequently by people discussing the newspaper. Knowing these terms will help you understand and actively participate in this part of the unit.

On a separate sheet of paper, write the terms that follow and their definitions. Then locate an example of each term in the newspaper of your choice. The terms listed below will appear in the Unit Review, so be sure your notes on them are complete and accurate.

1. Banner Headline: a headline that stretches across the newspaper page from one side to the other.
2. Headline: large type above an article indicating the content of the article.
3. Byline: a line at the beginning of an article listing the author's name.
4. Dateline: a line indicating where the event described in the article took place.
5. News Agency: an organization that sends news stories by wire. Two of the most well-known news agencies are the Associated Press and Reuters.
6. AP: the abbreviation for *The Associated Press*.
7. Lead: an article's first paragraph, in which the questions *who, what, when, where,* and *why* (the five Ws) are answered.
8. Caption: the words beside or below a photograph or illustration that give information about the picture.
9. Jump: words informing a reader that an article continues on another page.

Sections of the Newspaper

Take a minute and try to name all the sections you would find in an average newspaper. If you are the type of reader who skips from the front page to the sports section to the comics, you might have trouble with your list. This activity will help you discover *all* of the sections in your newspaper.

First, from the following list read the name of your newspaper section and its description. Add this information to your notes. Then, using a newspaper and its index, find that particular section. In your notes, write down the location in your newspaper of each of the sections given.

Sections of the Newspaper

Front Page: the page a reader sees first. Its format, appeal, and contents often influence a reader's decision about whether to buy the paper. Thus, the front page helps sell the paper; it also carries the most important stories of the day.

Editorial Section: Presents opinions through editorials by staff writers; editorial cartoons; letters to the editor (written by readers); and syndicated columns.

Feature Section: Entertains and appeals to readers' interests through comics; information on and reviews of movies, plays, concerts, and celebrities; homemaking hints; fashion news; and so on.

Sports Section: Covers a wide variety of sporting events and includes analyses of player and team performances; coaching strategies; scheduled games; statistics; predicted winners; and so on.

Business Section: Consists of articles that discuss and analyze economic activity; personnel; business strategies; and companies of note. It also includes stock quotations and interest rates.

Advertising Section: Pays those who produce the newspaper; allows businesses to communicate with consumers; informs readers of products and services available in the marketplace.

Weather Section: Includes local or regional forecasts; describes road conditions; lists national temperatures and extended forecasts.

Obituary Section: Contains notices of the deaths of prominent persons, usually members of the community, but sometimes national or international figures. It usually includes brief accounts of the persons' lives and may include lists of surviving family members and funeral information.

Analyzing the Newspaper

Too often people limit their newspaper reading to only a couple of sections. For example, when you read a newspaper, you may consistently read only the front page, the comics, and the list of automobiles for sale. But you may be missing valuable information by doing this, as Activity 10.4 will show you.

Using a newspaper and its index, locate the sections of the newspaper discussed in Activity 10.3 in order to discover what type of information is contained in each section. Then, on a separate sheet of paper, answer the following questions.

Front Page

1. What is the title of the most important story on the newspaper's front page?
2. Does the front page have one or more pictures? Does it include an index?
3. How many articles appear on the front page?

Editorial Section

1. Does the editorial section contain letters to the editor? Editorial cartoons? Syndicated columns?
2. List the topic of one of the editorials written by a staff writer.

Feature Section

1. Does the feature section include a TV schedule? A movie schedule? A review of a movie? Comics? Hints for homemakers? Fashion news? Advice columns such as "Dear Abby" or "Ann Landers"?

Sports Section

1. Does the sports section include a sports cartoon? Team standings? Reports of past games? A story about an important person in sports? A column by a sports writer?
2. On what pages do you find sports information?

Business Section

1. Does the business section list stock quotations from the New York Stock Exchange? The American Stock Exchange? The NASDAQ?
2. Does the section contain articles about important people in business? Specific companies? List the names of the companies featured.
3. Does the section contain syndicated columns? A report on grain prices? Money market rates?

Advertising

1. On what pages do you find the classified ads?

Weather

1. On what pages is the weather discussed?
2. Does the weather section contain forecasts? Road conditions? National temperatures?

Obituaries

1. On what pages do you find the obituaries?
2. Do any of the obituaries include pictures?
3. How many obituaries are listed in today's section?

Exploring the Front Page

Remember that a newspaper's front page is very important, especially on the newsstand. It must sell the paper. What do you know about the front page of today's newspaper? Use it to help you answer the questions that follow. Write your responses on a separate sheet of paper.

1. What is the headline of today's top news story?
2. How many columns does the front page of your newspaper have?
3. Does your newspaper print the weather news on the front page?
4. Does your newspaper print an index on the front page?
5. How many front page news stories contain a jump?
6. How many front page stories have been circulated by news agencies? How many are from the A.P.? How many are from Reuters?
7. How many photographs appear on the front page?
8. How many headlines on the front page of today's newspaper take up more than one column?
9. Does the front page contain a banner headline?
10. How many front page stories contain bylines?
11. How much does your newspaper cost?

Exploring the Editorial Pages

You probably take time to read your newspaper's front page, but its editorial pages may be new to you. The editorial pages present opinions of the newspaper's editorial staff, opinions of syndicated columnists from across the country, and opinions of the general public. By reading the editorial pages, you encounter new viewpoints. Whether you agree or disagree with what is being expressed, the editorials will make you think more about your position on the issue.

Using a separate sheet of paper and today's newspaper, turn to the editorial section and answer the following questions.

1. Find the editorials written by the newspaper's editorial staff. List headlines from two of them.
2. Choose one of the two editorials, explain the staff writer's viewpoint, and then discuss your viewpoint.
3. Find the *letters to the editor* and list the topics of two of the letters.

4. Choose one of the letters to the editor, explain how the author felt about the topic, and then discuss your feelings.

5. Study one of the editorial cartoons and then explain its theme.

6. Find two syndicated columns. List the headline, author, news agency, and topic of each.

ACTIVITY 10.7

Scavenger Hunt in the Classified Ads

Have you ever scanned the classified ads hoping to find a used car bargain or a part-time job? Perhaps you have written a classified ad of your own. Individuals who want to buy, sell, rent, or trade something can place classified ads in the newspaper. These ads produce revenue for the newspaper and serve as a clearinghouse for community commerce as well.

Using the classified section from a newspaper, answer on a separate sheet of paper the following questions. You will need to locate and use the classified ad index to find the appropriate section for each question. Have fun while you are on your scavenger hunt…some of the ads are very interesting!

1. What is the most unusual item that has been lost?
2. How many motorcycles are for sale?
3. Which used car would you buy if you had your choice?
4. Which "personal" ad do you find the most interesting?
5. What job would you apply for if you were job hunting?
6. How many yard sales are listed?
7. Which two pets would you adopt if you had room in your home?
8. Which business opportunity interests you most?
9. Which number(s) would you call for a day care center that welcomes "drop-ins"?
10. What should you do if you find an error in an ad you placed?

ACTIVITY 10.8

Writing a Classified Ad

Many people use classified ads to advertise items they would like to sell; many of these same people are surprised at the response their ads receive. A well-written classified ad can help you empty your garage and pad your wallet. To write an effective ad, there are a few basic principles you need to know, however. Above all, keep in mind that people skim ads quickly, so remember:

1. The first word of the ad should catch a reader's attention.

This:	Not This:
FIREWOOD, del. and stacked. Mixed pinion, oak, and pine. $72/cord. 555-6858	OLD So. Cntry. kindling, fat pine—great gifts. For free brochure write Brewton Inc. P.O. Box 555, Brewton, Pa.

2. Use as few words in the ad as possible, because the cost of placing a classified ad is determined by the length of the ad. However, you must be certain that the ad includes all necessary information.

This:	**Not This:**
1 BDRM, carpet, drapes, appls.; adults, no pets; $275 + utilities. 555-0425	CHEERFUL! Near bus, utilities, $185, 555-1064.

3. In a classified ad, abbreviations are fine—if a reader can understand them. A brief ad that makes no sense to its readers cannot be effective.

This:	**Not This:**
PENTAX C330 with 45mm, 60mm, 180mm lenses $595. Yashica with 85–250mm Zuika lens, $250. 555-1786	PENTAX 6x7, 35, 75, 105, 135 mm XT, WL, EL, $1,175. Mike 555-7373.

4. Finally, be sure your ad is placed in the appropriate category in the classified ads. If you have a car to sell, place your ad in the "Automobiles for Sale" category, not "Miscellaneous."

Using the Classified Index shown on this page and keeping in mind the principles for writing good ads, compose two classified ads for things you would like to buy, sell, or rent.

```
              CLASSIFIED INDEX
Real Estate . . . . . .1    Wanted  . . . . . . .8
Rentals . . . . . . .2      Help Wanted . . . . .9
Rentals Wanted  . . .3      Jobs Wanted  . . . .10
Service Offered . . .4      Lost & Found . . . .11
Household Goods . . .5      Personals  . . . . .12
Miscellaneous . . . .6      Motorcycles  . . . .13
Pets . . . . . . . .7       Automobiles  . . . .14
```

Sports Line

Thousands of avid sports fans read the sports section each day, and if you are among them you will surely enjoy this activity. Use the sports section of your newspaper to answer the questions that follow. Write your responses on a separate sheet of paper.

1. What is the headline of today's top sports story?

2. Does one sport receive more coverage today than the others? If so, what sport is it? Why do you think that sport is given more attention?

3. Do upcoming games get more coverage than those already played?

4. What are the titles of the standings and statistics columns?

5. List all the sports in today's sports section that are given any type of coverage.

6. Did you read any articles that you thought showed the bias of the sports writer? Which team does he or she seem to prefer? How could you tell?

7. Are there any feature stories in today's sports section? If so, what topic do they discuss?

8. Is there any coverage of women's sports? If so, which ones?

9. Is there any high school sports coverage?

10. Are there any predictions of winners? If so, for which sport? List the name of the column or article in which the prediction was made.

FIGURE 10.1
NBA Standings

NBA STANDINGS

WESTERN CONFERENCE
Midwest Division

	W	L	Pct.	GB	L10	Strk	H	A	Cnf
Houston	24	8	.750	—	4-6	L 2	12-6	12-2	17-5
Utah	23	8	.742	½	5-5	W 1	16-2	7-6	14-6
Minnesota	14	18	.438	10	6-4	W 2	10-4	4-14	10-12
Dallas	10	19	.345	12½	2-8	L 2	6-7	4-12	7-9
San Antonio	9	21	.300	14	6-4	L 1	5-9	4-12	7-16
DENVER	8	23	.259	15½	3-7	L 4	4-11	4-12	6-12
Vancouver	6	26	.188	18	3-7	L 4	5-12	1-14	4-13

Pacific Division

	W	L	Pct.	GB	L10	Strk	H	A	Cnf
L.A. Lakers	24	9	.727	—	8-2	W 5	14-2	10-7	15-5
Seattle	23	11	.676	1½	7-3	W 2	11-4	12-7	16-6
Portland	18	15	.545	6	5-5	W 4	9-6	9-9	15-10
L.A. Clippers	13	19	.406	10½	6-4	W 3	7-9	6-10	11-11
Golden State	12	18	.400	10½	5-5	W 1	8-8	4-10	7-12
Sacramento	13	20	.394	11	5-5	L 3	9-8	4-12	9-13
Phoenix	10	22	.313	13½	3-7	L 3	7-8	3-14	7-14

EASTERN CONFERENCE
Atlantic Division

	W	L	Pct.	GB	L10	Strk	H	A	Cnf
Miami	24	8	.750	—	7-3	L 1	8-5	16-3	14-6
New York	23	9	.719	1	7-3	W 1	14-4	9-5	14-6
Washington	16	15	.516	7½	6-4	W 1	8-8	8-7	9-11
Orlando	11	17	.393	11	2-8	L 1	7-7	4-10	9-11
New Jersey	8	21	.276	14½	3-7	L 3	5-9	3-12	4-17
Philadelphia	8	22	.267	15	1-9	L 4	4-10	4-12	5-13
Boston	7	23	.233	16	2-8	W 1	6-10	1-13	3-16

Central Division

	W	L	Pct.	GB	L10	Strk	H	A	Cnf
Chicago	28	4	.875	—	9-1	W 3	15-1	13-3	18-3
Detroit	24	7	.774	3½	7-3	W 4	15-3	9-4	20-5
Cleveland	21	10	.677	6½	8-2	W 3	15-4	6-6	11-9
Atlanta	18	11	.621	8½	7-3	W 2	11-1	7-10	12-10
Charlotte	17	14	.548	10½	5-5	L 1	9-5	8-9	11-11
Milwaukee	15	16	.484	12½	3-7	L 5	9-9	6-7	10-10
Indiana	14	16	.467	13	5-5	L 1	6-6	8-10	7-10
Toronto	10	21	.323	17½	3-7	L 3	9-8	1-13	7-16

Sports Scoreboard

In the sports section of your newspaper, you will find many tables like the one shown in Figure 10.1. As you can see, all the teams in the National Basketball Association (NBA) are listed with their standings. There are two divisions in each conference. The conferences are divided by geographic location. This table shows wins, losses, percent of wins, and the number of games back a team is from first place. Refer to the table to answer the following questions. Write your answers on a separate sheet of paper.

1. What are the names of the two divisions in the Eastern Conference?
2. List the names of the divisions in the Western Conference.
3. Which team is in first place in each of the four divisions?
4. What statistic do the San Antonio, New Jersey, and Toronto teams have in common?
5. Which four teams were "in the cellar" when these standings were current?
6. Which team in first place looks most impressive to you? Why?
7. Which of the teams in last place looks best at this point in the season? Why?

Forecasting the Weather

Are you going to a football game, baseball game, track meet, or tennis match? You can use the temperatures and forecasts given in the weather section of your newspaper to help you decide what clothing to wear to be comfortable. If you are going to travel across the state, or go on a vacation to another area of the country, the weather section's predictions and present temperature lists will help you choose what to pack. The weather is a constant source of news, and the following activity will help you discover what types of weather information your newspaper provides.

Often, on the front page of a newspaper you can find a brief summary of the local weather forecast. The summary shown in Figure 10.2 is typical, giving information about the weather forecast for the day and evening.

For more detailed information, you would consult the official weather maps distributed by the National Weather Service. These maps appear daily in most newspapers. Such things as areas of low and high atmospheric pressure, position and movements of large air masses, and storm activity are illustrated as in Figure 10.3. Usually, this same information is summarized in a paragraph that you can find somewhere near the map.

Weather

DENVER AREA: Variably cloudy, not so cold and a few snow showers today. Partly cloudy, snow showers ending and cool tonight. Highs, 33-38; lows, 15-20. Details on Page 12-C.

FIGURE 10.2
Weather Forecast Summary

FIGURE 10.3   Detailed Weather Forecast

NATIONAL WEATHER SERVICE FORECAST to 7 PM EST 12-11-84

UPI WEATHER FOTOCAST ®

Cold, snow showers predicted for area

The unseasonably mild temperatures that have graced the Denver area will be replaced Tuesday by cold air and snow showers, weather forecasters said.

Ron Kelly, the Rocky Mountain News forecaster, said a storm front would move through the metropolitan area Tuesday, bringing overcast skies and rain that would change to snow in the late afternoon.

The forecast called for 1 to 2 inches of snow in the area overnight, and from 4 to 8 inches in the mountains, Kelly said. Highs for Tuesday were expected to be in the high 40s, dropping to 18 to 20 degrees Tuesday night.

Kelly said the cold weather would remain at least through Wednesday.

ROAD CONDITIONS

U.S. 6 west — Loveland Pass: icy in spots, snowpacked. I-70 west — Eisenhower Tunnel (both approaches): wet. Vail Pass: icy in spots. Glenwood Springs: icy in spots. U.S. 24 Colorado 91 — Fremont Pass: icy in spots. Tennessee Pass: wet, icy in spots. U.S. 40 west — Rabbit Ears Pass: wet, icy in spots, snowpacked in spots. Steamboat Springs: wet, icy in spots. U.S. 50 & 550 west of 285 — Monarch Pass: icy in spots. Red Mountain Pass: wet, icy in spots, snowpacked in spots. U.S. 160 west — La Veta Pass: icy in spots. Wolf Creek Pass: icy in spots, snowpacked in spots.

For updated road conditions, call the Colorado Department of Highways at 639-1111 for Denver and roads west, and 639-1234 for I-25 and roads east.

For mountain and avalanche conditions, call 236-9435 in Denver and Boulder; 482-0457 in Fort Collins, 688-5485 in Frisco, 827-5687 in Vail, and 920-1664 in Aspen.

FIGURE 10.4   Local and State Data

LOCAL AND STATE DATA

Monday's temperatures
Airport observations

High	63 degrees
Low	23 degrees
Mean temp. was	3 degrees

For the record

Normal high for Monday	47
Normal low for Monday	20
Record high for Monday set in 1939.	74

Monday's air quality at 5:15 p.m.: 213.
Tuesday's air quality forecast: extremely poor.

Record low for Monday ..... -13 set in 1932.
Humidity high on Monday 74
Humidity low on Monday 16

Sun and moon
Tuesday's sunrise 7:12 a.m., sunset 4:36 p.m.
Tuesday's moon rises 7:33 p.m., sets 10:15 a.m.

Precipitation to 6 p.m.

Precipitation for Monday	0.00 inches
Precipitation this month	trace
Normal for month	0.55 inches
Precipitation since Jan. 1	16.03
Normal precip. since Jan. 1	14.96

Last qtr.   New   1st qtr.   Full
Dec. 15   Dec. 22   Dec. 30   Jan. 6

DENVER'S MONDAY HOURLY READINGS

Hour	Temp.	Humidity
midnight	35	59
1 a.m.	34	59
2 a.m.	31	66
3 a.m.	31	65
4 a.m.	31	63
5 a.m.	30	63
6 a.m.	26	74
7 a.m.	26	74
8 a.m.	31	58
9 a.m.	34	64
10 a.m.	43	51
11 a.m.	54	24
noon	58	20
1 p.m.	61	17
2 p.m.	62	16
3 p.m.	62	20
4 p.m.	57	25
5 p.m.	50	37
6 p.m.	44	43

nr — no report

COLORADO TEMPERATURES

City	Hi	Lo	Prc
Alamosa	48	5	
Boulder	nr	nr	
Colo. Springs	58	25	
Craig	nr	nr	
Denver	63	23	
Dinosaur	nr	nr	
Durango	54	nr	
Fort Collins	51	20	
Glenwood Spgs	38	21	
Grand Junction	38	32	
Greeley	55	21	
Gunnison	nr	nr	
La Junta	59	25	
Lamar	nr	nr	
Leadville	48	5	
Limon	58	23	
Pueblo	57	20	
Salida	nr	nr	
Sterling	nr	nr	
Trinidad	65	31	
Vail	nr	nr	

FIGURE 10.5   Temperature Listings

NATIONAL TEMPERATURES

	Mon Dec 10			Tue Dec 11			Wed Dec 12		
City	Lo	Hi	Prc	Wea	Lo	Hi	Wea	Lo	Hi
Albany	22	38	.00	Ptcldy	30	45	Ptcldy	27	48
Albuquerque . .	27	52	.00	Ptcldy	31	54	Ptcldy	34	53
Amarillo	29	66	.00	Ptcldy	29	72	Ptcldy	37	50
Atlanta	47	63	.00	Sunny	45	67	Sunny	43	68
Atlantic City . . .	47	53	.00	Ptcldy	40	50	Ptcldy	37	54
Austin	51	75	.00	Ptcldy	51	77	Cloudy	53	76
Baltimore	39	50	.00	Sunny	37	53	Sunny	34	58
Billings	38	56	.00	Snow	20	35	Ptcldy	15	44
Birmingham . . .	55	66	.00	Sunny	40	67	Sunny	45	70
Bismarck	19	40	.00	Windy	24	26	Ptcldy	01	28
Boise	28	42	.08	Ptcldy	27	40	Snoshw	31	40
Boston	31	49	.21	Ptcldy	40	48	Ptcldy	37	50
Brownsville	56	82	.00	Ptcldy	58	84	Ptcldy	60	84
Buffalo	36	46	.07	Ptcldy	35	48	Cloudy	39	49
Burlington Vt . .	31	40	.00	Ptcldy	29	41	Ptcldy	28	46
Casper	35	40	.00	Snow	27	39	Ptcldy	07	34
Charleston Sc . .	48	62	.00	Ptcldy	44	67	Sunny	45	71
Charleston Wv .	37	52	.41	Sunny	39	55	Ptcldy	34	60
Charlotte Nc . . .	30	48	.06	Sunny	36	60	Sunny	35	66
Cheyenne	23	55	.00	Cloudy	25	45	Cloudy	11	35
Chicago	33	46	.08	Sunny	31	55	Cloudy	32	32
Cincinnati	45	50	.13	Sunny	38	51	Cloudy	38	55
Cleveland	36	41	.22	Sunny	36	48	Ptcldy	36	52
Columbia Sc . . .	31	62	.00	Ptcldy	39	68	Sunny	40	72
Columbus Oh . .	39	44	.38	Sunny	37	50	Ptcldy	37	54
Dal Ft Worth . . .	43	71	.00	Sunny	47	72	Cloudy	54	69
Denver	23	63	.00	Snoshw	30	50	Ptcldy	20	40
Des Moines	29	45	.00	Ptcldy	32	57	Cloudy	19	28
Detroit	30	46	.12	Sunny	33	46	Cloudy	32	42
Duluth	30	34	.00	Cloudy	30	37	Sunny	06	15
El Paso	31	66	.00	Ptcldy	33	70	Ptcldy	37	69
Fargo	23	37	.00	Windy	26	28	Ptcldy	01	21
Flagstaff	19	18	.00	Snow	30	39	Ptcldy	20	47
Great Falls	42	53	.00	Snoshw	10	32	Windy	20	46

FORECAST FOR THE REGION

New Mexico — Variable clouds Tuesday and Tuesday night, chance of showers and mountain snow showers mainly west and north. Highs Tuesday, 40 to 50 mountains and northwest. 50s to mid-70s lower elevations. Lows, teens to 20s mountains, mid-20s to near 40 lower elevations.

Kansas — Partly cloudy and mild Tuesday. Mostly cloudy Tuesday night, chance of light snow northwest and north-central. Highs Tuesday, mid-50s to mid-60s statewide. Lows, low 20s northwest, mid-30s east.

Utah — Mostly cloudy north Tuesday, scattered rain and snow showers, variable clouds south both days, widely scattered showers. Locally gusty winds statewide Tuesday. Highs Tuesday, mid-30s to mid-40s north, 40s south. Lows, low 20s-low 30s north, low 20s to mid-30s south.

Nebraska — Considerable clouds and colder Tuesday, increasing winds in afternoon, slight chance of showers west and north.

FOREIGN CITIES

City	Hi	Lo	Wth
Acapulco	90	75	cdy
Amsterdam	50	46	clr
Athens	63	41	clr
Barbados	84	72	clr
Berlin	45	37	cdy
B'Aires	77	61	cdy
Cairo	66	48	clr
Calgary	39	18	cdy
Copenhagen	49	41	clr
Dublin	52	39	clr
Edmonton	32	0	clr
Frankfurt	46	32	cdy
Geneva	39	32	cdy
Guadalajara	80	41	clr
Hong Kong	73	64	clr
Jerusalem	54	39	cdy
Kingston	90	73	cdy
London	48	41	clr
Madrid	57	43	clr
Mazatlan	87	71	cdy
Manila	88	66	clr
Merida/Cancun	84	57	clr
Mexico City	73	46	clr
Montreal	39	32	cdy
Moscow	36	34	sn
New Delhi	81	52	clr
Ottawa	34	1	cdy
Paris	48	45	clr
Regina	24	−4	cdy
Rome	55	34	clr
San Juan	72	70	cdy
Stockholm	45	37	clr
Tokyo	57	43	cdy
Toronto	39	32	cdy
Vancouver	43	36	rn
Vienna	39	32	cdy

Some newspapers also include information about the condition of local highways. Travelers can use this information to plan their routes.

In addition, the weather section reports on precipitation, air quality, humidity, and hourly temperatures for cities throughout the state. And if you are interested in knowing the temperature in Tokyo, you can consult the detailed, alphabetized lists of temperatures in cities throughout the world. The National Weather Service compiles these lists for various major cities around the globe.

Consult the charts in Figure 10.5 and you will see that Brownsville, Texas, and Barbados both had temperatures of 84 degrees on December 12, although one city had partly cloudy skies, while the other had clear skies. Now, try doing some more weather research on your own. Use the charts in Figures 10.2–10.5 to answer the following questions. Write your answers on a separate sheet of paper.

1. What is the expected high temperature on Tuesday in the New Mexico mountains?

2. What is the expected low temperature on Tuesday in the northwest section of Kansas?

3. What was Monday's low temperature in Albany?

4. What was Monday's high temperature in Dallas/Fort Worth?

5. How much precipitation was recorded in Detroit on Monday?

6. Which two cities on the national chart recorded the lowest temperature on Monday? What was the temperature?

7. Which city on the national chart recorded the highest temperature on Monday? What was the temperature?

8. Which two cities on the foreign chart recorded the highest temperature? What was the temperature?

9. What kind of weather is predicted for Denver?

10. What was the record low for Denver on December 11th? (Hint: It was set in 1932.)

ACTIVITY 10.12

Understanding Stock Quotations

Read the business section in your newspaper and you can learn about the stock market. Why is stock market activity such important news? Because the buying and selling that happens on Wall Street affects many individuals' incomes, as well as the economies of the United States and the world. Perhaps you have invested in stocks yourself. If so, you probably turn quickly to the stock quotations whenever you pick up a newspaper.

If you do not yet know how to read stock quotations, you are about to enter the world of Wall Street. To read and understand the stock exchange pages found in the business sections of all metropolitan papers, you must first learn some essential terms. On a separate sheet of paper, take notes on these terms and their definitions.

Year's high: the highest price the stock reached in one year's time.

Year's low: the lowest price the stock reached in one year's time.

Day's high: the highest price the stock reached on a given day.

Day's low: the lowest price the stock reached on a given day.

Last price: the price at which the stock was selling when the market closed for the day.

Net change: the difference between a stock's last price today and the same stock's last price on the previous day of trading.

NYSE: New York Stock Exchange: one of the major stock exchanges.

$7/8$ = 87.5 cents

$3/4$ = 75.0 cents

$5/8$ = 62.5 cents

$1/2$ = 50.0 cents

⅜ = 37.5 cents

¼ = 25.0 cents

⅛ = 12.5 cents

Now, look at the stock quotations that follow and answer questions one to four. Use the terminology you just learned to find the answers.

52-week High	Low	Stock	Div.	Yld.	PE	100s	Sales High	Low	Last	Chg.
$32^1/_2$	$21^5/_8$	Mattels					$27^1/_4$	$26^5/_8$	27	$-^3/_8$
53	$41^1/_2$	Goodyr					53	$51^7/_8$	$52^7/_8$	+1
$36^3/_8$	$25^5/_8$	Chryslrs					$35^5/_8$	$35^1/_4$	$35^3/_8$	...

1. What were the year's high, year's low, day's high, day's low, last price, and net change for Chrysler stock?

2. Using the stock quotations for Goodyear, provide the same information requested in Question 1.

3. Using the stock quotations for Mattel, provide the same information requested in Question 1.

4. Finally, survey the stock quotations for several companies whose names are familiar to you. Using a metropolitan newspaper, look up the year's high, year's low, day's high, day's low, last price, and net change for the following stocks: Alcoa, Campbell's Soup, Delta Air Lines, Exxon, and K-Mart.

Stock Quotation Worksheet

ACTIVITY 10.13

Are you a Wall Street wizard? Using the New York Stock Exchange (NYSE) quotations from a metropolitan paper, look up the following stocks and, on a separate sheet of paper, record these statistics for each stock listed below: the abbreviation for the stock, year's high, year's low, day's high, day's low, last price, and net change.

Ford Motor Company	Kellogg's	Texas Instruments
General Electric	Penney's	United Air Lines
Honda	PepsiCo	Wendy's
Motorola	Kimberley Clark	Xerox

After you find all the information requested above, answer, the following questions:

1. Which of the stocks has the highest *last* price per share?

2. What was that stock's *last* price?

3. Which of the stocks has the lowest *last* price per share?

4. What was that stock's *last* price?

5. Which stock recorded the largest *net gain* from the previous day?
6. How much did that stock gain?
7. Which stock recorded the largest *net loss* from the previous day?
8. How much was that stock down?
9. If you were buying one of these twelve stocks, which would you buy? Why?

ACTIVITY 10.14

Magazine Preferences

Reading for pleasure certainly must include magazines. You probably enjoy browsing through a favorite magazine relating to a hobby or a sport or cars or fashion. Some magazines are funny or inspirational; some magazines are interesting and informative. No matter what your reason for reading a specific magazine, you need to recognize that reading magazines is an important part of reading for pleasure.

And reading for enjoyment is important for developing reading speed, reading comprehension, and vocabulary. The more you read, the more practice you have improving your reading skills, the more contact you have with words and word meanings, and the more your reading speed improves. Although reading a magazine may seem like nothing but pure enjoyment, you benefit by doing it.

Let's begin by surveying your magazine reading habits. On a separate sheet of paper, number from one to five, skipping every other line. Answer the following questions regarding your leisure reading preferences.

1. Which magazine(s) do you enjoy reading most? Why?
2. Do you read the entire magazine, or do you read only parts of it? If you read only parts of it, which parts do you read?
3. Do you read entire articles in the magazine, or do you simply skim them? Why?
4. Where and when do you read magazines? Why do you choose this time and location?
5. Do you enjoy reading magazines more than reading books? Why?

ACTIVITY 10.15

Magazine Survey

There are hundreds of magazines on newsstands and library shelves today. Select a magazine you have never read before and skim through it. Choose an article that catches your interest or makes you curious and read it. Next using a separate sheet of paper, write down the name of the magazines you selected and the title of the article you read. Then briefly state the article's main idea. Do the same survey with a second magazine and, if you have time, a third magazine as well. (Remember, don't be tempted by your usual favorites—choose a magazine that's new to explore.) Be prepared to explain why you selected the magazines you did and to discuss whether you would like to continue to read those titles.

Magazine Summary

Bring to class a magazine you enjoy reading. Choose an article and, simply for pleasure, read it. Now, on a separate sheet of paper, write a short paragraph summarizing the gist of the article.

Was reading and summarizing easy or difficult for you? If it was easy, you are comprehending well enough during leisure reading to get the main idea of the content. Did you find yourself skimming the article, selectively skipping sentences or sections you did not enjoy, or did you read the article word for word? Were you still able to get the gist of the article using the skimming and skipping reading technique?

You do not have to feel guilty skimming and selectively skipping passages as you read for pleasure. After all, you are not reading for specific details; you are not going to be tested on the material. Reading for pleasure in your leisure time should be enjoyable!

Repeat this activity frequently. On a separate sheet of paper prepare a chart similar to the one shown. Each time you complete the exercise, log it on your chart.

Name of magazine	Title of article	Summary
1.		
2.		

Selecting an Enjoyable Book

Have you read any good books lately? For some people, sitting back and getting lost in a book is the most relaxing thing they can do.

Rediscover the joy of reading a book for pleasure. Your instructor will set aside some class time for leisure reading. Your task is to choose a book to read that you will enjoy. If you start a book and don't like it, select another. It defeats the purpose of this activity to have you suffer through a book you don't like.

The first step, then, is to find a book you will enjoy. You might ask your librarian to suggest some books other students have liked. Or, your instructor may have some ideas that interest you. On the other hand, you may prefer to browse independently, skimming covers and summaries to find a book that suits you. However you go about finding your books, enjoy this opportunity to get reacquainted with reading for pleasure.

Reading for Pleasure

Keep a record of your reading progress by making a chart like the one that follows. Each time you read your book, log on your chart the date and the number of pages you read.

Remember, as you read, your reading speed is increasing, your comprehension is improving, and your vocabulary is growing. Not bad, since reading a book you enjoy is a pleasure, anyway!

	Date	Number of pages read		Date	Number of pages read
1			4		
2			5		
3			6		

ACTIVITY 10.19

Creative Book Projects[1]

If your instructor says *book report*, she or he is likely to hear a loud groan in response. This activity gives you the opportunity to do something much more creative and fun than writing a typical book report. From the list that follows, choose the format for a creative book project that appeals to you. Be sure to include your book's title and author somewhere in your project.

1. Create a crossword puzzle based on you book. Include at least forty *Across* clues and forty *Down* clues and make certain that most of your clues are related directly to your book. The only exceptions to this rule are words or definitions that you have to use as "fillers." Include a key for the crossword puzzle.

2. Construct an exam of at least fifty questions based on your book. Include multiple-choice, matching, true-false, and completion questions on your exam. Try to use approximately the same number of each type of question. You may include other kinds of questions, such as short essays, but provide an outline of possible essay answers along with an answer key for the objective questions.

3. Design an oversized poster based on your book. Include in the design a 300-word recommendation "advertising" the book. This format lends itself very well to sports stories and mysteries.

4. Draw a detailed map of the book's primary setting and then explain in sequence the important action that occurred at the various places illustrated on your map. Completeness, creativity, and neatness are important here.

5. Choose either a major or minor character from your book and explain his or her part in the plot or sequence of events. Then, explain how you would have reacted or behaved differently.

6. You are a literary critic. Choose one of the following and discuss the statement, reflecting and amplifying on your book.

   A. "Authors are people behind masks."

   B. "The biographer is a maker of heels or heroes."

   C. "Show me what the age is reading, and I can tell you the nature of the times."

---

[1]The suggestions in this activity are taken from Isabelle M. Decker, *100 Novel Ways with Book Reports*. New York: Scholastic Magazines, Inc., 1969.

    D. "This book should be included in a capsule buried today, to be dug up in 100 years."

    E. "This book should be read by every young adult and his or her parents."

7. Condense the action in your book into various articles and present them as though they made up the front page of a newspaper. Use a standard six-column newspaper format. Include human interest stories, sports events, obituaries, editorials, want ads, advertising, and so on. Make sure all of your articles reflect the book you read and the era in which its story action took place. (For example, Tom Sawyer would not be riding a mountain bike.)

8. Write a television commercial about your book. Include all necessary dialogue, as well as descriptions of the story action. Draw pictures or use magazine illustrations to convey your ideas. The illustrations should reveal what your commercial would look like if shown on television.

9. If you choose to read a collection of short stories, you may wish to do one of the following:

    A. Write your intellectual reactions to five stories, rather than analyzing them. Discuss the type of reader who would enjoy or find satisfaction in reading each story. To justify your position, present at least three positive aspects of a story you like and three negative aspects of one you disliked.

    B. Write an essay on the significance and importance of titles, referring to the titles of ten specific stories to support your generalizations.

Traditional Book Projects

ACTIVITY 10.20

Some students feel more confident following a more conventional form for a book project, and some books lend themselves to this type of report format. If you are one of this group, or if you feel that the book you chose fits the traditional project category, try the following:

1. In the center of the page on a separate sheet of paper, write the title of the book you read and underline it. Beneath the title, write the author's name.

2. For Part One of your report, begin by describing the action in the book. In other words, what was the plot of the story?

Choose three of the following to conclude your book project.

3. Describe in detail the main character of the book you read. Include a description of his or her appearance, personality, motivations, and so on. Point out whether this character changed though the course of the story.

4. Describe what you consider the climax of the plot and tell why.

5. Discuss whether you think the book is true to life and, if not, why not.

6. Tell about the incident or aspect of the book that you either really liked or really disliked.

7. Give your general evaluation of the book, including what you liked and dislike about it. Would you recommend it to anyone else?

Review

Unit 10

Number a separate sheet of paper from one through twenty-five. Read the following questions and write the correct answers beside the corresponding numbers on your answer sheet.

I. Sections of the Newspaper (1–7)

Identify the section of the newspaper being described by writing the name of the section in the corresponding space on your answer sheet.

1. The _____ section deals with entertainment. It includes information about movies, plays, concerts, and nightlife. It also includes the comics.

2. This section is essential for the paper because it provides the money to publish the paper. It is called the _____ section.

3. The _____ is what the reader sees first. It influences his or her decision about whether to buy the paper.

4. _____ focus on individuals who have died and give accounts of occupation, relatives, funeral information, and so on.

5. The _____ section focuses on opinions of staff writers, the general public, and syndicated columnists.

6. The previous night's basketball game, the top sports statistics, and news of a player trade are covered in the _____ section.

7. Stock quotations are found in the _____ section, along with articles on new products, marketing strategies, and companies of note.

II. Newspaper Jargon (8–16)

Match the terms given with their correct definitions.

8. Banner headline
9. Headline
10. Byline
11. News agency
12. A.P.
13. Dateline
14. Lead
15. Caption
16. Jump

A. Continued on page _____.
B. The first paragraph of a story
C. Associated Press
D. The line indicating who wrote the article
E. Words beside or below a photograph or illustration
F. The line indicating when the described event took place
G. An organization that sends news stories by wire
H. Large type above and article indicating the content of the article
I. A headline that stretches from one side of the newspaper page to the other

III. Business and Financial Section (17–23)

Study the stock quotation given below and identify each numbered section with the term that describes it.

17.	18.	19.	20.	21.	22.	23.
$13\frac{7}{8}$	$4\frac{7}{8}$	Mattel	$11\frac{1}{2}$	$11\frac{1}{4}$	$11\frac{1}{2}$	$-\frac{1}{4}$

IV. Classified Ads (24)

Since you pay for Classified Ads by the word, it is your advantage to use as few words in an ad as possible. Rewrite the following classified ad, making it brief, yet complete. (Hint: thirty-five to forty words will supply all the necessary information.)

24.   FOR SALE—I would like to sell for $75 the Victorian sofa my husband says is like new. I also have a dining room table and four chairs for $160 that I really want to get rid of. Because we have a new color TV set, I will also sell my 7-year-old portable TV for $24. Last year we bought a new G.E. Electric range for $750, but I really don't like it. I will be willing to let it go for $300. Anyone who is interested in any of these terrific bargains should call me at 123-4567. Be sure not to call until after 5:00 P.M. because I won't be home from work until then.

V. Reading for Pleasure (25)

No matter what you prefer to read—newspapers, magazines, or books—reading for pleasure is good for you.

25.   In a short essay explain the benefits of reading for pleasure.

Getting It Together

So what do you want to do with your life? Graduate from high school? Go to a post-secondary school? Get a job half way around the world? Make a million dollars? Post-secondary education is costly these days, career possibilities are endless, international employment is often lucrative, and planning for your future is a must. This chapter focuses on life after high school and *you!* It will begin with an interest inventory, expand to career research techniques, and include steps for preparing for post-secondary education. By the time the chapter is complete, you should have some good techniques for *preparing for your future.*

An Inventory of Your Interests

ACTIVITY 11.1

Ever thought of being a member of the cyber patrol and looking for high-tech criminals and cyber thieves? Maybe you are great at a foreign language and would like to become a corporate representative for a major company in a foreign country. Or perhaps science is your thing, and you would like to be on the team that discovers the cure for the next threatening virus. What are your interests? How much do you know about yourself? What would you choose to do after high school that would fit your skills, guarantee an income to meet your preferred lifestyle, and keep you happy and challenged as well?

Let's find out more about you! Read the following forty-eight items and place a check beside those activities and career fields that interest you.

1. Work on a farm
2. Solve complicated math problems
3. Act in a movie or play
4. Study social groups in society
5. Interview strangers for the TV news
6. Learn about and study the economy
7. Study "how-to" mechanics manuals
8. Perform science lab experiments
9. Manage an art gallery
10. Conduct a religious service
11. Bargain at a flea market
12. Analyze statistics
13. Build cabinets or furniture
14. Study nature or trace the effects of pollution on the environment
15. Write a movie screenplay
16. Lead a club or scout troop
17. Buy merchandise for a store
18. Work nine to five in a corporate office
19. Operate heavy machines
20. Play chess
21. Work on an art or music magazine
22. Get involved in a charity
23. Do fast-paced, high pressure sales

24. Design computer games and programs
25. Work outside in a national park
26. Research a law case
27. Play a musical instrument
28. Work with babies or children
29. Run for class office
30. Work after school to save money
31. Set up a stereo system
32. Read science fiction
33. Write a short story, play, or novel
34. Entertain at a party
35. Work in a politician's office
36. Keyboard documents into computers
37. Build a jet aircraft model
38. Use an electronic microscope or a high-tech medical instrument
39. Design a new line of clothes
40. Read and discuss literature
41. Debate political and social issues
42. Keep accurate records of a business
43. Repair a car engine
44. Identify constellations of stars
45. Take pottery classes
46. Work with senior citizens
47. Sell products on commission
48. Set up a budget for running a large company or government agency

ACTIVITY 11.2

Evaluating Your Interests

So, what does the inventory of interests mean? Are you going to be the next Georgia O'Keefe? Albert Einstein? Or maybe a protege of Martin Luther King? Let's find out about you!

Step One:

Circle every number that you checked off. For example, if you checked *Work on a farm*, circle *1*. After you have circled all the items, count the total numbers you circled in line A. (If you circled three numbers, you would write three beside *Total Circled*.) Repeat for lines B through F.

A. 1   7   13   19   25   31   37   43   Total Circled _____
B. 2   8   14   20   26   32   38   44   Total Circled _____
C. 3   9   15   21   27   33   39   45   Total Circled _____
D. 4   10 16   22   28   34   40   46   Total Circled _____
E. 5   11 17   23   29   35   41   47   Total Circled _____
F. 6   12 18   24   30   36   42   48   Total Circled _____

Step Two:

Compute your response by taking the total circled for letter A and writing it in the space below; repeat for B through F.

_____ A. Doer   _____ C. Artist   _____ E. Enterpriser
_____ B. Investigator   _____ D. Helper   _____ F. Detailer

In which two personality types did you score highest? Write the personality types below.

First personality type   _____
Second personality type   _____

Step Three:

Now let's see how those personality types relate to possible careers. Using your top personality type, refer to the following list and write down three jobs from that personality type that would interest you. Do the same for your second personality type.

First Personality Type   _____
Career Choices: _____
                             _____
                             _____

Second Personality Type: _____
Career Choices: _____
                             _____
                             _____

Doers

If you like working with your hands and being physically active, you may be a doer. Doers are often practical, stable, self-controlled, and independent.

Some Careers for Doers

Landscape Architect
Police Officer
Forester
Recreation Administrator
Vocational/Agricultural
Military Officer
Teacher
Mechanic
Fish and Game Warden
Hairdresser
Dental Technician
Physical Therapist
Electrician
Construction Worker
Drafter
Truck Driver
Cartographer
Athletic Trainer
Firefighter
Machinist
Locksmith
Carpenter
Computer Repairs/Engineer
Licensed Practical Nurse
Chef
Surveyor
Caterer
Air Traffic Controller
Plumber
Archaeologist
X-Ray Technician
Farm Manager

Helpers

Helpers like jobs that let them interact with people. Helpers are good communicators who love to listen as well as talk. They work well in groups, too.

Some Careers for Helpers

Youth Services Worker
Parole Officer
Recreation Director
Attorney
Physical Therapist
Sales Representative
Occupational Therapist
Fitness Instructor
Extension Agent
Cosmetologist
Therapist
Paramedic
Counselor
Mental Health Specialist
Teacher
Social Worker
Personnel Director
Nurse
Funeral Director
Dietician
Religious Worker
Information Clerk
Chamber of Commerce
Child Care Worker
Travel Agent
Athletic Coach
Airline Personnel
Claims Adjuster
Receptionist
Waiter/Waitress
Office Worker
Home Health Aide
Career Counselor

Investigators

Investigators are observant and curious about things around them. They are inquisitive, self-confident, and logical. They like to think independently, so often they like to work alone, too.

Some Careers for Investigators

Computer Analyst
Pharmacist
Science/Math Teacher
Ecologist
Technical Writer
Nurse
Science Lab Technician
Biologist
Computer System Analyst
Engineer
Medical Technologist
Paralegal
Research Analyst
Librarian
Reporter
Dietician
Physician
College Professor
Police Detective
Lawyer
Veterinarian
Consumer Researcher
Meteorologist
Astronomer
Horticulturist
Computer Security Specialist
Dentist

Enterprisers

Enterprisers are self-confident, sociable, and adventurous. They like making decisions, selling products, leading groups, and politics. This type is outgoing and will start projects involving a lot of people.

Some Careers for Enterprisers

Banker
Sales Person
Real Estate Appraiser
Entrepreneur
Florist
Stock Broker
Lawyer
Police Officer
TV/Radio Announcer
Campaign Manager
Lobbyist
Insurance Manager
Personnel Recruiter
Office Manager
Travel Agent
Advertising Agent
Advertising Executive
Politician
Business Manager

Artists

Artistic people value creative self-expression. Artists tend to be innovative, imaginative, and out-of-the-ordinary. They love working freely and often put their emotions into their work.

Some Careers for Artists

Artist
Cartographer
English Teacher
Dance Instructor
Drama Coach
Entertainer
Music Teacher
Graphic Designer
Architect
Advertising Manager
Musician
Writer
Painter
Florist
Interior Decorator
Illustrator
Photographer
Landscaper
Journalist
Recording Technician
Reporter
Lighting Specialist
Cosmetologist
Librarian
Museum Curator

Detailers

Detailers are conventional people who enjoy collecting and organizing. They work well within a system and are efficient and practical. Detailers often like being part of large companies, though not necessarily in leadership positions. They enjoy steady routines and following clearly defined procedures.

Some Careers for Detailers

Accountant
Business Teacher
Bookkeeper
Personnel Clerk
Actuary
Secretary
Librarian
Proofreader
Administrative Assistant
Credit Manager
Estimator
CAD Operator
Reservations Agent
Bank Manager
Cartographer
Cost Analyst
Court Reporter
Medical Secretary
Auditor Statistician
Financial Analyst
Safety Inspector
Tax Consultant
Insurance Underwriter
Corrections Officer
Computer Operator
Paralegal
Medical Lab Technologist
Cashier
Hotel Clerk

Exploring Career Paths

Environmental Auditor? Sanitation Engineer? Genetic Researcher? Web Master? Computer Animator? Geriatric Case Manager? Online Content Project Manager? How do these careers fit your interests and personality types? What do you know about these seven careers? What do you know about other careers? It is time to go exploring!

It is never too early to begin researching possible careers paths. Even elementary schools host career fairs so that young students can begin career explorations at an early age. It used to be that career choices were fairly limited: secretary, nurse, teacher, waitress, and stewardess for women and fireman, policeman, farmer, assembly line worker, doctor, lawyer, engineer, or business executive for men. How things have changed! The career choices for young people today are endless, and experts in the field predict that most people will have not one, but five to seven careers during their lifetimes. It appears, then, that researching career paths for most people will be a lifelong activity instead of a "What will I do after high school?" task.

There are many resources available to help you in your search for a career. Your school guidance counselor, school vocational clubs, schools internship program, local job service, library, and even the Internet can provide some helpful information about careers. It would be foolish to head down a career path without doing some research. What if you completed four years of college only to find the career path you had selected was oversaturated, and there were far more applicants than there were jobs? Or worse yet, what if you prepared for a career only to find that career being slowly phased out by technology?

ACTIVITY 11.3

Investigating "Hot Job Tracks"

Each year toward the end of October, *U.S. News and World Report* devotes a magazine issue to careers. They cover the latest and the greatest in terms of career paths, trends in careers and facts to consider for the future. The excerpts from the article "20 Hot Job Tracks" in Figure 11.1 will give you a good idea of the type of material you can expect to find when you do career research. Choose one of the careers and, on a separate piece of paper, answer the following questions based on the information contained in the article. Then do the same exercise with another career.

1. List the name of the career that you have selected.
2. Why is it predicted to be a good career choice?
3. On average, what is the entry level salary?
4. What is the mid level salary?
5. What is the top salary?
6. What kind of training do you need?
7. List three other careers in that field and what they pay.

FIGURE 11.1   Career Paths

ACCOUNTING

International Accountant

As far as the economies in Eastern Europe, Latin America and China have opened up, U.S. companies have rushed in to capitalize: exporting, buying firms, building plants, planning joint ventures. The North American Free Trade Agreement provided $20 billion in new trade with Mexico alone in 1994. To make the deals happen, comapnies need accountants who know international financial-reporting standards, merger-and-acquisition protocol and foreign business customs. The number of international accountants at the accounting firm Deloitte & Touche has increased more than fourfold in the past five years and is expected to double again in the next five.

Hot Track Salaries (average)
Entry Level: $28,000–$32,250
Manager: $43,000–$62,500
Partner: $55,000–$84,500

Training. An accounting or business degree and another language. Overseas experience helps.

Runner-up Hot Track. Forensic accountant. Companies and law firms hire them to check financial reports for signs of fraud or evidence of criminal conduct.

What Accounting Jobs Pay

ACCOUNTING CLERK	**$19,500–$24,500**
INTERNAL AUDITOR*	**$24,000–$30,000**
ASSISTANT CREDIT MANAGER	**$24,500–$42,000**
SENIOR BUDGET AND COST ANALYST	**$38,000–$46,500**
MANAGER, PUBLIC ACCOUNTING FIRM	**$42,000–$62,500**
CORPORATE TAX MANAGER†	**$67,000–$105,000**

Note: Average salaries for 1995.
*Entry level.
†At companies with more than $250 million in volume.

Sources: AICPA Job Bank, American Institute of Certified Public Accountants, Deloitte & Touche, International Trade Administration of the U.S. Department of Commerce, KPMG Peat Marwick, Robert Half International

HOSPITALITY

Food Service Manager

A study by the National Restaurant Association found that when a woman works outside the home, she and her family are more apt to dine out or order in than to have a home-cooked supper. Little wonder the food service industry now takes about 44 cents of every dollar spent on food. The Bureau of Labor Statistics predicts that by 2005, jobs in food service management will jump by 44 percent; besides restaurants, hotels, hospitals and contract food service companies will be recruiting. Food service managers purchase food and supplies, hire, plan menus and oversee operations.

Hot Track Salaries (median)
Entry Level: $30,000
Midlevel: $37,000
Top: $48,000

Training. More than 60 percent of restaurant owners and managers began as dishwahers, servers and cooks, so experience is important. A degree in hotel or restaurant management may mean faster advancement.

Runner-up Hot Track. Hotel general manager. The travel industry is booming—by year's end, there will be 40 percent more hotel jobs than there were in 1992. Managers oversee all hotel employees, operations, and sales and marketing.

What Hospitality Jobs Pay

FLIGHT ATTENDANT (ENTRY)	**$13,700**
TRAVEL AGENT (3–5 YEARS'S EXPERIENCE)	**$19,500**
GENERAL MANAGER (FAST-FOOD RESTAURANT)	**$27,000**
EXECUTIVE CHEF	**$37,000**
HOTEL GENERAL MANAGER	**$56,000**
HOTEL CHIEF FINANCIAL OFFICER	**$95,000**

Note: Median salaries for 1994–95.

Sources: American Hotel and Motel Association, Association of Flight Attendants, Council on Hotel, Restaurant and Institutional Education, National Restaurant Association, *Travel Weekly*

ENTERTAINMENT

Computer Animator

Anyone who has experienced the roaring dinosaurs of *Jurassic Park* or Jim Carrey's facial contortions in *The Mask* will understand why computer animation is a sizzling medium. Filmmakers, television show creators, video game producers and advertisers are rushing to add dazzling computer effects; Industrial Light & Magic in San Rafael, Calif., one of the top computer effects shops, has seen its computer graphics staff grow from two in 1985 to more than 295 today. Much of the demand will be at smaller firms focused on television and video game animation, which are springing up rapidly as equipment prices plummet. (One complete top-of-the-line package of animation hardware and software has gone from as much as $100,000 in price three years ago to less than $20,000.)

Hot Track Salaries (average)
Entry Level: $27,000–$40,000
Midlevel: $40,000–$80,000
Top: $80,000 and up

Training. A two- or four-year degree from a computer animation or graphics program. Two years of experience is desirable at top firms.

Runner-up Hot Track. Entertainment lawyer. Changing technology has made copyright and trade issues devilishly complex. Entertainment companies need lawyers with the know-how to protect their products.

What Entertainment Jobs Pay

DANCER/CHOREOGRAPHER	**$24,200**
ART DIRECTOR	**$33,800**
STAFF VIDEO EDITOR	**$45,430**
CHIEF VIDEO ENGINEER	**$47,300**
STAFF DIRECTOR (COMMERCIALS)	**$57,250**
VICE PRESIDENT (ENTERTAINMENT COMPANY)	**$86,100**

Note: Average salaries for 1994; dancer/choreographer salary is for 1992–93

Sources: Alias/Wavefront, Alliance of Motion Picture and Television Producers, California Arts Council, *Entertainment and Media Industry Commentaries, Entertainment Marketing Letter,* Hope Reports, Industrial Light & Magic, RitaSue Siegel Resources

---

FIGURE 11.1 Career Paths (continued)

TELECOMMUNICATIONS

Computer Security Expert

The rapid move by corporate America to computer networks, pluse the explosive surge in Internet traffic, has created real opportunities for high-tech snoops and cyberthieves. The annual loss to U.S. businesses is estimated at $6.5 billion to $9 billion and is expected to swell by 25 percent in 1996. Result: Companies want computer security pros to design and monitor protections for computer-stored trade secrets, employee data, etc. They might install software that mandates password changes every so often, say, or develop an encryption technique that converts all sensitive information into code

Hot Track Salaries (average)
Entry Level: $30,000–$40,000
Midlevel: $65,000–$78,000
Top: $90,000 and up

Training. A degree in computer science, engineering or telecommunications, plus an understanding of networking and communication systems, is required. To reach the top, security experience is the key.

Runner-up Hot Track. Wireless specialist. Desire for ever smaller, more sophisticated cellular phones and pagers drives demand for these designers and technicians.

What Telecommunications Jobs Pay

SALES REP (ENTRY LEVEL)	**$22,000**
JUNIOR TECHNICIAN	**$25,500**
MIDLEVEL TECHNICIAN	**$29,400**
ENTRY LEVEL ENGINEER	**$40,600**
SALES/ MARKETING EXECUTIVE	**$53,100**
TOP-LEVEL ENGINEER	**$59,100**
ONLINE CONTENT PROJECT MANAGER	**$80,000**

Note: Average salaries for 1995

Sources: Career Press, Communications & Toll Fraud Specialists, Inc., MultiMedia Telecommunications Association

HEALTH CARE

Information Specialist

Any hospital, clinic, health maintenance organization or medical practice that wants to work cheaper and faster —all health care providers, in other words—either has scrapped or soon will scrap paper medical records in favor of digital data. Advantages: Electronic data can be updated and retrieved quickly; specialists can tap into a patient's records and consult on a case long distance; and research can be conducted more easily. According to one estimate, the need for staffers conversant with medical information and computer databases is expected to outstrip supply by 54 percent by the year 2000.

Hot Track Salaries (average)
Entry Level: $27,500
Midlevel: $47,500
Top: $82,500

Training. A two- or four-year health information management degree is required, as is passage of a national certification exam.

Runner-up Hot Track. Physical therapist. According to the American Hospital Association, there's a 15 percent vacancy rate—at least—in the field.

What Health Care Jobs Pay

MEDICAL TECHNICIAN	**$19,000–$20,000**
MEDICAL TECHNOLOGIST	**$23,000–$24,000**
DIETITIAN	**$27,924**
STAFF NURSE, RN	**$35,464**
SPEECH THERAPIST	**$36,036**
PHARMACIST	**$49,608**
PHYSICIAN ASSISTANT	**$50,000–$55,000**
NURSE PRACTITIONER, RN	**$50,000–$55,000**

Note: Median salaries for 1994

Sources: American Health Information Management Association, American Hospital Association, Bureau of Labor Statistics

SPORTS MANAGEMENT

Corporate Sales Representative

It costs $3,500 to be top sponsor of the Hoopla Aurora Youth Basketball Tournament in Colorado; $200,000 buys the honors for college football's Peach Bowl. At all levels of play, sporting events, teams and the arenas they compete in are aggressively selling sponsorships as a way to make money: Companies in North America will spend a stunning $3.05 billion as sponsors this year, up 44 percent since 1992. The sales force cuts the deals, which generally give a company logo rights (San Francisco's Candlestick Park is now 3Com Park after the computer maker, for example), TV advertising during an event and free tickets.

Hot Track Salaries (average)
Entry Level: $18,000
Midlevel: $60,000
Top: $80,000 and up

Training. A business degree with an emphasis in marketing is helpful but not necessary. A background in sales or media plus knowledge of the sports industry should open doors

Runner-up Hot Track. Sports marketer. These pros battle for spectators by devising the right PR and advertising message. The number of sports-marketing firms has grown from 110 in 1980 to about 800 today.

What Sports Management Jobs Pay

PUBLIC RELATIONS STAFFER (ENTRY)	**$19,000**
ASSISTANT ATHLETIC DIRECTOR (COLLEGE)	**$45,710**
GENERAL MANAGER (MINOR LEAGUE)	**$60,280**
TICKET SALES DIRECTOR	**$75,000**
CHIEF FINANCIAL OFFICER (PRO TEAM)	**$90,000**
EXECUTIVE VICE PRESIDENT (ARENA)	**$191,670**

Note: Average salaries for 1993–94 (latest available)

Sources: IEG Sponsorship Report, Chicago, Regional Sports Report, Sports Careers Inc., Sports Market Place, Team Marketing Report, Inc., TeamWork Consulting Inc.

ACTIVITY 11.4   Exploring Other Types of Career Information

It is often not enough to know which careers have a promising future and what training is needed for those careers. Knowing how many people are employed in that field, the annual demand for new employees, and the average hourly wage for that career in different fields can be helpful information. The following chart, giving statistics for a single state during a single year, is a sample of what you might find. On a separate sheet of paper, answer the questions based on the information given in the chart.

ADMINISTRATIVE SUPPORT OCCUPATIONS, INCLUDING CLERICAL WORK

Occupation	Average Hourly Wage in Each Category			Yearly Employment	Annual Demand
	All Industries	Hospitals	Manufacturing		
Bank Tellers	$6.51			6,138	325
Bookkeepers and Accounting Clerks	$8.74	$9.70	$9.30	36,627	744
Clerical Supervisors and Managers	$9.84	$13.70	$13.20	21,119	828
Computer and Peripheral Equipment Operators	$8.74	$10.00	$10.20	4,148	81
Data Entry Keyers	$7.21	$8.30	$7.80	`5,306	139
File Clerks	$6.87	$7.20	$6.90	4,378	241
General Office Clerks	$6.70	$9.00	$8.20	38,962	1,328
Insurance Claims and Policy Processing	$9.95			3,936	39
Postal Clerks and Mail Carriers	$12.30		$7.10	6,588	152
Receptionists and Information Clerks	$6.55	$7.90	$7.40	15,069	713
Reservation and Trans. Ticket Agents	$8.24			4,210	148
Secretaries	$10.92	$10.40	$10.30	40,408	1,614
Statistical Clerks	$8.18	$7.80	$10.40	798	19
Stenographers	$9.73	$10.50		1,368	36
Stock Clerks	$7.62	$8.40	$9.40	19,006	807
Telephone Operators	$7.02	$7.80	$7.80	3,423	99
Traffic, Shipping, and Receiving Clerks	$7.28	$8.20	$9.10	10,070	226
Typists and Word Processors	$7.59	$9.80	$8.60	9,869	201

1. Which career has the highest average hourly wage for all industries?
2. What is the average hourly wage for that career?
3. Which career has the lowest average hourly wage for hospitals?
4. What is the average hourly wage for that career?
5. Which career has the highest average hourly wage for manufacturing?
6. What is the average hourly wage for that career?
7. Which career has the highest yearly employment?
8. Which career has the lowest yearly employment?
9. Which career has the highest annual demand?
10. Which career has the lowest annual demand?
11. If you were choosing one career from this chart, which would you choose and why would you choose it?

Researching Other Sources

Now it is time to go beyond the textbook for your career search. You have a good idea of your interests, your personality type, and possible career choices. Go to one of the resources cited previously: your school guidance counselor; local job service; library; Internet; or *U.S. News and World Report* (the issue published the last week in October) and on a separate sheet of paper answer the following questions about your career choice.

1. List the name of the career that you have selected.
2. Why did you select it?
3. Explain why it is predicted to be a good career choice.
4. On the average what is the entry level salary?
5. What is the mid-level salary?
6. What is the top salary?
7. What kind of training do you need?
8. List one "pro" for having this career.
9. List one "con" for having this career.
10. List other valuable information you discovered when you researched that career.

You should now have a good idea of the type of training needed for your possible career path(s). Will an apprenticeship or internship give you that extra advantage? Is a vocational/technical education a requirement? How about the armed services? Or maybe college is a must? Will you need a masters degree or a doctorate? What kind of prerequisites are there, and how are you going to prepare yourself for those?

Designing a Resume

It doesn't matter whether you are planning to enter an apprenticeship, the working world, a vocational/technical school, the armed services, or college after high school, people with whom you interview or to whom you talk are going to want to know specifics: *what you have done in the past, what are you doing now,* and *where you are headed?* Even if you are just interested in getting a part-time job while you are still in school, you will be asked to fill out applications and forms. Starting a resume of this type of information early on is a must!

Fill in the following form; it will be the first step in designing a resume. After you have completed it, you may type it and input the information on computer using different fonts, type sizes, styles, and/or lines to make it more eye-catching. Or, you may elect to take it to a print shop or secretarial service and ask them to prepare it for you. Remember that your resume is an important part of selling yourself. It must be accurate, complete, and neatly done.

Resume Form

Name _____

Address _____

City _____ State _____ Zip Code _____

Telephone (   )_____ Birth Date _____

Social Security # _____

G.P.A. (optional) _____ ACT Composite Score (optional) _____ Class Standing (optional) _____

Educational
Goal   To _____

Career Goal   To _____

Education   Junior High_____ Location _____ Years Attended _____

                 Senior High _____ Location _____ Years Attended _____

Academic &   Senior _____
Other Awards
                 _____

                 Junior _____

                 _____

                 Sophomore _____

                 _____

                 Freshman _____

                 _____

Activities &   Senior _____
Offices Held
                 _____

                 Junior _____

                 _____

                 Sophomore _____

                 _____

                 Freshman _____

                 _____

Sports, Letters, & Awards

Senior _____

_____

Junior _____

_____

Sophomore _____

_____

Freshman _____

_____

Job Experience (Hours/week & Position Held)

Senior _____

_____

Junior _____

_____

Sophomore _____

_____

Freshman _____

_____

Volunteer Work

Senior _____

_____

Junior _____

_____

Sophomore _____

_____

Freshman _____

_____

Interests/Leisure Activities/Hobbies

_____

_____

References

Name _____ Address _____

Phone # _____

Name _____ Address _____

Phone # _____

Name _____ Address _____

Phone # _____

It is safe to say almost everyone will go job hunting at one time or another. Many will find themselves job hunting several times during their lives. Designing a resume is just the first step. Keeping the resume up to date is next. Throughout school and beyond, you will need to keep a copy of your resume on file and periodically revise the information. While you are in school, you should update it regularly.

ACTIVITY 11.7

What's Next? Is a Full- or Part-time Job in Your Future?

You already know the importance of designing a good resume. Another essential step in getting a job is filling out the application. Since the application and your resume may be the only items an interviewer or a prospective employer initially may see, you will need to sell yourself well on paper. Your application should be neatly written or typed with no misspellings. If you show up at the place of employment and quickly fill out the application, you risk having inaccurate or incomplete information, spelling errors, erasures, and/or a sloppy-looking document. It would be a shame to lose the opportunity for employment on that basis alone! Instead, try to pick up an application ahead of time, take it home, and use your resume to fill out the information neatly and carefully. This will improve your chances of selling yourself on paper and becoming employed!

Go to a local place of employment. Select a business for which you might actually be interested in working. Ask them for an application, take it home, and fill it out. This will be excellent practice in preparing for that all important job.

ACTIVITY 11.8

Are You Applying for a Vocational/Technical School?

As with a job, a carefully prepared resume and a neatly typed application are essential elements in applying for a post-secondary vocational/technical school. Once you have written for or picked up an application, it is a good idea to photocopy it and fill out a practice form. Get all the information down on your practice copy before you begin the final draft. Go to your school guidance office and look at the selection of vocational/technical school catalogs they have. Choose one school, explore the information on it, and then, on a separate sheet of paper, write down the answers to the following.

1. What program does the school have that is of interest to you?
2. What are the costs to attend the school?
3. What are the admission requirements?
4. What are the graduation requirements?
5. What are the job placement statistics once you have graduated?
6. Select a school that interests you and write to them requesting a catalog and an application form.
7. Photocopy the form and fill it out. Submit it to your instructor.

Is a College Degree in Your Future?

Let's assume a college degree is required for your career path. The first step in getting your degree is getting admitted to a college. Admissions requirements vary from college to college; some schools have very difficult admissions standards while others are less stringent. Most of them use a chart similar to the one in Figure 11.2 which matches your grade point average (GPA), with your scores from the American College Testing Assessment (ACT), or Scholastic Assessment Test (SAT). Let's see where *you* would be placed!

Admission Qualifications:

- Students with an admission index of 100+ will be admitted in good standing.
- Students with an admission index of 90–99 are likely to be admitted in good standing.
- Students with an index of 85–89 will be *considered* for admission on an *individual basis as space is available.*
- With an index below 85, students will not be admitted. An appeal for provisional admission may be made.

Look at the admission index chart and find your GPA. (If you don't know your GPA, visit your school guidance office and request a copy of your school transcript and your GPA.) See where you would be placed on the chart and what

FIGURE 11.2   Admission Index Chart

ADMISSION INDEX

TEST SCORES

ACT	Enhanced Recentered SAT	GPA 4.0	3.9	3.8	3.7	3.6	3.5	3.4	3.3	3.2	3.1	3.0	2.9	2.8	2.7	2.6	2.5	2.4	2.3	2.2	2.1	2.0	1.9	1.8	1.7	1.6	1.5	1.4	1.3	1.2	1.1
36	1600	142	140	139	137	135	133	132	130	128	126	124	123	121	119	117	116	114	112	110	108	107	105	103	101	100	98	95	94	93	91
35	1580	140	138	137	135	133	131	130	128	126	124	122	121	119	117	115	114	112	110	108	106	105	103	101	99	98	96	94	92	91	89
34	1530	138	136	135	133	131	129	128	126	124	122	120	119	117	115	113	112	110	108	106	104	103	101	99	97	96	94	92	90	89	87
33	1460	136	134	133	131	129	127	126	124	122	120	118	117	115	113	111	110	108	106	104	102	101	99	97	95	94	92	90	88	87	85
32	1410	134	132	131	129	127	125	124	122	120	118	116	115	113	111	109	108	106	104	102	100	99	97	95	93	92	90	88	86	85	83
31	1360	133	131	130	128	126	124	123	121	119	117	115	114	112	110	108	107	105	103	101	99	98	96	94	92	91	89	87	85	84	82
30	1320	131	129	128	126	124	122	121	119	117	115	113	112	110	108	106	105	103	101	99	97	95	94	92	90	89	87	85	83	82	80
29	1280	129	127	126	124	122	120	119	117	115	113	111	110	108	106	104	103	101	99	97	95	94	92	90	88	87	85	83	81	80	78
28	1240	127	125	124	122	120	118	117	115	113	111	109	108	106	104	102	101	99	97	95	93	92	90	88	86	85	83	81	79	78	76
27	1210	126	124	123	121	119	117	116	114	112	110	108	107	105	103	101	100	98	95	94	92	91	89	87	85	84	82	80	78	77	75
26	1170	124	122	121	119	117	115	114	112	110	108	106	105	103	101	99	96	95	94	92	90	89	87	85	83	82	80	78	76	75	73
25	1140	122	120	119	117	115	113	112	110	108	105	104	103	101	99	97	96	94	92	90	88	87	85	83	81	80	78	76	74	73	71
24	1100	120	118	117	115	113	111	110	108	106	104	102	101	99	97	96	94	92	90	88	86	85	83	81	79	78	76	74	72	71	69
23	1060	118	116	115	113	111	109	108	106	104	102	100	99	97	95	93	92	90	88	86	84	83	81	79	77	76	74	72	70	69	67
22	1030	117	115	114	112	110	108	107	105	103	101	99	98	96	94	92	91	88	87	85	83	82	80	78	76	75	73	71	69	68	65
21	990	115	113	112	110	108	106	105	103	101	99	97	96	94	92	90	89	87	86	83	81	80	78	76	74	73	71	69	67	66	64
20	950	113	111	110	108	106	104	103	101	99	97	95	94	92	90	88	87	85	83	81	79	78	76	74	72	71	69	67	65	64	62
19	910	111	109	108	106	104	102	101	99	97	95	93	92	90	88	86	85	83	81	79	77	76	74	72	70	69	67	65	63	62	60
18	860	109	107	106	104	102	100	99	97	95	93	91	90	88	86	84	83	81	79	77	75	74	72	70	68	67	65	63	61	60	58
17	820	108	106	105	103	101	99	98	96	94	92	90	89	87	85	83	82	80	78	76	74	73	71	69	67	65	64	62	60	59	57
16	770	106	104	103	101	99	97	96	94	92	90	88	87	85	83	81	80	78	76	74	72	71	69	67	65	64	62	60	58	57	55
15	720	104	102	101	99	97	95	94	92	90	88	86	85	83	81	79	78	76	74	72	70	69	67	65	63	62	60	58	56	55	53
14	670	102	100	99	97	95	93	92	90	88	86	84	83	81	79	77	76	74	72	70	68	67	65	63	61	60	58	56	54	53	51
13	600	100	98	97	95	93	91	90	88	86	84	82	81	79	77	75	74	72	70	68	66	65	63	61	59	58	56	54	52	51	49
12	540	99	97	95	94	92	90	89	87	85	83	81	80	78	76	74	73	71	69	67	65	64	62	60	58	57	55	53	51	50	48
11	480	97	95	94	92	90	88	87	85	83	81	79	78	76	74	72	71	69	67	65	63	62	60	58	56	55	53	51	49	48	46
10	430	95	93	92	90	88	86	85	83	81	79	77	76	74	72	70	69	67	65	63	61	60	58	56	54	53	51	49	47	46	44
9	400	93	91	90	88	86	84	83	81	79	77	75	74	72	70	68	67	65	63	61	59	58	56	54	52	51	49	47	45	44	42
8	380	92	90	89	87	85	83	82	80	78	76	74	73	71	69	67	65	64	62	60	58	57	55	53	51	50	48	46	44	43	41
7	350	90	88	87	85	83	81	80	78	76	74	72	71	69	67	65	64	62	60	58	56	55	53	51	49	48	46	44	42	41	39
6	320	88	86	85	83	81	79	78	76	74	72	70	69	67	65	63	62	60	58	56	54	53	51	49	47	46	44	42	40	39	37
5	290	86	84	83	81	79	77	76	74	72	70	68	67	65	63	61	60	58	56	54	52	51	49	47	45	44	42	40	38	37	35

ACT or SAT scores you would need to gain admission to this university based on its admission qualifications listed on page 185. Answer the following questions on a separate sheet of paper.

1. My GPA is _____.
2. I would need an ACT score of _____ or above to be assured admittance in good standing. (An admission index of 100 or better is required for this category.)
3. I would need an SAT score of _____ or above to be assured admittance in good standing. (An admission index of 100 or better is required for this category.)
4. I would need an ACT score of _____ or above for likely admittance in good standing. (An admission index of 90–99 is required for this category.)
5. I would need an SAT score of _____ or above for likely admittance in good standing. (An admission index of 90–99 is required for this category.)
6. I would need an ACT score of _____ or above to be considered for admission on an individual basis as space is available. (An admission index of 85–89 is required for this category.)
7. I would need an SAT score of _____ or above to be considered for admission on an individual basis as space is available. (An admission index of 85–89 is required for this category.)
8. If I had an ACT score of _____ or below, I would not be admitted. (Admission index below 85.)
9. If I had an SAT score of _____ or below, I would not be admitted. (Admission index below 85.)

It is important to note that colleges not only look at your GPA and ACT or SAT scores, they also look at the classes you took during high school in considering you for admission. It would be unfortunate if you took the easy route through high school and then found yourself on the rejection list(s) of the college(s) of your choice. The best advice is to be informed when it comes to college entrance requirements. Again, it is never to early too begin your research.

ACTIVITY 11.10

Taking the ACT or SAT

Again, times are not what they used to be. It used to be that only students certain of going to college took the college entrance exams. But guidance counselors today find that many students are uncertain of their career plans, or they find that students' career plans change and then the students find themselves having to take the ACT or SAT several years after graduation when much of the information has been forgotten. School counselors now encourage most students to take the college entrance exams whether they have immediate plans to go to college or not.

When to Take the ACT or SAT

For those certain of going to college, planning ahead is a must. Some scholarships or more selective colleges require ACT or SAT scores be submitted in December or January. Many students wait until October or November of their senior year to take their first exam and then face time constraints if they need to take additional exams to raise their scores. Since college entrance exams measure what you should have learned by the end of your junior year, that is the best time to begin taking the tests.

Most guidance counselors recommend taking the Preliminary Scholastic Aptitude Test (PSAT) in the first semester of the junior year, the SAT or ACT during the second semester of the junior year to gain practice in taking the test, and the SAT or ACT again at the end of the junior year when all the junior level courses have just been completed and the material is fresh in your mind. That leaves early in the senior year for retakes to improve scores if necessary. And remember, you must send in your registration material at least a month in advance to avoid late fees or, worse yet, being too late to take the exam at all.

1. Decide which of the following tests you are going to need to take for the school(s) of your choice. Circle the acronym for those tests.

2. Next, visit your high school guidance counselor and enter the specific sign-up dates for each of the tests you need to take, the dates each will be given, and the basic cost of each test.

Test	General Time	Registration Date	Test Date	Cost
PSAT	1st semester - Junior year			
1st SAT or ACT	2nd semester - Junior year			
2nd SAT or ACT	End of Junior year			
Follow-up Tests	1st semester - Senior year			

3. Begin preparing for the exam by reviewing the tips in Unit 4 of this book, Taking Tests. Focus your attention and take notes on Activity 4.4, Relieving Test Anxiety. Since ACT and SAT tests are anxiety producers for most students, you'll need some strategies to deal with the test stress. Then go on to Activity 4.5, Strategies for Taking Tests. The tips in this activity will be helpful reminders of the proper way to take a test. Activity 4.6, covers Tricks for Taking Tests, strategies that are helpful for specific types of test questions. Finish up with Activity 4.9, Preparing for the ACT/SAT test.

ACTIVITY 11.11

Organizing Your Approach

Whether you have decided to look for a job, go to vocational/technical school, or pursue a college education, an organized approach is needed. And second semester of your senior year is *not* the time to begin! Job internships or apprenticeships, school visitations, and applications for schools need to be planned well in advance. The following steps will help you organize your approach.

1. Create a Four-Year Plan of the classes you need to take.

   By the end of eighth grade, you should have visited your school guidance counselor and mapped out a four-year schedule of the classes you need to take to reach your goals. If you have not done this yet, do it now!

2. Arrange job internships or apprenticeships in your sophomore or junior years if possible.

   More and more schools are providing students opportunities to explore careers during their high school years through internships or apprenticeships. Students are able to get a better feel for their level of interest and aptitude by actually being at the job site. Without this experience, students might spend thousands of dollars and several years preparing for a career for which they are not well suited.

3. Organize a post-secondary notebook.

   As you begin your search for vocational/technical schools or colleges, set up a notebook so you can keep all the essential information together. Include a separate divider for each school, ACT/SAT scores, transcripts, and recommendations. Also, folders with pockets for loose materials or forms that will need to be completed should be included. Each time any paperwork has been filled out or sent to you, photocopy it and place it in your notebook. Doing so will ensure that you do not have to rely on memory.

4. Keep a spreadsheet of vital information.

   This spreadsheet should show you the following at a glance.

   - the information you need to know about the schools you are considering
   - the paperwork you have completed and the paperwork you still need to do
   - the responses you have received

Visit your school guidance office and browse through their school catalogs. Select several schools you are interested in visiting or attending. Copy the following chart and write in information you gained about those schools. Place the sheet at the front of your new notebook, and continue to chart your progress as you work through the application process.

	School 1	School 2	School 3
Name			
Location			
Size			
Tuition Cost $			
Room & Board $			
Books & Fees Cost $			
Personal Expenses $			
Application Fees $			
Housing Application Fee $			
Application Due Date			
Housing Due Date			
Scholarship Due Date			
Item and Date Submitted:			
Application			
Application Fee			
Resume			
Transcript			
ACT/SAT Scores 1			
ACT/SAT Scores 2			
ACT/SAT Scores 3			
Letter of Intent			
Scholarship Application			
Letters of Recommendation			
Picture			
Housing Application			
Housing Fee			
Other			
1			
2			
3			
4			
5			
6			

Review

Unit 11

1. In this unit I learned that my two strongest personality types were:

_____ A. Doer _____ C. Artist _____ E. Enterpriser
_____ B. Investigator _____ D. Helper _____ F. Detailer

2. The career choices that interested me the most in these two categories were:

First Personality Type: _____
Career Choices: _____
_____
_____

Second Personality Type: _____
Career Choices: _____
_____
_____

3. In my own career search I found the following careers interested me:

_____ Why:
_____ Why:
_____ Why:

4. To prepare for these careers I need:

_____ a high school diploma

_____ a degree from a vocational/technical school

_____ an associate degree (2 year) from a junior college/community college

_____ a bachelor's degree (4 year) from a college or university

_____ a master's degree from a college or university

_____ a doctorate degree from a college or university

5. In order to plan well, I must do (check if you have done) the following:

Freshman Year

_____ Create a four-year plan of the classes I need to take in high school to prepare for my career and/or college.

_____ Begin my resume.

Sophomore Year

_____ Check into apprenticeships/internships in the career fields of my choice.

_____ Monitor my class choices and my GPA.

_____ Update my resume.

Junior Year

_____ Take the PSAT first semester.

_____ Begin my apprenticeships/internships.

_____ Take the ACT/SAT at the beginning and end of second semester junior year.

_____ Continue to monitor my GPA.

_____ Continue to update my resume.

Summer following Junior Year

_____ Ask four teachers to write recommendations for me.

_____ Write to vocational/technical schools, colleges, or universities for applications.

_____ Fill out and return applications.

_____ Visit schools I am interested in.

_____ Set up notebook and spreadsheet for post-secondary schools.

_____ Update my resume.

Senior Year—First Semester

_____ Retake the ACT/SAT if necessary.

_____ Update resume and notebook.

_____ Begin applying for scholarships.

_____ Finish visitations.

_____ Finish applications.

_____ Continue internships/apprenticeships.

Senior Year—Second Semester

_____ Continue to update resume and notebook.

_____ Continue to apply for scholarships.

_____ Choose school and send in housing application.

You have now Gotten It Together, and you should have a very complete plan for your future! Good Luck!

Summing It Up

This is the final unit in your student worktext. Take a moment to consider what you have learned. Think about changes you have made in your study setting, your study techniques, your test-taking strategies, and your note-taking methods. Have your reading speed and comprehension improved? What do you know about the dictionary, the newspaper, and the library that you did not know before?

To assess your progress, you'll need to answer all these questions; this unit will help you accomplish that. In addition, you'll understand that the skills you learned in this worktext will benefit you not only in other classes, but throughout your life. Even after you leave school, you will be reading and learning. You must continue to do both in order to adapt to and live in our ever-changing world.

Preparing for the Worktext Review

ACTIVITY 12.1

To assess your progress, we will begin by evaluating how much *information* and *knowledge* you have gained in the areas mentioned in the unit introduction. You will need to study and prepare for a worktext review, which will be similar to the unit reviews that which you are already familiar.

1. Begin by creating a good study setting for yourself. (See Unit 2 to review what a good study setting consists of.)

2. Create a budget for your time; allow enough time in the day over several days for proper review of the material. (See Unit 2 for tips on budgeting your time.)

3. Review your text using the techniques described in Unit 2, Previewing Your Text, to refresh your memory on the information this worktext covers.

4. Review your notes. Begin by using a highlighter to mark important material you anticipate will be covered on the review. Write margin notes identifying main points. Then, look at your margin notes and recite the material to be learned. (See Unit 3, Note Taking.)

5. Remember, you should study for brief periods each day over several days; that way your memory will absorb the material and give you reliable recall. (See Unit 4, Taking Tests.)

6. Prepare for your review using the techniques listed in Activity 4.3 in Unit 4.

7. Assess your anxiety and practice the techniques that work for you. You will find suggestions in Unit 4, Activity 4.4, to help you control your anxiety.

8. Finally, when you do the worktext review, use the technique outlined in Unit 4, Activities 4.5 through 4.7, to achieve the best possible results.

Material to Cover

Unit 2: Developing Study Skills.
- Previewing your textbook: What is involved? Why do it? What are the seven steps in the process?
- Study setting: List seven tips.
- Budgeting time: What should a time budget include, and how do you make one up?
- Study sequence: What choices do you have?
- SQ3R: Describe the process by explaining what each letter and number stands for.
- Sizing up your instructor: Explain the steps and the benefits of sizing up your instructor.

Unit 3: Note Taking
- Methods of note taking: List five methods and draw illustration or write an explanation for each.
- Shortcuts: List five shortcuts and give two examples of each.

Unit 4: Taking Tests
- Memory: Explain the four layers of memory, what happens in each layer, and how you prepare for each.
- Preparing for a test: List the steps.
- Relieving anxiety: List tips that work for you.
- Test-taking strategies: List the steps.

- Test-taking tricks: List tips for answering true-false, multiple-choice, matching, and completion questions.
- Test terminology: Explain what is required for each of the twelve test terms listed in the unit.

Unit 5: Improving Your Understanding
- Define and be able to apply the following:

main idea	comprehension	cause and effect
gist	sequence	inference
key words	cloze	predicting

Unit 6: Increasing Speed
- What three factors determine reading speed?
- List five ways to build a good vocabulary.
- Describe how your eyes move when you read; explain what happens when your eyes fixate.
- Discuss four common reading problems and one way to correct each.

Unit 7: Skimming and Scanning
- Define and explain when to use:

skimming	overview	slow and careful rate
scanning	study rate	rapid rate
preview	average rate	very rapid rate
review		

- What three factors determine reading rate?
- What two factors determine the ability to read fast?

Unit 8: Using The Dictionary
- Define and be able to identify:

main entry	guide words
etymology	homograph
syllabication	diacritical marks
variants	parts of speech
inflected forms	

Unit 9: Exploring the Library/Media Center
Unit 9 perused the material and services provided by the library/media center. Be able to define these reference tools found in the library/media center that students find useful when they are doing research.

automated periodical indexes	biographical references
Reader's Guide	maps and atlases
almanacs	vertical files
encyclopedias	

Unit 10: Reading for Enjoyment
- Define and be able to identify:

byline	net change	day's low
dateline	headline	two national news agencies
caption	banner headline	editorial
jump	year's high	news story
lead	year's low	two stock exchanges
last price	day's high	five Ws

- Be able to recognize the type of story found in the business section, editorial section, sports section, and feature section.
- Be able to read stock market quotation sheets.
- Know the four criteria of a good classified ad.

Unit 11: Getting It Together
- Explain which career(s) are the most promising for you and why you feel these careers hold the most potential.
- Explain the education/training you will need for the career(s) listed above.
- Beginning with your freshman year and continuing through your senior year, list the steps you should take (or have taken) to stay on track and adequately prepare for life after high school.

ACTIVITY 12.2

Worktext Review

Number a separate sheet of paper from 1 to 133. This activity will assess your comprehension of the material and activities in this worktext.

I.   Study Skills: Previewing Your Text

1.–7.   Skim the following seven steps in previewing a text and decide in what order they should be done. Place the letter of the step that should be done first beside number 1 on your paper, the letter of the step that should be done second beside number 2, and so on.

A. Page through the book and look at the charts, pictures, graphs, and so on.
B. Look at the appendixes (glossary, index, and so on).
C. Skim the table of contents.
D. Evaluate the difficulty of the material.
E. Look at the title, author, and date of publication.
F. Know your purpose for reading the text.
G. Read the preface or introduction.

8. Why is it important to preview your text? Place the letter of the correct answer beside number 8 on your paper.

   A. To become acquainted with the material to be covered in class before the class actually starts.
   B. To determine how difficult the material will be for you.
   C. To explore the type of information, study aids, and so on available in the text before actually using it.
   D. All of the above.

Study Skills: Note Taking

Write *true* if the statement is true and *false* if the statement is false beside the appropriate number on your paper.

9. The *outline* system of note taking consists of Roman numerals followed by capital letters, numbers, small letters, and so on.

10. The *listing* system of note taking resembles a diagram or a pattern, the shape of which is determined by the information.

11. Signal words point you to important information in a text. *Full signals* are words such as *next*, *then*, *last*, and *moreover*.

12. *Half signals* are words such as *first*, *second*, and *third*.

13. One shortcut in note taking is the *no vowel* technique. It involves leaving the last letter, if it is a vowel, off the word.

14. A useful shortcut in note taking is using *technical symbols*. An example of this would be using = in place of the word *equals*.

15. A note-taking shortcut is to use the beginning of a word in place of the entire word. An example *Intro* for the word *Introduction*.

Study Skills: Study Setting

There are several ways to improve concentration while studying, and these involve the study setting. For example, if you study in the same place each day, concentration improves.

16.–20. List five other tips for improving study setting.

Study Skills: Additional Material

21. There are several choices for determining the order in which you should study subjects. Which is *not* a correct study sequence?

   A. As the books come out of your backpack
   B. Hardest to easiest
   C. Most important to least important
   D. Alternating activities

22.–26. Explain what each of the letters stands for in *SQ3R*.

Study Skills: Taking Tests

27.–30. Explain the four layers of memory, what happens in each, and how you prepare for each.

31.–35. List five methods for relieving test anxiety that work for you.

Match the following descriptions with the test terminologies they describe. Place the letter of the correct answer beside the proper number on your answer sheet.

36.	Give your judgment or opinion based on reasons; good and bad points should be included.	A.	contrast
37.	Give details, progress, or history of the topic from beginning to end.	B.	trace
		C.	diagram
38.	Include a chart, graph, or drawing with labels and a brief explanation if needed.	D.	criticize
39.	Give both similarities and differences.	E.	compare
40.	Give differences only.		

Choose the letter of the answer that is *not* a trick for the type of test given, and write the letter beside the appropriate number on your paper.

41. On a *true-false* test:
   A. Beware of qualifying words such as *all*, *none*, and *never*, which usually make the statement false.
   B. Beware of qualifying words such as *usually*, *sometimes*, and *generally*, which usually make the statement true.
   C. Watch for four *true* or *false* responses in a row; the next response will always be the opposite of the previous four.
   D. Be aware of false logic that makes the statement false.

42. On a *multiple-choice* test:
   A. Watch for patterns in the answers, such as A, A, B, A, A, B.
   B. Look for the longest answer; it is frequently the correct one.
   C. Pay attention to "all of the above"; it is frequently the correct response.
   D. Eliminate first the answer that is obviously incorrect.

43. On a *matching* test:
   A. Read the list on the right first.
   B. Read the list on the left first.
   C. Read the entire list of choices, because an answer may appear to be correct, but a more correct answer might appear farther down the list.
   D. Answer the questions you are sure of first, and use the process of elimination to answer those you are unsure of.

44. On a *completion* test:
    A. Read the question several times; the key word to complete the statement may pop into your head.
    B. Look for the context clues within the question that may provide you with the correct answer.
    C. Look for *a* or *an*; *a* will be followed by an answer beginning with a consonant and *an* will be followed by an answer beginning with a vowel.
    D. Never go by first instinct on completion; give the question a lot of thought, and leave it blank if you don't know the answer.

45. On an *essay* test:
    A. Plan your time carefully.
    B. Never write the outline for your essay answer on the paper; the instructor might think you are cheating.
    C. Understand the test terminology; if you are asked to *compare*, make sure you list similarities and differences.
    D. Write neatly, leave suitable margins, and allow space between answers.

46. In preparing for a test:
    A. Anticipate what material might be on the test.
    B. Reread the entire text material thoroughly.
    C. Find out what type of questions might be on the test so you can use the appropriate study techniques.
    D. Discover how much material is based on your notes.

47. In preparing for a test:
    A. Skim the material on the first night.
    B. Skim the material, look at margin notes, and recite aloud on the second night.
    C. Look at your margin notes and recite important points on the third night.
    D. Take a break on the fourth night.

48. The day of the test:
    A. Eat a small breakfast so you don't upset your stomach; coffee and donuts are good.
    B. Get you mind and body stimulated with exercise.
    C. Wear something comfortable that makes you feel confident.
    D. Build your self-confidence.

49. When taking any test:
    A. Arrive early in order to compose yourself.
    B. Bring all materials with you.
    C. Sit by a friend; it will make you feel better.
    D. Listen carefully to the instructor's directions.

50. When taking any test:
    A. Begin with the first question and work through the test in the order the questions appear.
    B. Answer the easy questions first to build your confidence.
    C. Answer objective questions before essay questions; they may provide you with responses for the essay.
    D. Guess at the answers you don't know, unless there is a penalty for guessing.

II. Comprehension

Match the following descriptions with the terms that identify them. Place the letter of the correct answer beside the corresponding number on your answer sheet.

51. The point the author is trying to make

52. An exercise in which you bring closure to a statement by supplying the missing word

53. Understanding the point(s) the author is trying to make

54. Putting things in order

55. Meaning is not clearly stated; you must look at clues to gain it by _____.

56. What happens next is not clearly stated; you must _____ it.

A. inference
B. predicting
C. cloze
D. main idea
E. sequence
F. comprehension

III. Increasing Speed

Determine which answer fits the blank in the statement and write that answer beside the corresponding number on your answer sheet.

Three things determine your reading speed. They are __57__ , __58__ , and __59__ .

Two factors influence your ability to read material rapidly. They are __60__ and __61__ .

The best readers know reading rates are __62__ ; they know you do not read everything at the same __63__ .

When you read, your eyes make an __64__ rather than moving in a straight line.

When you read, your eyes pause or stop to take in words; this pause or stop is called a __65__ .

__66__ is saying words aloud as you read them; it slows down reading speed.

67.–71. Improving your vocabulary will improve your reading speed. List five ways to improve your vocabulary.

IV.   Skimming and Scanning
Place the letter of the correct definition for the term given beside the corresponding number on your answer sheet.

72.   skimming   A.   used when reading for pleasure
73.   scanning   B.   follows a previous reading; used to go back
74.   preview   over material
75.   review   C.   quickly passing over the entire selection to
76.   overview   get the gist of it
77.   average rate   D.   an end in itself; gives an overall impression of
78.   study rate   the material
                         E.   looking over material rapidly to find a specific piece of information; then reading stops
                         F.   followed by a second, more thorough reading
                         G.   the slowest rate; used for difficult material and provides a high degree of understanding

V.   Using the Dictionary
Place the letter of the correct definition for the term given beside the corresponding number on your answer sheet.

79.   main entry   A.   pronunciation marks
80.   etymology   B.   spellings that are irregular
81.   syllabication   C.   the history or origin of a word
82.   variants   D.   the word you are looking up
83.   inflected forms   E.   found in italics following the word you are
84.   homograph   looking up
85.   diacritical marks F.   words that are spelled the same, but have
86.   guide words   different meanings or origins
87.   parts of speech   G.   division of a word into syllables
                         H.   the first and last words on a page; these words are found at the top of a dictionary page
                         I.   two or more spellings of the same word
                         J.   none of the above

FIGURE 12.1
Dictionary Entries
Exercise

camisole | candescent

The operator of a motion-picture or television camera.

cam·i·sole (kăm'ĭ-sōl') *n.* A woman's short, sleeveless undergarment. [< LLat. *camisia,* shirt.]

cam·o·mile (kăm'ə-mīl') *n.* Var. of *chamomile.*

cam·ou·flage (kăm'ə-fläzh', -fläj') *n.* A means of concealment that creates the effect of being part of the natural surroundings. —*v.* **-flaged, -flag·ing.** To conceal by such means. [< Ital. *camuffare,* to disguise.] —**cam'ou·flag'er** *n.*

camp¹ (kămp) *n.* 1. a. A place where a group of people is temporarily lodged in makeshift shelters. b. The shelters in such a place or the persons using them. 2. A place consisting of more or less permanent vacation cabins. 3. A group favorable to a common cause, doctrine, or political system. —*v.* To shelter or lodge in a camp; encamp. [< Lat. *campus,* field.]

camp² (kămp) *n.* Artificiality of manner or style, appreciated for its humor, triteness, or vulgarity. —*adj.* Having the qualities of such a manner or style: *a camp movie.* [Orig. unknown.] —**camp'i·ly** *adv.* —**camp'i·ness** *n.* —**camp'y** *adj.*

cam·paign (kăm-pān') *n.* 1. A series of military operations undertaken to achieve a specific objective within a given area. 2. An organized activity or operation to attain a political, social, or commercial goal. —*v.* To engage in a campaign. [< OItal. *campagna,* battlefield.] —**cam·paign'er** *n.*

cam·pa·ni·le (kăm'pə-nē'lē) *n.* A bell tower, esp. one near but not attached to a church. [Ital.]

camp·er (kăm'pər) *n.* 1. A person who camps outdoors or who attends a camp. 2. a. A vehicle resembling an automobile-and-trailer combination, designed to serve as a dwelling and used for camping or long motor trips.

be excused? Yes, you *can.* [< OE *cunnan,* to know how.]

Usage: In speech *can* is used more frequently than *may* to express permission, even though traditionalists insist that *can* should be used only to express the capacity to do something. Technically, correct usage therefore requires: *May I have the car tonight?* Because the contraction *mayn't* is felt to be stilted, however, the negative form of this question is usually expressed as *Can't I have the car tonight?*

can² (kăn) *n.* 1. A metal container. 2. a. An airtight storage container usu. made of tincoated iron. b. The amount that a can holds. —*v.* **canned, can·ning.** 1. To seal in a can or jar. 2. *Slang.* a. To dismiss; fire. b. To dispense with: *can the chatter.* [< OE *canne,* water container.] —**can'ner** *n.*

Canada goose *n.* A common wild goose of North America, with grayish plumage, a black neck and head, and a white face patch.

Ca·na·di·an French (kə-nā'dē-ən) *n.* French as used in Canada.

ca·naille (kə-nī', -nāl') *n.* The common people. [< Ital. *canaglia.*]

ca·nal (kə-năl') *n.* 1. A man-made waterway. 2. *Anat.* A tube or duct. [< Lat. *canalis,* channel.] —**ca·nal·i·za·tion** *n.* —**ca·nal·ize** *v.*

can·a·pé (kăn'ə-pā', -pē) *n.* A cracker or small, thin piece of bread or toast topped with a spread or a tidbit, and served as an appetizer. [Fr.]

ca·nard (kə-närd') *n.* A false or unfounded story. [Fr.]

ca·nary (kə-nâr'ē) *n., pl.* **-ies.** A usu. yellow songbird popular as a cage bird. [< the *Canary Islands.*] —**ca·nary** *adj.*

ca·nas·ta (kə-năs'tə) *n.* A card game related to rummy and requiring two decks of cards. [Sp.]

Consult the dictionary entries provided in Figure 12.1. Write the answer to the question beside the corresponding number on your paper.

88.   What are the two guide words for this page?

89.   Give the etymology of the word *camouflage.*

90.   What is the etymological meaning of the word *camouflage?*

91.   What is the syllabication of the word *camouflage?*

92.   *Camomile* is the variant spelling of what word?

93.   Give the inflected form of the word *canary.*

94.   There is a set of homographs in these entries. Write the words that are homographs.

95.   Which homograph entry is more commonly used by all of us?

96.   Write the word *campaign,* including its diacritical marks.

97.   Give all the parts of speech of the word *campaign.*

VI.   Reading for Enjoyment—Newspaper Terms
       Choose the term(s) at the right that best fit(s) the sentence and place the
       letter(s) beside the corresponding number on your answer sheet.

98. and 99.   The two national news agencies that provide
               stories for newspapers across the country are
               called _____ and _____.

100.   A _____ tells the author of the arti-
        cle.

101.   A _____ tells where the story takes
        place.

102.   The _____ consists of words under a
        photograph or illustration giving information
        about it.

103.   A line stating that a story is continued on an-
        other page is called the _____.

104.   The line in bold print above a story telling
        briefly what the story is about is called the
        _____.

105.   A headline that stretches across the newspa-
        per page from one side to the other is called a
        _____.

106.   The first paragraph of a story is called the
        _____.

107.   Articles expressing opinions are called
        _____.

108.   The name of a major stock exchange is called
        _____.

109.   The highest price a stock reached in a year's
        time is called the _____.

110.   The lowest price a stock sold for in a year's
        time is called the _____.

111.   The highest price a stock sold for on a given
        day is called the _____.

112.   The lowest price a stock sold for on a given
        day is called the _____.

113.   The price a stock was selling for when the
        market closed for the day is called the
        _____.

114.   The difference between today's closing price
        and the previous day's closing price is called
        the _____.

A. New York
    Stock
    Exchange
B. headline
C. last price
D. day's high
E. year's high
F. jump
G. caption
H. Associated
    Press
I. byline
J. editorials
K. day's low
L. Reuters
M. dateline
N. year's low
O. banner
    headline
P. lead
Q. net change

Leads

Each sentence listed below represents the lead of a front page story, feature story, sports story, or editorial. Beside the appropriate number on your answer sheet, write the letter of the section in which the lead would be found.

A. Front page
B. Feature section
C. Sports section
D. Editorial section

115. To the delight of area fishermen, the State Department of Conservation released 5,000 two-pound bass in Lake Neoga today.

116. Five passengers in a convertible were seriously injured today in a three-car crash on Route 88.

117. The time has come for the United States government to take a long hard look at its tariff laws.

118. Everyone who saw the long-awaited showing of *Breakfast in Berlin* last night witnessed a first in film history.

119. A missed seven-foot putt almost cost Don Sawyer the top prize in the Coles County Open on Sunday.

120. This newspaper feels that the best qualified candidate for governor is Nick Donley.

STOCK QUOTATIONS

Stocks				
AT&T	$48^3/4$	$47^1/2$	$48^3/4$	$+^7/8$
Campbell's Soup	$81^7/8$	81	$81^1/2$	$+^1/4$
Eastman Kodak	$71^1/2$	$69^1/2$	$71^1/4$	$+1^1/2$
Hershey's	45	$43^7/8$	$44^7/8$	$+^7/8$
Motorola	73	72	$72^1/4$	$-^3/4$
Sears	$46^3/4$	$45^3/8$	$46^1/2$	$+1^1/4$
Coca-Cola	$54^3/8$	$53^5/8$	$53^7/8$	$+^1/2$
Reebok	$41^5/8$	41	$41^3/8$	. . .

Using the stock market quotations shown, determine the correct answer and write it beside the corresponding number on your answer sheet.

121. Which stock costs the most per share?

122. What is that stock's closing price?

123. Which stock costs the least per share?

124. What is that stock's closing price?

125. Which stock recorded the greatest gain form the previous day?

126. How much did that stock gain?

127. Which stock recorded the greatest loss from the previous day?

128. How much did that stock lose?

129. Which stock was unchanged from the previous day?

Classified Ads

130.–133. List the four criteria used in writing a good classified ad.

VII. Essay
      What was the most valuable skill you learned in this class? Why? (Explain
      in a short paragraph.)

Progress Chart

So that you have a composite picture of how your skills have improved and your
speeds increased, on a separate sheet of paper create a chart resembling the one
that follows. Next, begin by turning back to your Rapid Discrimination Drills
chart. Record your fastest speed and your slowest speed; determine your progress
by subtracting the slower figure from the faster one.

    Turn now to your Comprehension Activities chart and make the same
calculation. Follow that with calculations for Speed-Reading Activities (if you did
them). Finally, record the information from your Assessment Test.

    Now look at the total picture. How did you do?

PROGRESS CHART

Rapid Discrimination Drills
Fastest Speed _____
Slowest Speed _____
Progress _____

Comprehension Activities
Fastest Speed _____
Slowest Speed _____
Progress _____

Speed-Reading Drills
Fastest Speed _____
Slowest Speed _____
Progress _____

Assessment Test

Level at which you last tested:	Comprehension _____	Vocabulary _____
Level at which you first tested:	Comprehension _____	Vocabulary _____
Progress:	Comprehension _____	Vocabulary _____

Summing It Up

Reflect now on all the activities you have done in this worktext and how you
benefited from each. On a separate sheet of paper, create the following charts,
mark the columns appropriately, and answer the questions at the end of each
section.

Units Covered

Unit	very interesting	helpful	not helpful	poor	omit
Developing Study Skills					
Note Taking					
Taking Tests					
Improving Your Understanding					
Increasing Speed					
Skimming and Scanning					
Using the Dictionary					
Exploring the Library/ Media Center					
Reading for Enjoyment					
Getting It Together					

1. Which of the units did you enjoy most and why?
2. Which of the units did you benefit most from and why?
3. Which of the units did you like least and why?

Reading Speed and Comprehension Activities

Type	very interesting	helpful	not helpful	poor	omit
Rapid discrimination					
Comprehension					
Speed-Reading					

1. Which of the activities did you enjoy most, and why?
2. Which of the activities did you benefit most from, and why?
3. Which of the activities did you like least, and why?

Study Skills Covered

Skill	very interesting	helpful	not helpful	poor	omit
Previewing your text					
Study setting					
Controlling your time					
Sizing up your instructor					
SQ3R					
Note-taking techniques					
Streamlining notes					
Memory					
Preparing for tests					
Test-taking anxiety					
Taking tests					
Interest inventory					
Career search					
Resume preparation					
Post secondary school search					

1. Which of the skills did you enjoy most, and why?
2. Which of the skills did you benefit most from, and why?
3. Which of the skills did you like least, and why?

Now you have a composite picture of what you have gained from taking this class. Keep your worktext and notes to refer to—they will help you with your reading rate and comprehension, provide you with test-taking strategies, and more. The skills you have learned are valid now, while you are a student in the classroom, and years from now, as you train for a new job. As a student, as an employee, as an adult, you will have many opportunities to apply what you have learned in this class.

Glossary

Almanac volumes published annually that summarize the previous year's events.

A.P. the abbreviation for *The Associated Press*, a well-known news agency.

Banner headline a headline that stretches across a newspaper page from one side to the other.

Byline a line listing the author of the article.

Call numbers numbers and letters indicating classifications of nonfiction books which determine the books' positions on library shelves.

Caption the line beneath or beside a photograph or illustration providing information about it.

Card catalog a filing system consisting of alphabetically arranged cards bearing the call numbers of each book in the library/media center.

Cloze from the word *closure*; meaning to bring completion to a sentence.

Comfortable reading rate the rate preferred by the reader.

Compare to give both the similarities and the differences; a term used in essay questions.

Comprehension the ability to understand what is read and pick out the most important ideas or facts.

Contrast to give the differences only; a term used in essay questions.

Cramming studying only the night before a test.

Criticize to give a judgment or opinion based on reasons; good and bad points should be included; a term used in essay questions.

Dateline a line indicating where the newspaper story action took place.

Day's high the highest price a stock reached on a given day.

Day's low the lowest price a stock reached on a given day.

Define to give meanings but no details; often a matter of giving a memorized definition; a term used in essay questions.

Describe to give details or a verbal picture of the topic; a term used in essay questions.

Dewey decimal system a method of classifying nonfiction; it uses numbers to identify ten major subject categories.

Diacritical marks dots, dashes, and other symbols that show correct pronunciation of a word.

Diagram to include a chart, graph, or geometric drawing with labels and a brief explanation, if needed; a term used in essay questions.

Discuss to give reasons pro and con with details; a term used in essay questions.

e-mail an Internet tool that allows the user to send messages to other people across the room or around the world.

Etymology the origin of a word.

Fiction writing that is based on imagination—writing that is not true; novels and short stories arranged alphabetically by the author's last name.

Fixation in reading, a pause of the eyes to take in words.

FTP (File Transfer Protocol) an Internet tool used in retrieving information.

Full signals obvious word "flags" such as *the first, the second, the third,* and so on.

Gist the central or main idea.

Guide words the words at the top of a dictionary page indicating the first and last entries on the page.

Half signals less obvious word "flags" such as *the next, the last, in summary,* and so on.

Headline large bold type above a newspaper article indicating the content of the story.

Highlighter a marker that allows print to show through; used in note taking to identify key information. When used with textbooks, the books must be student-owned.

Homograph words that have the same spelling but different meanings and origins.

Inferences sentence(s) in which the meaning is not directly stated.

Inflected form changes in the spelling of a word due to a tense change or a plural form.

Infotrac   a library system that consists of a computer and a compact disk; it lists available material for specific topics.

Internet   a collection of computer networks which supply information on a variety of topics to people around the world.

IRC (Internet Relay Chat)   an Internet tool that allows many people at different locations to instantly respond to the thoughts of others via their keyboards.

Justify   to prove or give reasons; a term used in essay questions.

Key words   important words in a sentence.

Lead   the first paragraph of a well-written story which answers the questions *who, what, when, where,* and *why* (the five Ws).

List   to write a numbered list of words, sentences, or comments; a term used in essay questions.

Listing   a form of note taking that uses main headings and lists to record information succinctly.

Jump   a line stating that an article is continued on another page.

Last price   the price at which a stock was selling when the market closed that day.

Library of Congress   a method of classifying nonfiction; it uses letters to identify twenty-one major categories.

Mailing lists   an Internet tool which sends specific topical material to the user's e-mail address.

Main entry   the word you look up in the dictionary.

Main idea   the point the author is trying to make.

Margin notes   a form of note taking in which key points are written in the margin. When used with textbooks, the books must be student-owned.

Microforms   information from newspapers and magazines that has been photographed and reduced in size to be stored on microfiche or microfilm.

Net change   the difference between a stock's last price on a given day and its last price on the previous day.

News agency   an organization that sends news stories by wire. Two well-known news agencies are the Associated Press and Reuters.

Nonfiction   material that is true; all books that are not novels or short stories; nonfiction is classified using either the Dewey decimal or Library of Congress classification system.

NYSE   the abbreviation for the New York Stock Exchange, one of the major stock exchanges.

Outline   a system of note taking that involves recording main ideas and supporting details in a concise manner.

Overview   a comprehensive view of all the material; usually it is not followed by another reading.

Parts of speech   italic type in the dictionary indicating whether a word is a noun, pronoun, verb, adverb, and so on.

Patterning   a form of note taking that uses drawings, diagrams, charts, graphs, and so on.

Periodicals   newspapers, magazines, and digests that are published periodically.

Preview   a form of skimming; a view of the material before actually beginning to read, usually followed by a more thorough reading.

Push reading rate   a rate at which the reader sacrifices comfort to read as quickly as possible without diminishing comprehension.

Reading rate   the speed at which material is read.

Readers' guide   *Readers' Guide to Periodical Literature;* a reference book that indexes articles on specific subjects.

Reference books   books such as dictionaries, encyclopedias, almanacs, and so on that are valuable sources of information for researchers.

Review   a form of skimming; to view material again; it follows a previous reading.

Scan   to glance at a selection for specific information; not a true reading rate.

Sequence   arranging items in their proper order.

Signal words   word "flags" that indicate main points within sentences or paragraphs.

Skim   to pass quickly over an entire selection to get a general idea of its contents; not a true reading rate.

SQ3R   a study technique that uses the steps of survey, question, read, recite, and review to aid comprehension and retention.

Summarize   to give a brief, condensed account of the main ideas; omit details; a term used in essay questions.

Syllabication   a division of a word into syllables.

Telnet   an Internet tool that allows the user to access other computers.

Test anxiety   nervousness prior to taking a test.

Trace   to include details, progress, or history of a topic from beginning to end; a term used in essay questions.

Underlining   a method of note taking in which a student underlines key information as he or she reads. When used with textbooks, the books must be student-owned.

Usenet newsgroup   an Internet tool that is a public access bulletin board.

Variants   two or more correct spellings of a single word.

Verbal clues   like signal words; they "flag" what a lecturer thinks is important and may include on a test.

Vertical file   filing cabinets used in libraries for storage of small pamphlets, booklets, catalogs, and clippings on a variety of topics.

Words per minute (wpm)   the number of words read in one minute.

Year's high   the highest price a stock reached in one year's time.

Year's low   the lowest price a stock reached in one year's time.

WWW (World Wide Web)   an Internet feature which allows access to huge databases of information and retrievable files.

Acknowledgments

Grateful acknowledgment is made to the following for permission to reprint copyrighted materials:

Jamestown Publishers, for "How Your Memory Works" from *How to Study in High School* by Jean Snider, copyright 1983. Reprinted by permission of the publisher.

Judy McKenna and Carole J. Makela, for "It's Your Money—Managing Credit," Colorado State University—Cooperative Extension Service, Fort Collins, CO.

Employment & Training Administration, U.S. Employment Service, Washington, DC 20210, for "Merchandising Your Talents."

Kendall Slee, for "One Night in the Woods."

J. Weston Walch, Publisher, for excerpts from *Speedreading for Better Grades* by Ward Cramer. Copyright 1978 by J. Weston Walch, Publisher; Portland, Maine. Used with permission. All further reproduction prohibited.

J. Patrick Hooley, for "Creating Successful Study Habits."

Mary Lael Van Riper, for "Mary Had a Little Lamb."

Metra Commuter Rail, Chicago, Illinois, for excerpts from the Metra (Union Pacific/Northwest Line) timetable, 1996.

Fred Matheny, for "Cycling Risks" from *Beginning Bicycle Racing* by Fred Matheny, copyright 1983.

Houghton-Mifflin, for dictionary excerpts. Copyright © 1994 and 1983 by Houghton-Mifflin Company. Adapted and reproduced by permission from *The American Heritage Dictionary, Third Paper Edition*, and from *The American Heritage Dictionary, Second Paperback Edition*.

The H. W. Wilson Company, for *Readers' Guide* excerpts. *Readers' Guide to Periodical Literature*, July 1988 issue, copyright © 1988 by The H. W. Wilson Company, reproduced by permission.

Information Access Company, for excerpts from Infotrac®.

The Denver Post, for excerpts from selected sports and weather sections from *The Denver Post*, and *The Denver Post* Newspaper in Education Department, for excerpts from the *1994 Colorado Career Guide*.

U.S. News & World Report, for excerpts from "20 Hot Job Tracks," Copyright October 30, 1995, *U.S. News & World Report*.

Utah State University, for the "Admission Index" from the *Utah State University Bulletin*.

Index